India Under Pressure

[illegible]
December 1, 1986
Washington DC

Westview Replica Editions

The concept of Westview Replica Editions is a response to the continuing crisis in academic and informational publishing. Library budgets for books have been severely curtailed. Ever larger portions of general library budgets are being diverted from the purchase of books and used for data banks, computers, micromedia, and other methods of information retrieval. Interlibrary loan structures further reduce the edition sizes required to satisfy the needs of the scholarly community. Economic pressures on the university presses and the few private scholarly publishing companies have severely limited the capacity of the industry to properly serve the academic and research communities. As a result, many manuscripts dealing with important subjects, often representing the highest level of scholarship, are no longer economically viable publishing projects--or, if accepted for publication, are typically subject to lead times ranging from one to three years.

Westview Replica Editions are our practical solution to the problem. We accept a manuscript in camera-ready form, typed according to our specifications, and move it immediately into the production process. As always, the selection criteria include the importance of the subject, the work's contribution to scholarship, and its insight, originality of thought, and excellence of exposition. The responsibility for editing and proofreading lies with the author or sponsoring institution. We prepare chapter headings and display pages, file for copyright, and obtain Library of Congress Cataloging in Publication Data. A detailed manual contains simple instructions for preparing the final typescript, and our editorial staff is always available to answer questions.

The end result is a book printed on acid-free paper and bound in sturdy library-quality soft covers. We manufacture these books ourselves using equipment that does not require a lengthy make-ready process and that allows us to publish first editions of 300 to 600 copies and to reprint even smaller quantities as needed. Thus, we can produce Replica Editions quickly and can keep even very specialized books in print as long as there is a demand for them.

About the Book and Author

India Under Pressure: Prospects for Political Stability

Robert L. Hardgrave, Jr.

India, as the dominant power in South Asia, is the region's keystone for stability. Contending that the Indian government is under ever-increasing pressure as a result of internal social and political conflict, Dr. Hardgrave provides a broad survey of the sources of conflict: regionalism, particularly demands for separation and autonomy in Assam and the Punjab; enmity between religious groups, manifested in increased Hindu-Muslim tensions; caste violence; peasant unrest in the countryside; and protests among students and labor groups in the cities. The author analyzes the capacity of India's political parties, the bureaucracy, and the military to cope with change and to manage the country's social diversity and the potential for conflict. In particular, he examines the ruling Congress party, the leadership style of Prime Minister Indira Gandhi, the problem of succession, prospects for unity among opposition parties, and the potential impact of a coalition government on political stability. In considering the role that foreign relations play in India's political stability, Dr. Hardgrave discusses India's relations with South Asia, the Middle East, the Soviet Union, China, and the United States.

Robert L. Hardgrave, Jr., professor of government at the University of Texas at Austin, is the author of *India: Government and Politics in a Developing Nation* (1980).

India Under Pressure
Prospects for Political Stability

Robert L. Hardgrave, Jr.

Westview Press / Boulder and London

A Westview Replica Edition

Published in 1984 in the United States of America by
Westview Press, Inc.
5500 Central Avenue
Boulder, Colorado 80301
Frederick A. Praeger, Publisher

Library of Congress Catalog Card Number: 84-50862
ISBN 0-86531-860-3

Printed and bound in the United States of America

10 9 8 7 6 5 4 3

Contents

Chapter 2

The Prospects for Political Stability in India:
A Five-Year Perspective

Chapter 3

Continuity and Change in India's Foreign Policy: The Next Five Years

Preface

American interests in South Asia, in the broadest sense, are political, humanitarian, economic, and strategic. They involve support and promotion of democratic values, human rights, prosperity, and peace. The most pressing and immediate interest, a projection of American global concerns and an extension of vital strategic interests in the Persian Gulf, is the containment of Soviet power within the region. With the Soviet invasion of Afghanistan in December 1979, Pakistan may have become a "frontline state" (a description rejected by Pakistani President Zia-ul-Haq), but India, as the preeminent power of the subcontinent, is the keystone of stability in South Asia. Major unrest threatening India's national integrity or its political stability would provide new opportunities for the extension of Soviet influence. India's stability and economic strength, far more than a rearmed Pakistan, constitute the major force for limiting Soviet influence within the region. American interests are best served by a policy that enhances India's sense of security and supports its efforts for economic development.

Whatever Government may be in power in New Delhi over the next five years, there will likely be little substantive difference in foreign or domestic policy from that of the Congress Government today. The pluralism of Indian society, with its multiplicity of competing interests, is a major force for holding politics and public policy on the middle ground. The Congress embraces this pluralism within itself, as does the Janata Party in the opposition, and any alliance of opposition parties necessary to form a coalition Government would, in balancing its divergent tendencies, blunt more radical change.

India is under pressure, and with increasing social unrest, parliamentary elections, and (if Congress is returned to power) the matter of leadership succession, the next five years will be critical. In exploring the prospects for political stability, this study examines the forces, both domestic and international, that are likely to shape India's near future.

Robert L. Hardgrave, Jr.
March 1, 1984

Acknowledgments

I wish to thank those who read the draft manuscripts and offered their valuable suggestions and insight: Walter K. Andersen, Craig Baxter, Stephen P. Cohen, Rodney Jones, Pauline Kolenda, Douglas C. Makeig, Jagat Mehta, James R. Roach, Leo Rose, Lloyd I. Rudolph, Eliza Van Hollen, Myron Weiner, and W. Howard Wriggins. I owe special thanks to Edward G. Griffin, Senior Research Analyst in the Office of Long-Range Assessments and Research, U.S. Department of State, for his guidance and encouragement. I wish also to express my gratitude to Betty McEuen for her work on the word processor and for her sharp eye to syntax and style. For all my appreciation to those who assisted me and stimulated my effort, however, I alone am responsible for what appears here.

The research upon which this book is based was supported under contract by the United States Department of State. Views or conclusions contained in this study should not be interpreted as representing the official opinion or policy of the Department of State.

Robert L. Hardgrave, Jr.

1 Social Change and Political Stability in India

Predictions of national disintegration, the collapse of democracy, social chaos, and revolutionary violence have accompanied the processes of change in India from the time of independence. In the face of illiteracy, poverty, and the "fissiparous tendencies" of caste, religion, language, and region, there are many who have seen democracy as a system that India could ill afford. Cassandras--both Indian and foreign--have greeted each parliamentary election as inevitably its last. The Emergency (1975-1977) was widely mourned as the death of democracy. Some viewed it, no doubt, as proof apparent that democracy cannot work in India.

The "restoration" of democracy in 1977, with the squabbling Janata Government, and the return of Indira Gandhi in 1980, witnessed heightened expectations, sharpened social conflict, and increasing political malaise. In January 1982, India Today, the nation's leading news magazine, diagnosed India's political institutions as "in an advanced state of decay and degeneration." A year later, in the wake of the Congress defeats in the 1983 Andhra and Karnataka assembly elections, Prem Shankar Jha of the Times of India foresaw the imminent disintegration of the Congress party and, in consequence, "a new and dangerously unstable phase" which will put the survival of Indian democracy to a severe test.[1]

Dire predictions, if made often enough, may ultimately find fulfillment. Yet India has survived its "dangerous decades" reasonably well, and its political institutions, perhaps somewhat worse for wear, have demonstrated remarkable resilience. Of more than 60 nations that have emerged from colonial rule since World War II, India is one of the few that has retained free elections and democratic institutions. But India does face enormous problems. It is a nation under pressure, and its stability is by no means assured.

DEFINING POLITICAL STABILITY IN THE INDIAN CONTEXT

The notion of stability is central to an assessment of socio-economic and political conditions and the projection of trends for any nation. Yet, as is so often true for the most important concepts, it eludes precise definition. Indeed, attempts to define it rigorously--typically in terms of various statistical indicators--have more often than not left the analyst in a conceptual straightjacket. It is not enough, however, to say, with Justice Potter Stewart in his view of obscenity, "I know it when I see it." We need a clearer sense of what we are looking at.

Political stability is approached most frequently at the level of the regime and is defined in much of the literature in terms of the prolonged absence of seizures or attempted seizures of power by force--coups, uprisings, and revolution--and by the absence of any common expectation that such seizures are likely to occur. But in the context of South Asia, such gross measurements of stability provide little discrimination other than to place India securely in the "stable" column.

In the broadest sense, political stability refers to the continuity of government--in structure, process, and policy. It is not static, but dynamic, involving the capacity to cope with change--to absorb it, to shape it. Political stability in India involves three forms: ministerial stability at state and Center levels and regime stability.*

The stability of the ministry (or Government, in the European sense) involves the capacity of the ruling party or coalition to retain the confidence of a parliamentary majority. To do so, it must successfully resist outside pressure and overcome internal dissension that would bring the Government down. Within the Indian federal system, ministerial stability of states and Center are distinct and, to considerable degree, insulated from each other. Thus, a state may undergo periods of political instability while the central Government remains stable--as, in fact, we have seen in numerous cases since India's independence. Similarly, there may be periods where state Governments are stable

---

* In "The Prospects for Political Stability in India," we look more closely at each of these levels of political stability.

and effective, while the central Government is adrift--as in the Janata period, 1977-1980.

Regime stability refers to the continuity of the political order itself. It involves the capacity of the system to withstand and cope successfully with attempted coups, uprising, and revolution.

Sources of Indian Stability

India's stability stands in sharp contrast to most nations of the Third World. Since independence in 1947, the regime has never been seriously threatened by uprisings, coups, or revolution nor does such a prospect lie on the horizon. India's political order, parliamentary democracy, has a legitimacy paralleled in few nations of the Third World. On the death of two prime ministers, Nehru and Shastri, it witnessed orderly succession. Through free and competitive elections, India has twice undergone a peaceful transition of political power from one party to another. Indian national unity, once problematic, is fundamentally secure--bound by an increasingly national economy, a national system of communications, and (despite heightened regional sentiment) a growing national consciousness.

Popular images abroad--communal riots, atrocities against untouchables, agitation in the Punjab, massacre in Assam--belie India's fundamental political stability and national integrity. Moreover, these incidents of unrest must be put in perspective: India, a nation of some 700 million people, has a population greater than all of Africa and Latin America combined.

Having said this, the fact remains that social unrest is endemic in India, but it is--or, at least it has been--fundamentally manageable. It has been manageable for three principal reasons: the strength of India's institutions, particularly the Congress party; the nation's democratic political framework; and the sheer complexity of Indian society that with its multiplicity of social cleavages has tended to compartmentalize unrest.

It is ironic that the social complexity decried as the bane of national unity is one of the most important sources of India's stability. The cross-cutting divisions of caste, class, tribe, sect, religion, language, and region give to India the character of a vast mosaic. Each social compartment is, to varying degrees, insulated from the other. This pattern is reinforced by the federal system in which state boundaries follow, for the most part, major divisions of language and regional identity. Structurally quarantined, social unrest that arises in one state rarely spreads to other states. Thus contained, it is more readily managed and controlled.

Whether this will continue to be true remains to be seen. The sources of national unity, particularly the increasingly integrated economy and communications systems, may provide the basis for an expression of all India discontent. This has already been reflected in the remarkably uniform swings in the 1977 and 1980 elections,[2] with similar voting patterns in both urban and rural areas and across the Indian states. What happens in one part of India increasingly has an impact throughout the nation and invokes similar response. Whether it is a rise in the price of onions in Maharashtra, drought in Tamil Nadu, or strikes in the Bihar coalfields, few Indians are today unaffected. Newspapers, multiplied in their effect by word of mouth, bring to all India reports of conversions of untouchables to Islam in a Tamil village, the farmers' movement in Maharashtra, and demands from Andhra for greater state autonomy.

Social unrest, once contained within state boundaries, may spill over into a movement of all India dimension. The potential was witnessed in the "J.P. Movement"* of 1974-75 directed against Indira Gandhi. The movement, essentially limited to North India and largely urban, had in all probability passed its peak, but it served as the excuse for the imposition of Emergency rule in June 1975. From the vantage point of New Delhi, it is one thing to put out isolated brush fires as they occur, quite another to face many at the same time--especially as they may join in a national firestorm of social unrest.

Social unrest, as it grows in intensity and, even more critically, as it arises simultaneously in a number of states, places increasing strain on India's institutional capacity. The institutional strength of its party system (of which the Congress has been the nucleus), the bureaucracy, and the army is the bedrock of India's political stability. As those institutions are weakened, so too its capacity to accommodate and

---

* Named for Jayaprakash Narayan ("J.P."), who emerged from political retirement to lead the movement against Congress corruption.

reconcile political demands, to cope with change, and to control social unrest is inevitably reduced.

In contrast to most other nations emerging from colonial rule, India came to independence with three strong institutions. The Congress party, shaped and strengthened during the nationalist movement for independence, provided the political structure to accommodate a plurality of interests and to reconcile conflicting demands. The direct legacy of British rule, the bureaucracy--the "steel frame" of the Raj--provided a structure of administration that spanned the nation and reached down into even the most isolated village. The Indian Army, with a proud and honored tradition, provided not only for the defense of the realm, but "in aid to the civil" stood as the ultimate guarantor of internal security--maintaining at the same time a scrupulous non-involvement in politics.

There are those, enamored with authority, order, and discipline, for whom military rule would be a welcome alternative to democratic politics. But stability cannot be purchased through repression--as Pakistan, a powderkeg of pent-up forces, clearly demonstrates. Stability is to be found in the balance between order and liberty.

The strength and responsiveness of India's democratic political institutions undergird political stability. If the complexity of Indian society is at once a source of both conflict and stability, it is also the most compelling reason why some form of democracy is necessary to ensure that stability. There is in India a broad-based commitment to democratic politics which has been reinforced and extended with each successive election. Democracy in India provides the framework by which expanding participation can be absorbed and ordered; by which the nation's many interests can find meaningful expression; and by which conflicts can be reconciled. It does so imperfectly and incompletely--but the remedy is not less democracy. Censorship of the press, banning of political parties, postponement of elections, imprisonment of political opponents--in short, the closure of political access--may put a lid on the expression of discontent, but it does not enhance the capacity of the government to cope with change. Instead, it isolates those in authority, as it did during the Emergency, and deepens alienation and discontent within the society. The consequences, as dramatically witnessed in Iran, can be explosive.

In exploring the dynamics of stability in India, we have identified its sources in the pluralism of Indian society, the strength of its institutions, and in democratic politics--all three closely interrelated. But India's stability is also sustained by its culture and, surely with mixed consequences, by its relatively slow rates of economic and social change.

Indian culture, of which Hinduism is the core, has historically revealed a remarkable capacity to absorb change. Various cultural themes--*dharma*, the code of conduct particular to each person, and *karma*, the fruit of action (a doctrine of just deserts)--have given strength, continuity, and an essential conservatism to Indian society. In traditional Hindu society, the government is the repository of the collective dharma. The person who holds power is the instrument of that dharma through which the destiny of the state manifests itself. This concept of dharma--an important element in the legitimacy of India's government today--is a source of both strength and vulnerability. So long as the government acts in accordance with dharma, it is legitimate, and to oppose it is to jeopardize one's individual dharma. But if government violates the moral order, the king forfeits the right to rule.

There is in Indian society a tolerance for ambiguity that cushions the impact of change. Change is compartmentalized, the modern coexisting with rather than displacing the traditional. But it would be as great a misconception to assume that traditional society is impervious to change as it would be to portray the Indian masses as inert and unresponsive, bound in resignation to their fate. Under pressure of change, Indian society has responded variously by resistance, reaction, and transformation. That change in India has not been more traumatic is, in part, related to its pace.

Much to the frustration of the leaders of India's development efforts, the rate of social and economic change has been slow. In the years since independence, the annual rate of economic growth has averaged roughly 3.5 percent, leaving real growth, once the population increase is accounted for, of little more than 1 percent per year. Described by the economist Raj Krishna as the "Hindu rate of growth," it has severely limited India's capacity to meet the expectations and demands of its people for a better life. Yet, at the same time, it has blunted the impact of more socially disruptive rapid change. What may have been in the short term a contribution to stability is in the long term, however, one of the greatest threats to stability. Heightened expectations exceed the capacity of the system to respond, and growing frustration is already marked by sharpened social tension and political unrest.

The "Foreign Hand": External Sources of Instability

Few incidents of political or social unrest have occurred in India that have not been linked by accusation to outside interference. Blitz, a pro-Moscow weekly from Bombay, regularly reports the CIA at work in destabilizing India. The Hindu nationalist Rashtriya Swayamsevak Sangh (RSS) sees Pakistan or an even more sinister "international Islam" behind communal tension in India and periodic Hindu-Muslim rioting. Prime Minister Indira Gandhi alludes periodically to a "foreign hand"--usually unnamed but typically implying the United States or Pakistan--at the source of India's troubles.

In assessing external sources of instability, it is important to distinguish between influence, interference, and subversion, as well as between instability which is an unintended consequence of either influence or interference and instability as the intended result of activity directed against the state.

There have been few instances of actions taken by a foreign government that were, in design, intended to destabilize India--and these were directed less against regime stability than India's national integrity.

During the 1960s, Pakistani agents in Kashmir sought to stir disaffection among local Muslims, but there is nothing to suggest that after 1971, this has continued. In the ethnically volatile Northeast, tribal insurgency has been linked to China--and, indeed, during the 1960s and early 1970s, China did provide training and arms for Naga and Mizo guerrillas. In 1979, however, China informed the Government of India that it was no longer aiding the insurgents, and New Delhi has accepted Chinese assurances.

Bangladesh has surely been a source of instability in India's Northeast, as Bengalis--both Hindu and Muslim--have moved across the borders into the states of Tripura and Assam. But like the illegal immigration from Mexico into the United States, immigration from Bangladesh into India is a result of poverty, not political design.

Much lies in the eyes of the beholder. How both actions and consequences are perceived is critical. Any foreign contact with groups for whom external allies as a source of money or support could be important may be seen as potentially "destabilizing." Thus, Saudi assistance to Indian Muslims in refurbishing mosques or in establishing schools has been perceived by apprehensive Hindus as foreign interference in the sensitive area of communal relations. More directly, the RSS and others, including the Congress(I), have alleged (without evidence) that Gulf money financed recent "mass conversions" to Islam among untouchables at Meenakshipuram in Tamil Nadu--an incident that sharpened Hindu-Muslim tension and sparked rioting as far away as Gujarat.

India is an open society, and freedom of movement for foreigners--as for its own citizens--within India stands in sharp contrast to many Third World nations and to the Socialist bloc. Nevertheless, any foreigner in contact with minorities or groups nurturing special grievances is potentially suspect. The matter of conversion has always been a source of unease in India, and Christian missionaries--especially those working among the tribals of the Northeast--are often viewed as fermenting unrest. The Government of India has restricted foreign scholars--especially Americans--in research on such topics as untouchability, Muslims, and tribals. (Yet, in fairness, it must be said that while India has restricted foreign research on designated sensitive topics and in certain border areas, few nations are as hospitable to foreign scholars as India and provide as far reaching access to government officials and archival sources.) International journalists--barred from such areas as the Northeast--are sometimes seen as a source of trouble insofar as their stories may come back into India to fuel the fires upon which they report.

Indians abroad may also be viewed with apprehension, as in the support for an independent Sikh nation of "Khalistan" expressed by a handful of Sikhs in Canada and the United States. Gandhi's talk of a "foreign hand" in the Akali agitation in the Punjab refers both to Pakistan and to these expatriate Sikhs, and India has registered its official displeasure with those governments admitting Sikh dissidents--albeit in accordance with their own laws.

The spectre of the "foreign hand" goes back to the 1950s and such publications as American Shadow Over India,[3] a catalog of American activities alleged to have been taken against India. But it was not until the late 1960s and early 1970s that Mrs. Gandhi regularly accused the United States--and the CIA in particular--of attempts to destabilize India. The Indian press often met such allegations with skepticism and sometimes with ridicule, as in a cartoon suggesting that India was so vulnerable to outside interference that even the weather was under foreign control. Whether Indira Gandhi really believed what she was saying or whether it was scapegoating for domestic consumption or Soviet appeasement is a matter of debate. But, according to Daniel Patrick Moynihan, then Ambassador to India, revelations in 1974 of CIA involvement in the overthrow of Allende in Chile, confirmed Indira Gandhi's "worst suspicions and genuine fears" about American policy toward India.[4]

Over the past decade, Gandhi's distrust of the United States has been tempered by her own sense of realpolitik and (one hopes) by a more accurate assessment of American interests in South Asia. She no longer refers to the CIA as an omnipresent threat to Indian stability, but her speeches, as during the 1983 Andhra election campaign, continue to contain references to dark forces that encourage regionalism and disunity.

Mrs. Gandhi has been notably silent in public criticism of the Soviet Union, despite Soviet support for the Communist Party of India (CPI) and its various front organizations. She apparently has chosen not to regard such activity as "interference" in Indian domestic politics--at least until the CPI went into opposition against her Government. Since 1980, Mrs. Gandhi has attacked the CPI for its cynical opportunism in joining the forces of reaction arrayed against her, and it was widely reported that in her visit to Moscow in September 1982, she told Brezhnev to rein in the party and to end its opposition to her domestic policy.

The danger of subversion by a "foreign hand," like the imminence of war, may be raised to deflect attention from problems at home and to avoid responsibility. It may also be raised in genuine belief that the stability or unity of the nation is threatened, but India's vast size and social complexity reduces the capacity of any foreign power to do much mischief. At most, it can aid and abet dissident elements within Indian society. The challenge to India's political stability lies not in external interference, but in the internal processes of change and sharpened social conflict.

LINKAGES: SOCIAL CHANGE, SOCIAL UNREST, AND POLITICAL INSTABILITY

Over the past two decades, various theorists on mass violence have constructed models linking social change to revolutionary action. Sometimes the causal linkage has been direct, with change measured by selected statistical indicators (economic growth, inflation, unemployment, strikes, riots, etc.). But the approach has proven to have little explanatory value and even less predictive power. No one has demonstrated a direct link, for example, between economic performance and political stability. The indicators that "explain" social unrest in one nation cannot explain why a similar pattern of change did not result in unrest elsewhere. Some of the arguments are simply tautological.

In many theories of the etiology, or causation, of mass violence, the linkage between social change and social unrest is mediated by <u>frustration</u>. But frustration is not always the catalyst to social unrest. It can be dissipated in cinema, alcohol, or family violence. Indeed, wife beating and child abuse are more likely outcomes of the frustration of unemployment, for example, than is political action--but <u>how</u> frustration is released and directed is both culturally and individually variable. It need not be acted out socially, that is, in concert with others, and it need not involve violence--though it surely may, as the history of communal, caste, ethnic, and linguistic conflict in India clearly reveals.

In the processes of social and economic change, some individuals and groups benefit, others suffer. One group may feel threatened, another frustrated by a sense of relative deprivation, either by unfavorable comparison with others or in a widening gap between expectation and achievement.

Various changes are likely to contribute to frustration and potentially to social unrest. Later, we will examine some of the most important variables of change in the Indian context. Here it should be underscored that unrest--insofar as it is related to change--is most likely to be the product of rapid change or of a sudden drop or reversal in the rate of change. But significant changes may be lost in aggregate data. All-India averages, for example, may conceal rapid changes in a state or locality that might bear critically on the emergence of social unrest within the region. Given the regional diversity of India and the federal system which both reflects and contains it, the variables of change must be monitored not only for India as a whole, but for each of the states and major urban areas. Indeed, regional disparity is itself a potential source of unrest.

Whether social unrest is directed against the Government or the regime depends upon a receptive climate of opinion: basic political attitudes and orientations. Most fundamental is the question of political legitimacy--the judgment as to whether the government is rightfully constituted, whether (in terms of Hindu tradition) it acts in accordance with dharma. Public opinion surveys tap these orientations through a variety of questions relating to confidence in government, sense of political efficacy, political alienation, and so on. Surveys in India--whether by the Indian Institute of Public Opinion, academics, or by the newer polling organizations--tend to reflect an urban bias. But even with their methodological problems, they provide a reading of the political climate that may bear on the potential for political instability. They monitor changes over time and identify variations among groups and regions.

The analysis of social and economic change and of the climate of opinion is critical to an assessment of the prospects for political stability, but it is not sufficient in itself. Change must be placed in an organizational context. If frustration arising out of change is to take the form of social unrest, if it is to be more than an episodic and anomic expression of discontent, if it is to pose a threat to the stability of the Government or the regime, it must be organized. Just as political stability depends upon the institutional capacity of the government to cope with change, so the challenge to that stability depends upon the organizational capacity of the opposition to transform individual frustration into social unrest and to direct it against those in power.*

In relating social change to social unrest and, in turn, to political instability, a number of organizational factors must be assessed.

---

* Frustration and social unrest are not organized solely against the government. Indeed, the government itself may direct it against alleged enemies of the state--domestic or foreign. Scapegoating remains a classic diversionary tactic, used no less in India than elsewhere.

Is organizational activity within a given arena of social unrest sustained and does it increase? Or is it an episodic, cathartic movement?

What is the character of the organization and its leadership--its unity, size, skills, resources, strategy, and goals? Does it have a permanent full-time staff? How effective is it in securing financial support?

How widespread geographically is its organization activity? Does it cross state boundaries or have all-India scope? Does it have links with similar organizations in other states?

What is the social base of the organization's support? What support or sympathy for the protest position or the organization's goals is there within the ruling elite? What degree of support or sympathy, if any, is there in other states? How is the organization treated in the press, both English and vernacular? What positions have political parties adopted with respect to the organization and its goals?

Is the organization strictly domestic in its sources of support and funding, or does it have international ties?

Rather than in a single movement, all India in scope, social unrest is most likely to manifest itself regionally in response to local conditions. Insofar as serious unrest occurs only periodically and remains contained within state boundaries, it may be managed with varying degrees of success. It may bring down a state ministry, but it poses no real threat to the stability of the Center. But if unrest spreads to other states, if it is linked organizationally with unrest in other states, or if a number of states, albeit separately, face serious unrest at the same time, the capacity of the Center to respond may be severely strained.

A single charismatic individual could fuse disparate groups into a united protest movement. Jayaprakash Narayan played this catalytic role in 1974-75, but the "J.P. Movement" was itself limited almost wholly to urban areas of North India, and even in its major center of strength, Bihar, it had begun to lose momentum before the Emergency was declared. There is no figure comparable to Jayaprakash in India today, but such leaders have often emerged suddenly out of crisis.

POLITICAL CONSCIOUSNESS, PARTICIPATION, AND PROTEST

Education is among the most important determinants of political consciousness and participation. The adult literacy rate in India is 36 percent, with extreme regional variation, from Kerala at 69 percent to Bihar at 26 percent. In response to efforts in education, these figures will rise at an accelerating rate in coming years. Primary school enrollments have expanded rapidly, from 19 percent of all children ages 6 to 11 in 1950-51 to more than 70 percent in 1980-81. The rising rates of literacy and a corresponding expansion in media consumption will heighten political consciousness and widen the arena of political participation.

Voter turnout in India--one measure of political participation--corresponds roughly to the rank order of states by literacy and other developmental indices. But while voter turnouts are highest for more progressive states (an average of 68.6 percent in Kerala for the last three parliamentary elections, 1971, 1977, and 1980, compared to 53.8 percent for Bihar and 44.9 percent for Orissa), turnouts in the more backward states are still dramatically higher than rates of literacy. Literacy clearly does not impose a threshold on political participation.

A variety of factors (such as the degree of competitiveness) may influence voter turnout in any given election, but over the past 30 years, there has been a long-term trend toward increased voter turnout in all states. All-India turnouts have risen from 45.7 percent in 1952 to 65.2 percent in 1971, 71.3 percent in 1977, and 64.9 percent in 1980--turnouts substantially above those for American presidential elections (55 percent, for example, in 1980). More effective registration and a greater number of polling stations account for a portion of this increase, but the major factors influencing greater voter turnout in India are increased political consciousness and the greater capacity of political parties to mobilize support and get out the vote.[5] The two are closely related.

Heightened political consciousness is itself the product of a multitude of changes--the expansion of education; the more direct involvement of government in the lives of the people; the development of national systems of transportation and communication, opening people to a wider world of experience; and the extension of the mass media and of a vigorous free press. But more than any other factor, competitive democratic elections are the major force in raising political consciousness. The competition for support, as each party seeks to outbid the other, has drawn people out of their parochial worlds and raised their hopes and aspirations. But disappointment is an educating and sometimes disillusioning experience.

The voters have with each successive election come increasingly to appreciate the power of the ballot box and the stakes involved. They have become more sophisticated, but they have also become more cynical and perhaps more impatient. Electoral competition, the motive force of expanding participation, has drawn new groups into the political arena, but the capacity of the government to respond in their demands has not kept pace. Increasing competition has heightened consciousness and deepened animosities. It has made people more aware of their poverty or of their vulnerability to displacement by those pushing up from below. As the gap between expectation and achievement widens, as the sense of relative deprivation becomes more acute, frustration grows more intense. The greater the degree of political consciousness, the more likely it is that frustration will be expiated politically--in a vote "to throw the rascals out," as has become the recurrent pattern in Indian electoral politics, or in direct action--from demonstration and protest to revolutionary violence.

Direct action is not new to the Indian political scene. Indeed, it gained legitimacy during the nationalist movement, and no political leader is prepared to wholly condemn it. Mass political activity has often been violent, but disorder is frequently vindicated by success. "Only when public ordr is endangered by a mass movement is the government willing to make a concession," Myron Weiner writes, "not because they consider the demand legitimate, but because they then recognize the strength of the group making the demand and its capacity for destructiveness. Thus, the government often alternates between unresponsiveness to the demands of large but peaceful groups and total concession to groups that press their demands violently."[6] The capitulation of the government to the demands for linguistic states only in the wake of rioting and the reevaluation of official language policy only after prolonged agitation are classic examples of the efficacy of violence. That mass action has succeeded so often has given it a certain legitimacy.[7]

Protest in India takes many forms, and the various terms used to describe them are working their way into the English language, just as such words as thug and goonda did earlier.[8]

Satyagraha, Gandhi's "truth force" of civil disobedience is used by groups of every political hue, although it is offically viewed as unjustified in the context of an independent and democratic India.

Hartal, another Gandhian technique, is a general strike involving cessation of all public activity.

Dharna, a strike with flags, pickets, and placards, is a common scene in front of government offices and companies in both public and private sectors. In a "sitting dharna," prominant persons--typically politicians--seat themselves before the building of the offending party. They sometimes dramatize their protest by a hunger strike and, more recently, have taken to "relay hunger strikes," in which the protesters take turn skipping meals to demonstrate their grievances.

The threatened "fast unto death", used by Gandhi with such effectiveness, remains a potent weapon if the person is of sufficient prestige.* In 1975, Indira Gandhi yielded to the demand for elections in Gujarat in the face of Morarji Desai's fast. Were he to have died, serious rioting would surely have posed a major threat to Mrs. Gandhi's Government. Desai's fast as a form of political extortion, leading as it did to Congress' electoral defeat, was one of the many ingredients in Mrs. Gandhi's decision two months later to impose the Emergency.

Gherao involves the physical encirclement of the managerial staff--usually that of a company or university--to secure "quick justice."

Rasta roko, literally "block the road," involves the disruption of traffic in a gridlock by protest. Prosperous farmers in demands for higher crop prices have blocked roads with their tractors; striking university students have snarled traffic in Connaught Circus, the hub of New Delhi; and protesting Akali Sikhs have sought to close down the Punjab's highways.

Morcha, or procession, covers the wide range of protest marches that are a daily occurrence in Indian cities.

---

*The fast unto death can be a politically dangerous game if the government is prepared to call a bluff, as Akali leaders found in the 1960s to the loss of their credibility when they backed down.

On any given day, there are hundreds of such protests throughout India. Most proceed peaceably, but each carries the potential for violence. The tempo of violence has increased yearly in India. The Government of India officially defines a riot as involving five or more people. The category, which includes brawls, gives little indication of the intensity or seriousness of the dispute, and, obviously, the statistics do not record "official violence"--police repression, lathi charges, police firing. Hundreds of riots are recorded each year, with the widening perception that there is a breakdown of law and order. During the Emergency, periodic outbreaks of violence, like that at Turkman Gate in old Delhi, were repressed with a heavy hand. Rumors, often wildly exaggerated, circulated of police firings and heavy death tolls. After the Emergency was lifted in March 1977, and the euphoria of the Janata victory had subsided, incidents of mob violence again increased, as did the number of police firings. In what Prime Minister Morarji Desai described as a "scourge of violence," India was shaken by daily reports of campus unrest, communal clashes, attacks on untouchables, and police confrontations with landless laborers and striking workers.

THE PRESSURES OF CHANGE

Population

Of all change in India, none is more relentless than population growth. The 1981 census recorded 683 million people, with an annual growth rate of 2.23 percent during the 1970s, a slight increase over the 2.20 percent for the preceding decade. India's leaders, however, can find little consolation in the current growth rate of 2 percent, for at that rate, India's population will reach 1 billion by the year 2000. Indeed, in absolute numbers, India's annual population increase now exceeds that of China. Within the next five years, India's population, if present trends continue, will increase by 74 million. The demands of this expanding population for jobs, housing, services, and above all food will place a heavy burden on India's limited capacity.

Unemployment

The Indian labor force, about 70 percent of which is engaged in agriculture, is estimated to be 294 million and is expected to reach 324 million in 1988, an increase of 30 million in 5 years. Even in the most favorable conditions, employment opportunities have not kept pace with new entrants into the labor market, let alone absorbed the expanding backlog of unemployed and underemployed workers.

Unemployment in India is almost impossible to estimate, as--partularly in the rural sector--so much of it is disguised and partially absorbed into subsistence agriculture, household industry, and "unorganized" services. Unemployment often goes unreported, and available statistics are not reliable. The figures for registered unemployed by no means include all persons seeking jobs; they include some who already have jobs but are in the market for other employment; and they reflect an urban bias. Increases may be due in part to better record-keeping and to a greater willingness on the part of the unemployed to register. Even so, registration statistics provide a measure of change and some indication of the magnitude of the problem. Since 1961, the total registered unemployed has grown annually by 12 percent to the present number of some 20 million. Educated unemployment has grown at an even faster rate--20 percent for graduates and 14.7 percent for the educated in general.

Job prospects for high school and college graduates are grim. Even for many of those who find employment, depressed wages--often below those for manual labor--and jobs "beneath their dignity" breed alienation and discontent. The educated unemployed and those depressed workers who join them in spirit are susceptible to extremist appeals from both the right and the left and are a source of potential urban unrest.

Rural unemplyment blurs into underemployment and is less sharply defined than in the urban sector. Food for Work programs have eased unemployment in targeted areas, but its impact is at best temporary and limited. In India, unemployment in both urban and rural areas continues to grow at a faster rate than population. Industry, which accounts for 11 percent of the labor force (roughly the same as three decades ago), can provide jobs for only about 3 percent of the new entrants into the labor force each year. Agriculture, through extended irrigation and expanded production, has the potential to absorb far greater numbers--but that capacity is not limitless, and pressure on the land grows yearly.

A decade ago, dire prophesies of a green revolution turned red portrayed those areas of India experiencing rapid agricultural growth as the seedbed of rural unrest. The gap between the "haves" and the "have nots" was said to be widening as poor peasants, tenants, and agricultural laborers were turned off the land. Reality has, for the most part, proven otherwise. The green revolution has expanded employment both on the land and in ancillary industry and services. Opportunities draw the unemployed from depressed areas, and agriculturally prosperous Haryana and the Punjab have attracted more than a million workers from other states--some from as far as Bihar. But the pull of prosperity is itself a source of unrest, as "locals" see migrants threatening their jobs, status, and power.

Migration

Migration is an escape valve for rural frustration, but census data reveals relatively little movement. While some 30 percent of the population reside in a locality different from where they were born, three-quarters are women who moved in marriage, following traditional village exogamy, and most moved short distances. Out of state migration is even more limited--less than 4 percent for India as a whole--and much of this involves movement from contiguous districts across state boundaries. But what all-India statistics do not reveal is the impact of selective patterns of migration and their political implications--as the 1983 violence in Assam bears dramatic witness.

Language differences remain a formidable barrier to large scale migration in India, but major cities--notably Bombay, Calcutta, Delhi, and Bangalore--do attract large numbers of migrants. Nearly one-third of the residents of Bombay were born outside the state. Fear of competition with "foreigners" has spawned nativist "sons of the soil" movements in a number of states, including Maharashtra, Karnataka, Tamil Nadu, and Orissa. Recurrent agitation has perhaps slowed down interstate migration, but hard times might spur population movement and sharpen conflict in the competition for employment.

Urbanization

Urbanization in India has been slow, with the percentage of urban population increasing from 11 percent in 1901 to 23.7 percent in 1981. The decade 1971-1981 did experience a marked acceleration in the rate of urban growth (3.86 percent annual growth, as against 3.26 percent for the previous decade), but by world standards, it is still low. Moreover, much of this involves reclassification of villages as towns as they grow in size rather than movement from the countryside into the cities. Also, larger cities typically extend their boundaries as they grow, thus incorporating existing populations.

Over the past three decades, towns and cities of all sizes have grown at similar rates, and India's largest cities--despite widespread belief otherwise--are not distinguished by particularly high rates of growth. Indeed, over the past 30 years, Calcutta's annual rate of growth has averaged only 2.3 percent--hardly more than the population growth rate for the country as a whole. Only Delhi and Bangalore, with the highest rates, are growing because of high rates of migration.

Whether Indian cities have been able to cope with even this relatively low and steady rate of growth may lie in the eyes of the beholder. But the pressure of normal population growth, let alone an increase in the rate of growth, heightens competition for jobs and housing and imposes increasing strain on already burdened urban services.

Urban transportation ranges from reasonably well-served Bombay to the unreliability of Delhi and the chaos of Calcutta. But it is everywhere overcrowded and a source of despair to those who must depend upon it. Virtually every Indian city has major power problems, and "load shedding" may cut off the supply for hours at a time. Calcutta is among the cities most seriously affected, with power cuts for as long as 14 hours a day. The most serious consequence for city residents is lack of water, for it takes power to operate the pumps. A new power station soon to go on stream offers some hope, and Calcutta may be able to meet its energy needs in five years.

Water is critically limited in a number of cities. South Delhi during the summer is often without water for days at a time. Madras--facing water shortages for years--reached a crisis point in 1982-1983 as a result of prolonged drought. The city was put on alternate day rationing, but whole areas of the city were without water at all. The prospect for epidemic diseases--hepatitis, cholera, etc.--mounted as the city's poor, in desperation, drew water from polluted sources. In the fall, 1982, even before the situation became critical, there were "broken pot" demonstrations by women before government offices--the broken clay pots symbolic of their lack of water.

The decline of basic services could well create an explosive situation in India's cities. The capacity of the people to endure urban decay may seem virtually infinite--but there are limits to patience even in Calcutta. When people are prepared to riot over a penny's increase in tram fares, it would be unrealistic to assume that they will accept the breakdown of transportation, power, and water supplies with resignation.

Economic Growth

Over the past 35 years, the Indian economy has grown at an average rate of 3.5 percent, with fluctuations year to year largely as a result of the vagaries of the monsoon. (Taking population growth into account, per capita real national income grew at an annual rate of 1.4 percent.) During the period of the Fifth Plan (1974-79), the economy showed considerable strength, as expanded agricultural production--largely in food-grains--pushed the growth rate to an average of 6.1 percent. In 1979-80, however, as a result of the combined force of severe drought and a doubling in the price of imported oil, GNP declined 4.8 percent. The next two years brought a dramatic recovery, with 7.5 percent growth in 1980-81 and about 5 percent growth in 1981-82. But the vulnerability of the economy to poor monsoons was again revealed in the low 1.8 percent growth in 1982-83.

The moonsoon remains the most important factor in India's prosperity, affecting both agriculture and industry.* A decline in agricultural production resulting from drought throttles industry, both by shortages in the supply of raw products (e.g., cotton) and, even more critically, by a decline in demand for industrial goods. But drought also affects industry directly in power cuts resulting from reduced hydroelectric capacity. (Forty percent of India's total power supply is hydroelectric.) Drastic power cuts in 1982-83, for example, reduced industrial production in Madras by an estimated 30 percent.

Meteorologists and soothsayers alike have sought to determine patterns in monsoon, and some discern a 6-7 year cycle for serious drought, with the next forecast

---

* While the greater part of India depends upon the southwest monsoon, June to September, there are a number of distinct climatic regions in India. The rainy season in Tamil Nadu, for example, is October-November.

for 1985 or 1986. This is more folklore than scientific fact. Drought is recurrent, but a predictable pattern is not clear. Moreover, drought is typically regional rather than all India in scope. Thus, the impact of drought in one area may be offset by sustained agricultural production--or even bumper crops--elsewhere. With a national transportation system, the movement of food into drought-affected areas substantially reduces the possibility of famine. The full impact of drought (and the prospect of famine) has also been reduced by extensive irrigation and by improved dry agriculture. Two successive monsoon failures, however, could have a devastating impact on Indian agricultural production and could require massive import of foodgrains.

Agriculture. Accounting for roughly 40 percent of the GNP and 70 percent of the labor force, agriculture is the foundation of the Indian economy. During the 1970s, foodgrains production expanded rapidly in the Punjab, Haryana, and in regions of other states where the green revolution had taken hold. By 1978-79, total production reached 132 million metric tons--40 percent higher than the average annual production a decade before. So long dependent upon food imports, India had attained marginal self-sufficiency. But in the drought of 1979-80--one of the worst in the century--production fell by nearly 17 percent to 109.7 m. tons, an output still substantially above earlier production levels. India met the shortfall from its own buffer stocks, but the drought underscored India's continuing vulnerability. In the next two years, India regained pre-drought production levels, but in 1982-83, erratic weather--a late monsoon, flooding in some areas, drought in others--again took its toll. Foodgrains production fell to 123 m. tons, substantially below the Plan target of 139-141 m. tons. For the first time in four years, in 1981 and again in 1982, India imported foodgrains to control prices and to replenish buffer stocks. By 1983-84, however, with good monsoons and expected bumper crops of rice, wheat, and pulses, food grains production was projected to be a record 141 m. tons.

Many observers believe that the green revolution has reached a production plateau. Factors accounting for the current stagnation include the high cost of inputs, notably fertilizer, but significantly expanded production will depend upon the development of new high yielding varieties and the extension of irrigation into new areas. While the potential is great, prospects are problematic. Again it is a matter of regional variation. Much of Indian agriculture--particularly in eastern Uttar Pradesh, Bihar, Madhya Pradesh, and Orissa--remains essentially subsistence and feudal in character, and with a separation of ownership from cultivation and risk, it is relatively unresponsive to the pricing incentives of the market economy.

The productivity of Indian agriculture is widely variable among both regions and the types of crops grown. Since 1950, overall agricultural production has grown at an average rate of 2.7 percent annually, a third less than the 4 percent Plan target. Two major factors account for this growth: increases in the area under cultivation and increases in yield per acre. The scope for further expansion of cultivation is now limited, and yields per acre have shown little recent improvement. In consequence, the level of output has slowed to just over 2 percent, barely keeping pace with the population growth rate. Unless the deceleration in agricultural growth can be reversed by a major breakthrough in production, the implications for the economy as a whole are likely to be serious indeed.

Industry. Industry accounts for 24 percent of India's GNP and employs 13 percent of the labor force. Since 1950, industrial production (including mining and power) has grown at an average annual rate of 5.7 percent, well below the Plan targets of 8-10 percent. Moreover, the rate of growth has steadily declined from 7.4 percent for the decade of the 1950s to 6.4 percent for the 1960s and 4.3 percent for the 1970s.

Various factors have contributed to the slowdown in industrial growth--sluggish agricultural production; limited market expansion; infrastructural bottlenecks; labor indiscipline; and government regulations that have stifled initiative, protected inefficiency, and inflated costs. Current planning targets (especially in power, coal, and railways) and the new industrial policy, with selective relaxation of controls and incentives for expanded production, offer a prospect for increased growth. Whether that potential will be achieved is dependent, in part, on the speed with which the international economy recovers from world recession.

International Economy. No nation is impervious to influences from its international environment, and some are more vulnerable than others. The ups and downs of the international economy--commodity prices, the price of oil, market opportunities, access to loans--affect domestic levels of production, employment, prices, and income. They may, in turn, exacerbate social tension, but India--both by the sheer size of its economy and its relatively minimal dependence on the international economy--has been fairly well insulated from the impact of world markets. Petroleum, accounting for some 40 percent of India's total import bill, is the notable exception. Indian leaders may find a scapegoat in the international economy, but it is the domestic economy, conditioned though it may be by its international environment, that directly shapes the life chances of the Indian people.

Inequalities and Disparities

If we are to relate economic growth and the other indicators of change to social unrest and ultimately to political stability, we must disaggregate all-India statistics and look at the wide variability in Indian conditions. All-India data are a mean statistical gloss on social inequality and regional disparity.

India's per capita GNP--$215 in 1982-83--gives little indication of how people really fare. In a predominantly agricultural economy, much of it outside the market, GNP is not a very meaningful indicator of standard of living. But even in these terms, India's poverty is exaggerated by an inappropriate comparison of the price of goods and services between the U.S. and India. A more realistic estimate of per capita income, based on World Bank calculations, is roughly $650.

But all-India averages conceal extreme income inequalities. Statistics are not reliable, but they at least suggest the magnitude of the problem. By Ford Foundation estimates, the top 20 percent of the population appropriates close to half of india's national income; the bottom 40 percent have a share of some 17 percent.

The statistic most widely referred to is the percentage of the population falling below the "poverty line." Using a Government of India income threshold of Rs. 3,500 in 1978-79, 48 percent of the population fell below the poverty line--poor farmers, landless agricultural laborers, and most tribals and Harijans. A number of economists, by various means, draw the line at roughly 40 percent. Perhaps a more accurate assessment of real poverty is in terms of nutrition, and estimates place a third of the population below the minimum required caloric intake. Neither income nor nutritional data stand up to close statistical and methodological scrutiny. Yet by any measure, poverty is the most glaring fact of Indian life. It is both the greatest impetus and the greatest impediment to economic and social progress. But perhaps even more disturbing than the enormity of poverty itself is the fact that the percentage of those below the poverty line is basically unchanging.

Over the past 30 years, real per capita consumption expenditure--perhaps the best index for standard of living in India--has grown at an average of 1.2 percent annually. But even this minimal improvement has steadily declined from the 1.8 percent growth in the 1950s to 1.2 percent in the 1960s and 0.6 percent in the 1970s. Even at these rates, everyone has not benefitted equally: the upper portion of the population has improved its living standard at a rate higher than average, while those at the bottom have at best stood still.

The breakdown of all-India averages reveals sharp regional disparities both between states and within states. This is true for levels of income/development and for rates of growth, such that the gap between more advanced and backward regions continues to widen.

There are no dependable estimates of income by state and district, but various indices provide a fairly consistent reading of inter-state disparities. The Center for Montitoring Indian Economy (CMIE), for example, calculates per capital rural income* at an all-India average of Rs. 545, with a range from 1,158 and 969 for the Punjab and Haryana, respectively, to 434 for Uttar Pradesh and 360 for Bihar. Industrial activity is similarly skewed. Although massive industrial investments in states like Bihar, Madhya Pradesh, and Orissa have reduced disparities, these projects remain "islands in a sea of backwardness."

Disparities exist not only among states, but within most states. It is in terms of districts, not states, that variable levels of development are most clearly revealed. Disparities, whether inter-or intra-state, nourish a heightened sense of relative deprivation. They impose stress on the federal system, both in conflict between state and Center and among the states themselves. Within the state, regional disparities sharpen political conflict in competition for limited investment resources, but they may also engender demands for autonomy and separate statehood.

---

* The per capita rural income is the product of income generated per hectare by the gross cropped area per rural person. CMIE, Indian Economy Since 1950-51, Bombay, November 1981.

Change exacerbates inequalities and disparities because it is experienced differentially. Inevitably, some benefit as others are hurt. It is not in the most backward regions and among the most depressed classes that discontent is most likely to manifest itself. Rather, the sources of social unrest are most likely to be found in those regions and among those classes experiencing more rapid change. This change may involve improvement or decline (real or imagined), either in absolute or relative terms. As in the movement of the earth's tectonic plates, conflict occurs along social fault lines, between groups in competition for the scarce goods of prosperity and power. It occurs most sharply between those groups who are rising and those who feel themselves threatened.

ARENAS OF CONFLICT: SOURCES OF SOCIAL UNREST

Regionalism

From the time of independence, cultural politics--whether in the demands for linguistic states; in the controversy over Hindi as the national language; or in the nativism of the "sons of the soil"--has deepened regional identities. Episodic movements have been both the vehicle of politicization and its inevitable result. The government has typically met cultural demands with vacillation and indecision--sometimes by calculated neglect--only to be followed, in the face of prolonged agitation, by a combined response of force and accomoda-tion.

Regionalism is rooted in India's cultural and linguistic diversity. Projected in geographic terms, it is at the state level both an ethnic and economic phenomenon. It is an expression of heightened political consciousness, expanding participation, and increasing competition for scarce resources. Com-petition by the state is for central financial allocation and Plan investment; for the individual, it involves access to education and jobs. Economic grievances--expressed in charges of unfairness, discrimination, or Center neglect--may be fused with cultural anxiety over language status and ethnic balance. It is this fusion that gives regionalism its potency. Language and culture, like religion, are at the core of an individual's identity and when politicized take a potentially virulent form.

So long as most states were under the Congress umbrella, conflict between states and Center, among states, and within states could be accommodated within the framework of the party. Today regionalism increasingly manifests itself through opposition to Congress--in regional parties like the AIADMK and DMK in Tamil Nadu, the Akali Dal in the Punjab, and the Telegu Desam in Andhra Pradesh and in demands by opposition parties across the ideological spectrum for greater autonomy for the states.

The demand for greater state autonomy--viz., increased financial resources; decentralization of planning; more independence in administrative areas for which states are constitutionally responsible--reflects, at least in part, an aspiration to bring government "closer to the people." The arguments are familiar in the American context, for federalism by its nature is "an invitation to struggle." That struggle in India, however, is aggravated by gross regional disparities, both in levels of development and in rates of growth, such that the gap between more advanced and backward regions continues to widen.

Disparities mean that the struggle between the states and the Center necessarily involves a struggle among states. All states do not share the same interests. More prosperous states, such as the Punjab, may resist redistribution of income among states by the Center, claiming that they are being unfairly exploited or that they do not receive a fair share back for what they contribute to the national economy. Other states, like Assam, Bengal, and Kerala, claim to be victims of Center neglect or discrimination. The more backward states, especially those of the Hindi heartland, look to the Center to redress disparities.

There are cross-cutting interests, and alliances among the states are likely to be ad hoc and temporary. Nevertheless, regionalism, as it expresses itself culturally and in the demand for greater state autonomy, is almost wholly a phenomenon of the non-Hindi speaking periphery, and it is this that continues to arouse fears of national disintegration. The North-South dichotomy has also been underscored by the 1983 Congress losses in Andhra and Karnataka. Indeed, Congress (I) General Secretary C. M. Stephen viewed the March 1983 meeting of the three opposition chief ministers from the South as "highly dangerous because it panders to the rising regionalist tendencies. The meeting," he said, "seems to have set the stage for a north-south fight." The federal relationship involves a permanent tug-of-war, and "rising regionalist tendencies" are a predictable response to increasing centralization in both government and the Congress party under Indira Gandhi. Regionalism will likely impose increasing stress on the federal system as state movements seek to restore greater balance, but it does not pose a threat to the integrity of the Union. While we may be witnessing a regionalization of politics in India, there are countervailing forces of national integration. The development of a national system of communications and the growth and extension of a national market economy have increasingly bound India together. But greater interdependence sharpens consciousness of regional disparities and intensifies the struggle among states to protect and advance their interests. Greater national integration, ironically, may deepen stress on the federal system rather than alleviate it.

To say that India's national integrity is fundamentally secure is not to minimize the serious problems posed by disturbances in the Northeast and in the Punjab. These are strategically sensitive border areas, and prolonged agitation involves basic interests of national security. The Government of India will do whatever it takes to bring these areas under control. In both Assam and the Punjab, the government initially pursued a policy of purposeful neglect ("constructive inaction") in hope that the movements would burn themselves out. Instead, they have grown in intensity. More moderate agitation leaders are pressed by the extremists to harden their positions as options close and compromise becomes more difficult. Neither situation is beyond redemption, but how the government responds will have far-reaching implications for all India.

In the tribal regions of the Northeast, the government has faced periodic armed insurrection from the time of independence. The creation of Nagaland in 1963 and the reorganization of the Northeast in 1972, with the formation of Mizoram, were welcomed by most tribals. On the whole, insurgency has been contained, but guerrilla activity by various underground organizations has not been brought wholly under control. Tribal regions of the Northeast remain under a form of quasi-martial law, reflecting both the continuing danger of unrest and the strategically vulnerable nature of the region. The Chinese no longer provide arms and training to tribal insurgents, but the adjoining region of northern Burma lies effectively outside the control of Rangoon and is both a source of arms into the Northeast and a haven for guerrillas.

In the late 1970s, clashes between the Indian Army and insurgents of the Mizo National Army grew in intensity, and the Mizo National Front, supporting independence for Mizoram, was outlawed in 1979. In Nagaland and Manipur, secessionist groups engage in periodic terrorist attacks against civil and military authorities. In 1982, for example, 20 soldiers were killed in an ambush in Manipur. The attack is believed to have been by the People's Liberation Army (PLA) of Manipur and the Nationalist Socialist Council of Nagaland (NSCN) in a combined operation. The PLA also has ties with the new secessionist Tripur Sena in Tripura. All of these are tiny and with limited support. In 1980, underground elements in Assam, Manipur, Nagaland, Mizoram, Tripura, Meghalaya, and Arunachal Pradesh formed the Seven United Liberation Army (SULA). The organization calls for the creation of an independent federation of the Northeast by armed struggle. At this point, there is no reason to believe that SULA has coordinated the disparate tribal secessionist movements or affected a link between Assamese and tribal discontent--much less that it has gained any substantial support in the Northeast. Nevertheless, the prospect of a united insurgency, however weak it may now be, is unsettling both militarily and politically and gives added urgency to a settlement of the problems of the region.

The situation in the seven states and union territories of the Northeast is aggravated by the incursion of non-tribals onto tribal lands. Tribals--economically, culturally, and politically threatened--have responded in violence. The problem, which goes back well into the British period, has been exacerbated over the past decade as a result of immigration from Bangladesh and, to a lesser degree, from Nepal. In Tripura, the influx of Bengali refugees has shifted the ethnic balance and reduced tribals to a minority. Efforts to protect tribal lands and culture have not been successful, as the slaughter of 350 Bengalis in Tripura in June 1980 bears tragic witness. In Manipur and Meghalaya, student-led agitations against "foreigners"--Bengalis and Nepalese--have taken their lead from the movement in Assam.

The volatile situation in Assam is complicated by the unrest engendered by the occupation of tribal lands by both Assamese and Bengalis. Lalung tribals were responsible for the massacre of more than 1000 Bengali Muslims at Nellie during the February 1983 election violence. But tribal grievances are directed as much against the Assamese, as clashes between Boro tribals and Assamese villagers clearly reveal. The Plains

Tribal Council of Assam, with the probable support of a majority of the tribals, calls for the creation of a separate tribal state of Udayachal to be carved out of Assam.

It is not tribal demands, however, but the "foreigner" issue that is the center of the political turmoil in Assam today. Immigration--primarily involving Bengalis from Bangladesh, most of whom are Muslim--has aroused Assamese fears that they will be reduced to a minority in their own state, if this has not, in fact, already taken place. The issue is political power. The conflict, rooted in the old love-hate relationship between Assamese and Bengalis, has been fueled in this century by Assamese apprehension that their language and culture are threatened. Bengalis have long dominated Assam state administration, but the extension of their control over the economy since independence has stimulated demands--primarily by Assamese youth--for the protection of jobs for "the sons of the soil." Economic concerns have been compounded by grievances that the Center has neglected the state--grievances expressed in the current agitation by such slogans as "Assam is not India's colony."

There is no way in this brief discussion, nor is it really necessary, to recapitulate the history of the Assam conflict. Suffice to say that it was the discovery of "foreigners"--illegal aliens from Bangladesh--on the voter rolls in 1979 that was the catalyst for the movement that has engulfed Assam and confronted the Center with a seemingly intractable problem. Led by the All-Assam Students' Union and joined by other political organizations, including the All-Assam Gana Sangram Parishad, the agitation has mounted in intensity and has come to embrace in its support virtually the whole of the Assamese-speaking population. The leadership of the movement remains in the hands of the moderates, but the Sweecha Sevak Bahini, an extremist wing of the All-Assam Students' Union, proclaims violence against "foreigners" as the only solution to the Assam problem.

The conflict remains essentially ethnic, but it has taken an increasingly communal character as both Hindu and Muslim organizations have exploited mutual anxieties. Over the past three years' agitation, the Jamaat-e-Islami and the Tabligh Jamaat have become increasingly active among Muslims, and the Hindu nationalist Rashtriya Swayamsevak Sangh (RSS), warning that Assam is being overrun by Muslim infiltrators, has dramatically expanded its activities in the state.

Center delay and Assamese intransigence have made a "solution" more difficult, and any settlement is likely to entail troublesome dilemmas. Assuming that a compromise can be reached for the cutoff date on the acceptance of immigrants to legal residence--sometime between 1961 as demanded by the Assamese and 1971 as accepted by the Center--the problems of detection, deportation, and dispersal remain.

Deportation would raise serious difficulties with Bangladesh. Moreover, the border itself is porous, and it would be as difficult to prevent the return of deportees as it has been to stem the flow of continued immigration--although the violence against Bengalis has surely slowed the movement across the border into Assam. Deportation--even if it were physically possible--would likely generate serious communal tension throughout India. "Foreigners" include both Hindus and Muslims, and the forceable return of Hindus (typically described as "refugees") to Bangladesh is widely viewed as unacceptable--and it would be politically explosive. On the other hand, deportation of Muslims alone would deepen insecurity among Indian Muslims generally, no doubt to the electoral cost of the Congress party, and it would surely draw sharp criticism and possible reprisal from the Muslim world.

Dispersal, that is, the resettlement of immigrants outside Assam, has been held out both as an alternative to deportation and as a means to share the refugee burden. But the Constitution protects (with limited exceptions) the free movement of people, and it is unlikely that the immigrants would voluntarily uproot themselves for what would likely be an inhospitable reception elsewhere--although some are now doing so in fear for their lives.

As we look to the next few years, there will be enhanced efforts to prevent any further influx of foreigners--and to return those who do get through. But deportation and dispersal of those already in India are likely to be limited at best. If a settlement between the Assamese and the Center can be reached, it is likely to emphasize protective legislation and Constitutional safeguards for Assamese linguistic, cultural, and political identity. It would include, as the first priority, the detection of "foreigners" and their removal from the voter rolls. The map of the Northeast might again be redrawn, possibly with the creation of the Udayachal tribal state, adjustments in the border with West Bengal, and cutting off the Bengali-speaking Cachar district from Assam to become a Union territory. That Cachar might become a noncontiguous district of

West Bengal is a less likely alternative so long as the Communist Party (Marxist) is in power in Bengal.

In diminished size, an Assamese majority would be more easily assured, and cultural integrity could be buttressed by legislation for Assamese as the medium of instruction in the schools and as the sole language of state administration. Employment reservations and restrictions on the acquisition of property by foreigners would provide greater economic protection. An agreement between state and Center for a more favorable finance and Plan allocation for Assam--possibly involving a "royalty" to the state on petroleum production--would go a long way towards redressing past neglect. All of these raise potential constitutional questions and carry the danger of contagion--that demands for similar protection would be raised in other states or regions.

The settlement of the Assam question is fraught with difficulties, though none are insurmountable. But what if a settlement cannot be reached and the situation continues to deteriorate? The Northeast already has the heaviest concentration of armed forces anywhere in India, and they are augmented by an array of paramilitary units. Given the strategic vulnerability of the Northeast and its importance to the Indian economy as a major source of domestic petroleum, the government, in all likelihood, would be prepared to invoke the emergency provisions of the Constitution and to impose martial law if required to maintain order. Although martial law has never been imposed to quell domestic unrest, disturbed tribal areas of the Northeast have been brought under quasi-military rule by the Armed Forces Act. Under the Act, in any area declared "disturbed," military officers are empowered to shoot to kill, to destroy buildings, to arrest without warrant, and to enter and search any premises without warrant. Barring the most extreme circumstances this power is likely to be used most sparingly and only in those localities where civil authorities are unable to maintain order. But in the most extreme circumstances, the Northeast could become virtually an occupied territory.

The crisis in the Punjab is, like Assam, likely to be long term and far reaching in its implications. It involves a combination of economic, cultural, and religious issues, and at its core is the identity of the Sikh community. The current agitation led by the Akali Dal--the party of Sikh nationalism--is, in part, a continuation of the earlier movement for a Sikh-majority state of Punjabi Suba and for the protection of Sikh culture, religion, and the Punjabi language.

In 1966, the Center yielded to Sikh demands for a separate state, but the creation of the Punjab and Haryana left the question of Chandigarh, the capital, unresolved. The decision, taken in 1970, to award the city to the Punjab, with two northwestern Punjab tehsils (subdistricts) going to Haryana in exchange, was never implemented. This has become one of the major issues of renewed agitation--though the Akalis want Chandigarh now and the matter of the tehsils transfer to be decided by an independent tribunal. Another major issue involves the allocation of river water for irrigation among the Punjab, Haryana, and Rajasthan. The Akalis demand a greater share to meet the vastly greater needs of the Punjab, India's granary. This too would be placed before an independent tribunal.

The Akali demands, embodied in the 1973 Anandpur resolution, include virtually complete autonomy for the state, leaving to the Center only defense, external affairs, communications, currency, and railways. This demand--short of the call for an independent Khalistan sought by the outlawed Dal Khalsa--is more a talking point on Center-state relations than a serious aspiration, at least at this stage. But while few Sikhs today want Khalistan, the line between regional aspirations and support for secession could be crossed as extremists gain greater support. Other Akali demands address various grievances and express a basic concern for the protection of Sikh culture and religious values.

Given the success of the Sikh community, their representation in the public services and in the military, and the wealth of the Punjab (with a per capita income more than twice that of the all-India average), there is little sympathy in India for Sikh claims of discrimination. In addition, much to the outrage of Akali extremists, most Hindus do not regard Sikhism as a separate religion though they do hold the Sikhs in high esteem.

The Center has accepted the more symbolic religious demands, including the declaration of Amritsar as a "holy city" and a ban on the sale of cigarettes and liquor within the vicinity of the Golden Temple. It has also indicated a willingness to consider the establishment of tribunals to adjudicate the territorial and water issues, but not until the agitation itself is called off. (The Center, its representatives have declared, will not negotiate with a loaded gun pointed at its head.) And in March 1983, against the backdrop of rising regionalism but with the situation in the Punjab at the forefront of consideration, the government established a commission under retired Supreme Court

Justice R. S. Sarkaria (a Sikh) to review Center-state relations more broadly.

The problem in the Punjab, as in Assam, is political power, and it is partly a question of ethnic balance. The Sikhs constitute some 52 percent of the population in the Punjab--and the balance is shifting against them as a result of their own success as a community: Entrepreneurial spirit has led to an out-migration of Sikhs (there are more Sikhs in India outside the Punjab than within), while agricultural prosperity in the Punjab has drawn Hindu laborers into the state.*

The political problem of the Punjab involves the exclusion of the Akalis from power. Indeed, when the Akalis were in power during the period of Janata rule at the Center, they did not press their demands. The Akalis had struggled for Punjabi Suba (a separate Punjabi-speaking state), but after their goal was attained in 1966, they found themselves excluded from power except for brief interludes of coalition government. The Akalis themselves were factionally divided and engaged in continuous internecine struggle, but the Sikhs, divided by sect and by caste, were not wholly behind the Akali Dal. Non-Jat Sikhs joined with Hindus in support of the Congress, and given the ethnic balance in the state, the effect was to exclude the majority of Sikhs, represented by the Akali Dal, from power. A succession of Sikh Congress chief ministers ruled the state, but without the confidence of the larger number of their own community. Political stability in the Punjab requires Akali participation in government--either in coalition with Congress or the opposition. The only times that the Akali Dal has headed a Government has been with the coalition support of the former Jana Sangh and the Janata party. The Bharata Janata Party (BJP)--even with its aura of Hindu nationalism--remains a potential ally, but the Sikh-Hindu communal distrust engendered by the current unrest may force the Akalis into political isolation. A settlement of the Punjab crisis and the prospect of shared power with the Congress could split the Akalis, driving a wedge between the moderates and the extremists. But the agitation, while exposing divisions among the Sikhs, has strengthened Sikh revivalism, heightened political consciousness, and broadened the base of Akali support--especially among youth.

---

* Hindu-Sikh communal tension carries a danger for the Sikh farmer, for fewer migrant laborers from Rajasthan, Uttar Pradesh, and Bihar are coming to the Punjab.

There is a basis for compromise in the Punjab, but Center delay, insensitivity, and ineptitude have strengthened the hands of the Sikh extremists. And therein lies the problem, not just for the resolution of the current crisis, but for the future. The Sikh extremists are unlikely to be party to any settlement and may well raise the ante as the Center meets Akali demands. The key figure in the current agitations is Sant Jarnail Singh Bhrindranwale, a zealot, and it is unrest that has been his vehicle to power. Sikh revivalism has been stoked by his portrayal of the "Sikh nation" in danger, and there is widespread fear among Sikhs of merging back into Hinduism and of losing their separate identity. Sikh fundamentalism has been met by heightened Hindu consciousness. The RSS--always strong in the Punjab--has grown in power, and Hindu chauvinists have organized the Punjab Hindu Suraksha Samiti (League for Hindu Protection). Sikh-Hindu relations in the Punjab have never been worse or more volatile than they are today. A relatively minor incident (much less an act of desecration such as occurred in 1982 when the decapitated head of a bullock was placed before a Hindu temple--an act as offensive to Sikhs as to Hindus) could provoke widespread communal violence that could spill over into neighboring Haryana and to Delhi. Sikh-Hindu rioting in Patiala in May 1983 began as a bazaar dispute over noise from a loudspeaker. It ended with police firings and the army on alert to move in.

In October 1983, armed Sikh militants stopped a bus and shot its six Hindu male passengers. The same day, another band of Sikh terrorists killed two officials on a train. None too soon, the central government, invoking emergency powers under the Constitution, dismissed the state Congress ministry and imposed President's Rule. Police and paramilitary forces, with sweeping powers, sought to restore order as the new Governor and his advisers settled in for what is likely to be a long and difficult period of reconciliation.

Violence in the Punjab--whether it be communal or an Akali "holy war" for satisfaction of their demands--raises an ominous prospect. Punjabis--Sikhs and Hindus alike--have a well-earned reputation as a "martial race," and unrest will not be easily controlled. The capacity of police or even paramilitary forces to contol serious violence is limited, and the use of the army, given Sikh representation in the armed forces, would be a matter of great sensitivity.*

Any settlement in the Punjab must involve a substantive, not just symbolic, response to Akali demands if moderate leaders are to retain their credibility among Sikhs and if unrest is to be effectively controlled. But violence in the Punjab is unlikely to be wholly contained. On the defensive, Sikh extremists could continue to use terrorism to maintain visibility as a political force in the Punjab and as a means of drawing support from the most disaffected elements of the Sikh community.

No settlement will come without costs. While Prime Minister Gandhi would surely win kudos in reaching a solution to the problem, it could involve serious political costs to Congress in Haryana and Rajasthan--with implications for continued Congress control at the Center--and could even precipitate violent reaction. For the states involved, the territorial and (even more critically) water issues are critical. Negotiations for a Punjab settlement must involve the affected states, and the settlement must be broadly accepted as fair if unrest is not to spread to other states.

The implications of the Center response, whatever they may be, to Akali and Assamese demands will be far-reaching. Center delay in each case has made settlement both more difficult and more costly--yet failure to reach settlements soon will only deepen discontent in Assam and the Punjab and require ever greater applications of repressive force, surely a tragic consequence for the Indian democratic body politic. On the other hand, yielding to demands under pressure gives an efficacy to violence that carries the danger of contagion. Success in demands for protective legislation for language and culture and for greater state autonomy for Assam and the Punjab is likely to give impetus and strength to regional movements throughout India. This should not, as some fear, bring

---

* Among Sikh grievances is the belief that they are now subject to discrimination in armed forces recruitment. So as to make the military more generally representative of the population, a 1980 government order provides that recruitment be conducted proportionate to population by state rather than by merit strictly. The Akalis allege that the Sikhs, now numbering some 15 percent of the armed forces, will be the principal victims if the rule is applied.

on the disintegration of the nation, but pressure for greater administrative and political decentralization will surely impose stress on relations between the states and the Center and among the states themselves.

The rise of regional parties and the "regionalization" of national parties are expressions of the growth of mass politics in India. They are, as we said earlier, expressions of heightened political consciousness, expanding participation, and increasing competition for scarce resources. The next five years, in parliamentary and state assembly elections, will likely witness a further regionalization of politics. They may also witness new unrest in movements for the protection of language and culture; for greater state autonomy; for the formation of new states or autonomous regions; and for reservtions in education and employment for "sons of the soil."

In Sikkim, quasi-independent until 1975, Nepalis today constitute some two-thirds of the population and hold political power. The interests of the indigenous Lepchas and Bhutias, once guarded by the Chogyal (the former ruler of Sikkim), are now protected by the central government. But the Lepchas and Bhutias feel their culture threatened, and state elections, as in Assam, are likely to heighten anxieties and ferment unrest. Although easily controlled because of its small size, trouble in Sikkim has an international dimension given the state's strategic border location and the refusal of China to recognize Sikkim as a part of India.

The state of Jammu and Kashmir, geographically isolated and with a majority of Muslims, is the subject of international dispute with Pakistan. For this reason alone, any unrest in Kashmir is likely to be viewed in New Delhi with particular alarm. Kashmir has a special status under the Constitution, with an autonomy that distinguishes it from all other states. This status, the result of the conditions on which Kashmir acceded to the Union in 1947, is jealously guarded, and any action by the Center or by Kashmiri politicians perceived as diminishing that autonomy would deepen anti-Indian feeling. Some Kashmiris are avowedly pro-Pakistan and others, no doubt, are sympathetic, but few Kashmiris would trade their special status under the Indian Constitution for Punjabi domination in Pakistan. Yet most Kashmiris do not regard themselves as Indian, and the ruling party of the state, the National Conference, faces renewed pressure from the militant Muslim Jamiat-i-Islami and from those who call for the liberation of Kashmir from "Hindu India."

In the June 1983 assembly elections in Jammu and Kashmir, the Congress(I) party, as expected, lost to the incumbent National Conference. Although the Congress has some following among Kashmiri Muslims, the National Conference holds the allegiance of most Muslims. In the Hindu-majority constituencies of Jammu, however, Congress emerged as the winner--in part, some believed, because of the tacit support of the RSS. In its campaign appeal to Hindu sentiment, in which Indira Gandhi joined, the Congress deepened Hindu-Muslim enmity in the volatile state and drove state chief minister Farooq Abdullah--once a potential ally--firmly into the opposition camp. Election violence in both the Jammu and Kashmir regions was widespread, and in the capital of Srinagar, arsonists gutted the Congress headquarters. With the National Conference victory came a volley of Congress accusations that the polling had been rigged. In the following months, Congress-led agitation against the Farooq Government became increasingly serious, with a police-firing in January 1984 that left at least three Congress protesters dead. From Farooq's perspective, it was clear that the agitation was designed to precipitate central intervention and the imposition of President's Rule on the pretext of a breakdown of law and order within the state.

Within Jammu and Kashmir, the two religious communities are geographically as well as politically polarized. Jammu, the less populous of the two regions of the state, is predominantly Hindu, of whom the Dogras are the dominant group. Dogra pride is enhanced as the community of the former maharajahs of Jammu and Kashmir. Incipient Dogra "nationalism," fed by Hindu resentment against Kashmir's Muslim majority, has raised the demand for a separate state of Jammu. Although the demand at this point does not have great support, communal tension could enliven the movement.

The cultural distinctiveness and economic and social disparities that nourish regionalism at the state level are found within a number of states. With heightened political consciousness and increased competition, demands for the creation of new states or for autonomous regions within states may be the catalyst for social unrest. Separate statehood movements, varying greatly in support and intensity exist, throughout India. Frequently involving depressed regions, these include tribal areas of Bihar, Orissa, and Madhya Pradesh; the hill districts of Bengal; the eastern districts of Uttar Pradesh; the Vidarbha region of Maharashtra; and the Telengana region of Andhra. Of a somewhat different character is the demand by some in Haryana for adjacent districts of Rajasthan and Uttar Pradesh so as to create Vishal (greater) Haryana.

Such movements tend to be episodic, but they can be virulent, as the now dormant Telengana movement bears witness. Recent demands include those by Nepali-speakers in northern West Bengal for a separate Gurkhaland and by the Tibetan Buddhists of Ladakh, in Kashmir, for a Union Territory under central administration. Most serious, however, is the renewed demand for the creation of a tribal Jharkhand state co the Chota-Nagpur region of southern Bihar and the contiguous tribal districts in Orissa.

The forces of nationalization and centralization have reinforced in the non-Hindi states a consciousness of their distinct cultural identity. With it has come a plethora of chauvinistic movements, rivaled perhaps only by the chauvinism of the Hindi region itself. Such movements are nourished by heightened competition for resources aggravated by slow economic growth, by widening regional disparities, and the sense of relative deprivation they inevitably engender.

Nativist "sons of the soil" movements have arisen in regions where culturally distinct migrants from outside the state are perceived as blocking opportunities for "locals" to advance. It is almost wholly urban and expresses the frustrated aspirations of an expanding, educated lower-middle class. A number of states--Maharashtra, Karnataka, Tamil Nadu, West Bengal--have enacted legislation providing for educational and employment preferences for "sons of the soil." The most virulent movements have been the Shiv Sena in Bombay and the Kannada Chaluvaligars in Bangalore. Although now quiescent, they could again erupt in violence. Under pressure of competition for jobs, similar movements could grow in Gujarat or in Orissa, where the cultural Neel Chakra ("Blue Wheel") movement is gaining support. As educational opportunities continue to expand and aspirations rise, social conflict is likely to deepen.

Communalism

India was born in communal conflict, and Hindu-Muslim tensions are nurtured today by the bitter memories of partition, by jealousy and fear. Several hundred incidents of communal violence are offically reported every year. Beginning in the 1970s, the number of reported communal clashes declined, as did casualties. But by the end of the decade, it was on the increase, and in 1982, the Home Ministry reported 474 communal incidents--the highest since 1970--with 238 persons killed.

Most begin as a minor incident--typically a dispute arising over a Hindu procession near a mosque--but however minor in themselves, they have frequently turned into major riots. The pattern is familiar, from rumors to bloodshed, with police intervention and then accusations of police excesses. This is usually followed by more clashes, often over a fairly wide area. Then, like a plague of locusts, it passes and the situation returns to "normalcy."

Communal riots are fueled by change and by "the revolution of rising frustration," the product of the widening gap between expectation and achievement. Their sources are less religious than economic, and though there has been disputed evidence of organized preparation among both Hindus and Muslims in recent riots, they are essentially anomic, cathartic releases of rage.

Communal violence is primarily an urban phenomenon--perhaps because most rural Muslims are too weak to pose a threat or to offer resistence. Rioting tends to be ad hoc, intermittent, and normally limited to a single city or locality--and it thus is manageable with sufficient application of force. The possibility of widespread communal conflict (on the scale of the violence following partition, for example), even if unlikely, cannot be ruled out if Hindu-Muslim tensions deepen, and it would be very difficult to bring under control even with the full force of the army. Moreover, widespread rioting would have serious international implications for India, not only with Pakistan and Bangladesh, but with the Muslim world more generally.

That communal conflict involves one community against another rather than against the government reduces the threat communalism poses to political stability as such. Ineptitude in handling a riot, either in failure to take precautions or in excessive force in putting it down, however, can seriously embarrass the Government, state or Center, and can be very costly politically.

Government enters into the communal equation in a number of ways, and its policies as they touch each community differentially may be a source of resentment and discontent. Muslims, like other minorities in India, look to government as their protector, and they have, with the notable exception of 1977, given their support to Congress. Indeed, with a decisive vote in many closely-contested constituencies, Muslims are a crucial element in Mrs. Gandhi's base of support. That support can no longer be taken for granted. Muslims are today more politically conscious, more assertive. While the vast majority of Muslims remain backward and depressed in rural areas, there is a rising urban Muslim middle class, mainly small businessmen and entrepreneurs. New prosperity for many Muslim families has also come through remittances from the Gulf. The money sent home by Indian Muslims working in the Gulf has provided capital for the rising entrepreneurs, but it has also gone into the purchase of land, new houses, and the construction and improvement of mosques and Muslim schools.

Not surprisingly, the Muslim's visible success has aroused jealousy among Hindus who have done less well or who now feel threatened by Muslims who expect their rightful share of the economic pie--a pie that is not growing fast enough to satisfy the expanding members of claimants pushing up from below. The communal riots of recent years--in Moradabad, Meerut, Baroda, Travancore, Hyderabad--have been fed by economic competition and resentment.

Increased communal tension has, despite their new confidence, deepened the Muslim sense of vulnerability, and many Muslims feel that the government--and Congress--has betrayed them. Muslim voting is increasingly anti-government, with the police often the target of their enmity. In November 1982, 44 Muslim members of Parliament, drawn from various political parties including the Congress (I), submitted a petition to the Prime Minister stating that "the Muslim minority is losing faith in the neutrality of the administration and the credibility of the Government" as a protector of India's weaker sections. They called for a ban on all paramilitary and extremist organizations "preaching communal hatred," specifically naming the Rashtriya Swayamsevak Sangh (RSS) and the Vishwa Hindu Parishad.

Muslims have been the principal victims of communal rioting, both in numbers (with three times as many casualties as among Hindus) and in a deepened sense of insecurity. But ironically, Hindus, with 82 percent of the population, are reacting to new Muslim assertiveness like a threatened minority. Many Hindus have long resented government measures to protect and uplift the Muslim community. During the 1980 elections, there were rumors--wholly without substance--that Mrs. Gandhi had secretly promised the Muslims "separate electorates," and within Congress circles there was fear of a Hindu backlash. It did not occur, but in December 1982, in the course of the election campaigns in Andhra and Karnataka, the Prime Minister felt compelled to dismiss as ridiculous the allegation that she had reduced Hindus to the status of third class citizens. In June 1983, during the communally sensitive assembly elections in Jammu and Kashmir, Mrs. Gandhi reached out for the Hindu vote, winning the support of even RSS stalwarts. Indeed, many political observers saw a new Congress electoral strategy in North India based on an explicit appeal to Hindu sentiment--a dangerous game both for Mrs. Gandhi and for the integrity of India as a secular state.

The rise of Islamic fundamentalism in Iran, Pakistan, and Bangladesh has heightened Hindu consciousness, and fear of resurgent Islam in India has been deepened by the issue of religious conversion. In February 1981, more than one thousand Harijans in the village of Meenakshipuram in Tamil Nadu converted <u>en masse</u> to Islam. Picked up by the press, reports of "mass conversions" stirred fear of Hinduism in danger. The RSS alleged that a "foreign hand" was behind the conversions and that the goal was political power by expanding the numerical strength of the Muslim community. Gulf money, in its view, is today's Khyber Pass through which Muslims seek to gain domination over India.

The Director for Scheduled Castes and Scheduled Tribes, Government of India, Madras, in his report on Meenakshipuram concluded that "long standing social discrimination based on untouchability and indifference of the Hindu society at large towards them was the main cause for the conversions." It was not possible, he stated, to say "anything categorically about the involvement of foreign money."

The conversion issue has activated communal groups among both Muslims and Hindus. The revivalist Jamaat-e-Islami, banned during the Emergency, has enjoyed a resurgence since 1977. Along with activists of the Jamaat and the Indian Union Muslim League, proselytising organizations, such as the Ishatual Islam Sabha and the Tabligh Jamaat, have been associated with the Harijan conversions. These groups are believed to have increasing contact with Islamic fundamentalist groups in the Middle East and to have received financial assistance from Gulf countries and from pan-Islamic organizations.

The RSS and the Arya Samaj have responded by a call for a ban on conversions to Islam and Christianity, and the Vishwa Hindu Parishad has set about to reconvert the

Harijans at Meenakshipuram and, more broadly, to bring Indian Muslims back into the Hindu fold. The Parishad, closely associated with the RSS but with a wider base of support, was founded in 1964 by the former Maharana of Udaipur. It was the Meenakshipuram conversions, however, that spurred its activities and brought it to national prominence. Meenakshipuram was also the catalyst for the formation of the Virat Hindu Samaj by Dr. Karan Singh, former Maharaja of Jammu and Kashmir. Established in 1981 as an umbrella organization for various Hindu groups, its major aim is consolidation and reform directed toward a Hindu renaissance.

A ban on religious conversion--though not reconversion (paravartan)--is at the top of the agenda for most of these organizations. The states of Orissa and Madhya Pradesh have already enacted legislation, upheld by the courts, curbing conversions "by inducements and other unlawful means." There is likely to be increasing pressure for similar legislation in other states and at the Center. The anti-conversion bills are directed as much against the Christians and Muslims and have aroused anxieties within the Christian community. Christian tribals in the Northeast (majorities in the states of Nagaland and Mizoram) view the Arunachal Freedom of Religion Act, 1978, as an attempt to restrict missionary activity.

The Meenakshipuram conversions in raising Hindu consciousness and organizational activity in Tamil Nadu have sharpened Hindu-Christian conflict and contributed to the 1982 communal violence in the heavily Christian Kanyakumari district.

The volatility of religious sentiment--and its potential impact on electoral politics--was witnessed in November 1983 in the uproar over reports that vanaspati, the vegetable oil that is the staple of Indian cooking, was being adulterated by cheap imported beef tallow. Hindu revivalists, leading mass demonstrations, denounced the polution, invoking the memory of the greased cartridges that spurred the Mutiny of 1857. The opposition parties attacked Prime Minister Gandhi for her failure to safeguard the purity of the nation, as Congress leaders, in turn, accused the former Janata Government of having approved the beef tallow imports in the first place. In an atmosphere of growing militancy and confrontation, the Vishwa Hindu Parishad launched a series of marches--"ekatmata yagya yatras," or soul union pilgrimages--across the length and breadth of India. Mrs. Gandhi warned of the "rabid communal forces" behind the marches and the threat they posed in dividing the nation along religious lines.

Untouchability and Caste Violence

Hindu revivalism has a confrontational character, but in their commitment to reform, these organizations--the Arya Samaj, the Vishwa Hindu Parishad, the Virat Hindu Samaj, and the RSS--seek the eradication of untouchability as a scourge on Hindu society.

Since India's independence, Harijans (untouchables) have been victims of far greater violence than anything suffered by Muslims. But violence against Harijans, endemic over much of India, tends to be ad hoc, highly localized, and overwhelmingly rural. It is thus difficult to control and often passes publicly unnoticed. In recent years, there has been a marked increase in reported attacks upon Harijans. This may be due, in part, to more vigorous press coverage and to a greater willingness among Harijans to file complaints. But most observers believe that the reported increase is not a statistical artifact and that caste violence has, in fact, increased. In any case, the 10,000 to 15,000 incidents officially reported are but a fraction of the acts of violence committed against Harijans each year.

The sources of caste violence are fundamentally economic, and the attacks on Harijans are at once vengeance against those who have sought to assert their rights and better their condition and a warning to others not to stray from their traditionally assigned roles. The increase in violence is a measure of economic and social change--of the rise of Harijans through education, greater political consciousness and participation, and increasing economic and political power.

In rural areas, while the vast majority of Harijans continue to suffer severe disabilities, an increasing number have improved their position through government economic programs, land redistribution (however meager), and various benefits, concessions, and reservations. In Bihar and eastern Uttar Pradesh, for example, among the most economically and socially depressed regions of India, caste conflict has sharpened in competition for scarce resources. Typically involving disputes over land and wages, conflict is primarily between the "Backward Castes" (small peasants--Jats, Ahirs, Yadevs--who have gained a toehold on prosperity and fellow caste tenants who see the prospect of improvement) and upwardly mobile Harijans. In asserting their greater independence, Harijans often meet violence from those of higher caste--beatings by hired thugs; the destruction of crops and property; the burning of huts; rape, murder, and massacre. Such attacks number in the thousands each year, although they are perhaps fewer today than they were during the Janata years (1977-1979), when the backward castes regarded the rise of Charan Singh, their political mentor, as their chance to put the Harijans down once and for all.

Some 90 percent of all Harijans live in villages, but those in cities also face animosity and violence. Rather than isolated attacks on Harijans, caste riots characterize urban conflict. Like communal riots, they feed on frustration and grievances. Caste Hindus among the educated lower middle class typically view the Harijans with whom they now compete as a "pampered" lot. Any improvement in the lot of the Harijans is seen as a threat to the status quo and to their own potentially vulnerable position. The upper castes particularly resent the government policies of "protective discrimination" (affirmative action) reserving a percentage of public service jobs and admissions into universities and medical schools for Harijans.

Caste riots over reservations have occurred in urban areas of Bihar, but it has been in the more "progressive" states of Gujarat and Maharashtra that rioting has been most serious. (Gujarat also has the dubious distinction of leading India in the number of communal riots.) Of all the states in India, Gujarat has both the highest percentage of literacy among Harijans (28 percent) and the highest percentage of Harijan urbanization (27 percent). Together, they provide a fair measure of social mobility, and in the reservation riots in Gujarat in 1981, violence was greatest in those districts where Harijan literacy and urbanization were highest. The caste riots in Maharashtra three years earlier reflected a similar pattern.

Caste conflict in India, both urban and rural, is most intense among those who are closest in class terms and who find themselves in competition for scarce resources, for educational and employment opportunities. It is not so very different from the racial conflict in the United States that pits lower middle class whites against upwardly mobile blacks. In India, as the lot of the Harijan improves, as they become more assertive in demanding their rights, conflict is likely to become more intense, and it will be sharpest in those areas and among those groups where social mobility is highest.

Intermittent caste violence is unlikely to threaten political stability, but former Uttar Pradesh chief minister Vishwanath Pratab Singh was convinced that Harijan atrocities in U.P., such as the 1981 massacre of 24 Harijans in the village of Deoli, were part of a conspiracy against the state Congress administration. Opposition leaders certainly lost no time in seeking to discredit U.P.'s Congress (I) ministry for failure to protect Harijans, a critical element in the Congress party's base of support, and politicians of both the Government and the opposition accused each other of complicity in the killings.

There is a growing consciousness, even militance, among Harijans--as there is among India's tribals--but, with few resources and divided among themselves, they lack organization. The Dalit Panthers, drawn from urban educated and unemployed Harijan youth, is largely limited to Maharashtra and has never gained wide support. Efforts by the Communists to mobilize rural Harijans have been limited in success and perhaps even half-hearted. But the 100 million Harijans who make up a major portion of India's landless poor have been likened to a sleeping giant. Once aroused, they may shake the earth--but that prospect does not lie on the near horizon.

Agrarian Unrest

India's disparities are no more evident than in the highly variable conditions of Indian agriculture and in the nature of agrarian relations. In most regions of India over the past three decades, the center of political power has shifted from the landlords and upper peasants of the traditionally dominant castes to peasant cultivators of the middle castes. Once the high caste absentee landlords were effectively eliminated in the early 1950s, the principal political struggle until the mid-1960s was between the upper and the middle peasantry. As the middle peasants--many from the "Backward Castes"--consolidated their power, they formed an alliance with small peasants based on caste ties and reinforced by economic incentive. These middle and small peasants, numerically preponderant, have sought to resist the challenge from below by sharecroppers and landless laborers, most of whom are Harijans.

Land reform has been subverted in most states, and ceilings on land holdings frequently remain unenforced, for the state governments are unwilling to alienate their base of support among the peasantry. Kerala and, more recently, West Bengal have implemented modest reform measures, but the prospects for substantial land reform are minimal. The major hope for change is in the extension of the market economy and expanded production through the green revolution in irrigation, fertilizers, and high-yielding varieties. In most of the areas brought under the green revolution, while the gap between landowning cultivators and landless laborers may have widened, substantial improvement in the conditions of the lower classes and greater employment opportunities have taken the immediate edge off agrarian conflict.

Agitation by poor peasants and landless laborers has been sporadic and uncoordinated. In the late 1960s, inspired by the 1967 tenant revolt in the Naxalbari distict of West Bengal, Indian Maoists--"Naxalites"--called for armed revolution in the countryside. In pockets of West Bengal, Bihar, Kerala, Tamil Nadu, and Andhra (Srikakulam district), radical students joined the landless, Harijans, and tribals in terrorism and insurgency. Police and paramilitary operations crushed the uprisings within a year. What was left of the Naxalite movement was divided into more than a dozen factions. Through the 1970s, there were spasmatic outbreaks of violence, and in 1980, an upsurge of Naxalite activity in various parts of rural India was brought quickly under control.

It is in the more backward areas, such as eastern U.P. and Bihar, where the long term potential for unrest is greatest--but here too repression weighs most heavily. The larger region of eastern India sinks yearly deeper into poverty, and severe drought in 1982-83 has made the situation even more critical. But the long-awaited uprising has yet to occur. Bihar is locked in conflict between the rising backward castes and the upper caste non-cultivating landowners. The feudal character of the state is reinforced as the two blocs unite against the landless Harijans and tribals pushing up from below. A decade ago, northern Bihar was a center of unrest; today it is southern Bihar. Here increasingly aggressive Harijans, organized by former Naxalities, and more politically conscious tribals present the prospect for increased rural violence in the near future. But lacking an effective organizational base, there is little prospect for widespread or sustained agrarian revolt in India.

Rural unrest today is most pronounced in the protests and agitations staged by capitalist farmers. Constituting some 15 percent of all rural landholding households, they own 60 percent of the cultivatable land and, as producers of surplus, are the principal source of food and agricultural raw material for India's cities and industries. These farmers of the green revolution are dependent upon modern agricultural inputs--fertilizers, pesticides, electricity, and diesel for irrigation pumps and tractors--and are caught between rising input costs (due mainly to the price of petroleum) and low returns on cash crops.

In 1980, in the Nasik district of Maharashtra, Sharad Joshi--an international bureaucrat-economist turned cultivator--organized the Shetkari Sanghatana and launched what was to become "the farmers' movement." The issue in Maharashtra was the price for onions, sugar, and cotton. In demands for higher agricultural support prices and lower input costs, Joshi's farmers blocked roads with tractors and gheraoed officials--and won basic concessions from the state government. Taking the lead from the movement in Maharashtra, the Tamil Nadu Agriculturalists Association laid down a series of demands--higher prices for paddy, writing off loans, and a moratorium on electricity payments--and staged a violent agitation that left 8 dead and 8,000 arrested. In Gujarat, the Krishi Rakshak Sangh blocked roads and railways and battled police. The demands here were for better groundnut and milk prices. In Karnataka, the demand was for higher prices for foodgrains and tobacco.

By early 1981, agitation had spread to the more advanced regions of eight states, but the movement lacks over-arching organization and remains closely bound to the interests of particular districts. Moreover, while Joshi--who is now seeking to form a farmer-peasant party in Maharashtra--proclaims rural solidarity, the movement is primarily that of the more affluent farmers. It has not been able to bridge the conflicts of caste and class--between the upper and backward castes, between landowning peasants and landless laborers. The government has played one group off against the other. While expressing sympathy for the high risk situation of the farmer, the Center has resisted as inflationary demands for higher price supports. It has sought to avoid large agricultural subsidies and to achieve balance between incentive supports for farmers and price stability for consumers. From the farmers' perspective, it is a policy that favors the cities at the expense of the countryside.

The farmers' movement is often described in terms of urban-rural conflict, but India's industrial and agricultural economies are increasingly interdependent. Agriculture keeps industry on a short leash, both as a source of raw produce and as a market for manufactured goods--tractors, fertilizers, pumps, etc. And it is in rural prosperity that industry finds its potential for an expanding market for a wide range of consumer products. Similarly, while farmers might try to hold the cities hostage for higher prices, they too would be victims of the cycle of inflation. Agricultural prosperity in India cannot be sustained by subsidies. For all the urban-rural disparities in wealth and income, farmers have an increasing stake in industrial growth and urban prosperity. Not only are cities the market for agricultural surplus, but, as reflected in the sale of stocks in recent years, industry has begun to attract investment by more prosperous farmers.

The farmers' movement has lost much of its momentum, but the frustrations that brought it into being remain. The various agitations have demonstrated the farmers' capacity to bring enormous pressure on the government both at the state and Center.

Urban Unrest

Cities have been the locus of unrest in various regional movements, sons of the soil and linguistic agitations, in caste conflict over reservations, and in communal tension between Hindus and Muslims. Such unrest has been episodic and essentially phenomena of the vulnerable middle class. The urban poor, unorganized, without leadership and resources, have been less able to express their discontent. Theirs are lives of quiet desperation. But among the poor, especially in the slums that surround the major cities, are migrants from the countryside for whom the city represents opportunity and a chance for a better life.

Urban unrest is manifest most intensely among those who feel threatened by sharpened competition for jobs and among those who have suffered losses--real or imagined--relative to others. As educational opportunities widen the number of claimants for "middle class" jobs and raise aspirations in a situation of scarcity, unrest is likely to increase. Urban unemployment continues to grow, and unemployment among the educated grows at an even faster rate. The frustration of the educated unemployed and of students for whom prospects are dismal is an especially volatile ingredient in the urban situation.

Students have been at the forefront of protest movements and agitations from the time of independence. If the urban poor are politically inarticulate, students are loudly vocal. But while organized, they often lack direction and coherence. "Student indiscipline" is endemic, and at any time, a major portion of India's colleges and universities are closed because of campus disorder. "Indiscipline" embraces a wide range of disruptive activities, from demonstrations and strikes relating to university specific demands to involvement in political movements of the larger community.

Students looking for a cause--as, for example, in protests over the firing of a menial employee--have paralyzed universities. Campus disorder has become increasingly violent, with gheraos and physical attacks on administrators and faculty, the murder of a Vice Chancellor, and terrorism of fellow students. Warring student factions are armed with automatic weapons on some campuses in North India and at Benaras Hindu University, one of the worst afflicted, the hostels are believed to be virtual arsenals. By no means everyone involved is actually a student. Aligarh Muslim University, the scene of frequent turmoil, recently discovered that it had considerably more "students" living in the hostels than were formally enrolled in the university. Every campus has a sizeable number of hangers-on, a lumpen element readily activated for protest.

There are more than 4 million students registered in some 4,000 colleges and universities in India. Most students are not politically involved, but the activists provide a reservoir from which political parties and protest movements can draw leadership and support. Campuses have long been centers of political opposition, and student government elections are usually fought out along party lines. The RSS student movement, the Akhil Bharatiya Vidyarthi Parishad, is now the largest student organization in India. The Congress, the BJP, the Communist party (Marxist) all have their campus affiliates. At Delhi University, for example, the RSS-BJP student organization dominates campus politics, while across the city at Jawaharlal Nehru University, the Marxists struggle for control of the student union.

The campus, however, has rarely contained student politics or unrest. Activated by a mixture of idealism and frustration, students have sought a wider arena. They have played a central role in the anti-Hindi agitation in Tamil Nadu in the mid-1960s; in the Telengana movement; and in the Naxalite violence in West Bengal and Andhra. The All-Assam Students' Union spearheads the current movement against "foreigners" in Assam. Students were the major force in bringing down state Governments in Orissa in 1964 and in Gujarat in 1974. Student discontent in Gujarat initially focused on increased hostel fees, but the agitation widened as the student "Society for Reconstruction" tapped statewide economic and political grievances. In the wake of the violence following the Gujarat Bandh, or general strike, in January 1974, the Congress Government resigned and President's Rule was declared.

Because of their concentration on the campus, their frustration and political consciousness, and their availability, students are readily mobilized. With campus discontent again on the rise, students can be expected to be a continuing factor in urban unrest, and if the past is prologue, they will likely play a major role in new regional and cultural movements.

Strikes have been a contributing factor to urban unrest and in critical industry, such as coal and rails, can pose a serious threat to the national economy and, by implication, to political stability. The Government of India devotes considerable concern to industrial relations and handles labor disputes with a combination of the carrot and a stick.

No more than 10 million workers--less than 4 percent of India's labor force--are even nominally unionized. But because they are organized and are situated in strategic sectors of the economy, they command considerable power--if not to influence, at least to disrupt. There are some 25,000 unions in India, most tied directly to political parties and affiliated with one of the major trade union federations. The Indian National Trade Union Congress (INTUC), the largest federation, is associated with the Congress (I) and has often served as an arm of government labor policy. The fastest growing union is the Bharatiya Mazdoor Sangh (BMS), with ties to the BJP. Much of its growth has come at the expense of the two Communist party federations--the CPI's All India Trade Union Congress (AITUC) and the CPM's Centre of Indian Trade Unions (CITU). One of the more militant unions is the faction-ridden socialist Hindu Mazdoor Sabha.

Indian law, permitting any seven persons the right to form a union and to raise any dispute, has contributed to the proliferation of unions and to the fragmentation of the trade union movement. Inter-union rivalry has itself been a major factor in fermenting labor unrest, and this is most evident in the activities of independent labor leader Dr. Datta Samant.

Samant, a former Congress (I) politician, came to the labor scene in Bombay in the mid-1970s and infused the trade union movement with new militancy. Through his aggressive tactics and by his early record of success in winning wage increases, Samant gained control of hundreds of unions, with membership totaling some 600,000 (figures vary upwards of 1.5 million), nearly all in the Bombay industrial region. Since 1977, he has organized more strikes and negotiated more settlements than any other union leader in India. He gives the employer two options--either meet his often exorbitant wage demands or face closure by strike. The strikes led by Samant have often been both violent and prolonged. The Bombay textile strike--the longest major strike in India's history--dragged on for nearly two years. Involving 250,000 workers at its peak, the strike all but paralyzed the textile industry. Workers gradually began to return to the factories, and the final collapse of the strike in 1983 reduced Samant's influence and underscored the strength of industry and government in relation to labor unions. Moreover, Samant's defeat in the May 1982 Thane (Bombay) parliamentary bye-election set back his ambition to start a new political party.

Wages are the central issue in most industrial disputes. Wages vary greatly across industries and regions, but, on the whole, unionized workers are a "privileged class," commanding wages 10 to 15 times that of their rural counterparts. Their wages, however, have barely kept up with inflation over the past decade, and workers will continue to press for increases. Yet for all the rhetoric, the number of strikes, and the millions of man-hours lost, Indian industrial labor is basically conservative. Surrounded by poverty and unemployment, they at least have jobs--and few are prepared to risk losing them. Indeed, the high costs of the textile strike for the workers involved may be a banner of warning.

The government has the capacity to control labor unrest--as its suppression of the 1974 railway strike dramatically demonstrated. In 1981, the government enhanced its power through the Essential Services Maintenance Act (ESMA). The act empowers the government to ban strikes in such crucial sectors of the economy as defense, rails, coal, power, steel, fertilizers, and irrigation. In response to the act, labor unions associated with eight opposition parties, ranging from the BJP to the CPM, united in a call for nationwide one-day strike on January 19, 1982. Some 6,000 strike leaders were taken into preventive detention and arrested under the very law they were protesting. At least 12 people were killed in confrontations with police, but the opposition's challenge to Mrs. Gandhi went largely unobserved. Except for Calcutta, where the Marxist West Bengal Government supported the strike, it was for the most part business as usual.

Labor statistics do not point toward an upsurge in industrial unrest, but in coming years, in both factory and office, there may well be an increase in industrial slow-downs, "pen down" strikes (where people come to work but do nothing), "mass casual leave" (where people simply stay home), and lightening one-day strikes of the sort that plague Italy. If these labor protests do not entail mass agitation and violence, they take their toll economically in reduced productivity and contribute to the daily chaos of urban life in India.

Election Violence

Elections in India have generally been orderly. Given the size of the elections--the world's largest--instances of rioting and violence have been remarkably low. During the 1971 campaign, however, West Bengal erupted into widespread violence. Incidents, arising both from Naxalite activity and CPI-CPM warfare, led the press to write of "the great Calcutta killings." The Bangladesh crisis in December 1971 provided the opportunity for military suppression of Bengal's political violence.

In preparing the way for Mrs. Gandhi's return to power, Sanjay brought a number of young toughs into the Youth Congress--portending, many feared, violent election clashes. But the 1980 elections were conducted with only scattered incidents of "booth capturing" and violence. The situation in Assam--the anti-foreigner movement having just gotten underway--led the Government to postpone elections. In February, 1983, with the situation surely no better, elections were held under the guard of some 90,000 paramilitary troops and auxiliary police--too few, it proved, to control the ensuing violence.

In the earlier state assembly elections in 1982 and in Andhra and Karnataka in January 1983, there were isolated instances of violence, and during the Andhra campaign, there were riots and police firing in Hyderabad. Election violence in June 1983 in Jammu and Kashmir was the preface to continued political unrest in the state. But while elections may heighten tension, there is no apparent trend toward greater election violence. Nevertheless, whether forthcoming parliamentary elections can be peaceably conducted--or conducted at all--in Assam and the Punjab, and perhaps even Jammu and Kashmir, is problematic.

LAW AND ORDER

Over the past five years, Indian newspaper articles and editorials have described an increasing breakdown of law and order. But press coverage of specific incidents of violence tends to project a national image of widespread unrest that is not wholly true. Most of India's countryside and cities have a relatively low level of unrest and violence. Indeed, it may be legitimately asked whether violence has increased or whether there is simply more public awareness of its scope and intensity. But while levels of violence may be exaggerated, no region is wholly immune, and in some areas violence is a problem of serious consequence.

In much of the Hindi heartland--Bihar, major portions of Uttar Pradesh, and parts of Madhya Pradesh and Rajasthan--gang rule and dacoity (banditry) are on the rise. In this region of North India, country-made guns and automatic weapons are widespread, and the level of violence--official and non-official--marks a drift toward anarchy.

Rival gangs of armed young toughs, typically with some education and a strong dose of Hindi film romance, operate with impunity in many districts, smaller towns, and industrial areas. They are used by political parties to raise funds, intimidate opponents, and for protection against similar tactics by other groups. Often in connivance with police officials, they engage in various criminal activities and hold local areas under mafia-like control. The term mafia has come to be used in India most frequently in connection with the politically-linked gangster domination of the Dhanbad coalfields in Bihar.

There has been a rise in reported dacoit activity in North India, particularly in Uttar Pradesh--not only in robbery, but in its use against assertive Harijans and political rivals. For centuries, dacoity has been endemic in districts of southwestern UP, but today the gangs are extending their influence throughout the state and have established ties with police and politicians of all parties. In a vow to rid the state of its dacoit menace, chief minister V. P. Singh in the fall of 1981 unleashed official violence in a series of police "encounters" that left 310 alleged dacoits dead within six weeks. The body count for the year totaled 1,480. In the view of the opposition, the police had run amuck, settling old scores and killing innocent people in contrived encounters. In 1982, the "law and order" situation in U.P. continued to deteriorate, and in July, immediately following the murder of 21 persons by dacoits, the chief minister submitted his resignation.[9]

Ties between criminals, police, and politicians are not a wholly new phenomenon nor is it by any means distinctly Indian. But, as political scientist Rajni Kothari and others argue, criminals have now become politicians. While it is surely an exaggeration to speak of the "criminalization of politics" in India, it is widely believed that many U.P. politicians, including ministers, have dacoit connections and that Bihar's mafia gangs are closely linked to state political leaders. In both states, a number of members of the legislative assembly are reputed to have criminal records and many have pending cases against them.

The Police and Internal Security

The police in India are held in generally low esteem, and they in turn are demoralized, unreliable, and increasingly militant. In 1979, the report of the National Police Commission stated that "in the perception of the people, the egregious features of the police are--politically-oriented partisan performance of duties, brutality, corruption and inefficiency." The 1980 police blinding of prisoners in Bhagalpur, Bihar, and the jail deaths in Tamil Nadu are only the most recent cases of police brutality, but there is widespread belief that the police are getting worse and that they can no longer maintain law and order. Indeed, they are often the perpetrators of violence. In the communal riots in Moradaband and Meerut, the police are alleged to have entered the fray with unprovoked attacks upon Muslims.

In a recent survey of "The Image of Police in India" conducted for the Home Ministry, 77 percent of the people interviewed blamed the police for "protecting or shielding goondas or criminal elements in the country" and for such malpractices as "putting up false cases, non-registration of complaints, use of third degree methods, high-handedness and illegal detentions at police stations." Survey respondents gave "political interference" as the principal cause of police malpractice.[10] Police officers are under constant pressure from politicians and bureaucrats, with the threat of transfer used to secure compliance. Transfers are also used to open positions for caste and familial favoritism. Other factors contributing to low police morale are low pay, long hours, poor living conditions, and a shortage of manpower and logistical support--although there is considerable variation in conditions from state to state.[11]

The police have begun to demand improved pay, better working conditions, and unions to represent their grievances. The depth of discontent was first made clear in the 1973 mutiny of the Provincial Armed Constabulary in Uttar Pradesh, in which nearly 100 policemen were shot to death by the Army. Over the past four years, the military has been brought in again and again to control growing police unrest. In May 1979, police protests, beginning in the Punjab, spread to seven states. In Gujarat, the Army opened fire on 5,000 striking police demonstrators. A month later, the agitation spread to three centrally-controlled paramilitary forces: the Central Reserve Police Force (CRPF), the Industrial Security Force (CISF), and the Railway Protection Force. The Border Security Force (BSF) and regular Army units intervened to put down the unrest--in most cases without incident. But in the commando-style raid staged by the Sikh Light Infantry against the striking Central Reserve Police camp near Delhi, three CRP men were killed. On the same day, the Army moved in to disarm the striking CISF unit at the Bokoro steel mill in Bihar. In an exchange of fire lasting three hours, 24 people were killed. In October 1979, the BSF and the CRPF--this time on the other end of the lathi--were called in to crush a police strike in Tamil Nadu. In 1980 and 1981, there were incidents of police unrest at Ranchi, Indore, and Gwalior, and the All-India Policemen's Federation threatened nationwide agitation if the government took disciplinary action against the offending officers in the Bhagalpur blindings case.

In August 1982, the Maharashtra government's ban on the police union and arrest of its top leaders led to a strike by the 23,000 members of the Bombay constabulary. The government crackdown ignited serious rioting, in which police were joined by striking textile workers and local rowdies. The situation was brought under control by the CRPF, BSF, and the Army. At the same time as the Bombay police riots, 500 members of the Haryana Armed Police blocked the Grand Trunk Road in a violent protest over working conditions. And Delhi's 20,000 police, growing increasingly restless, threatened agitation over their treatment as virtual "bonded labor" by the government.

In controlling domestic unrest, the government has four layers of force to which it can turn:

1. the civil police (armed only with lathis).

2. the provincial armed constabulary.

3. the paramilitary forces.

4. the Indian Army.

Under various names, the provincial armed constabularies are organized and paid for by the states. With some 250,000 men, they are the first to be called in if the civil police are unable to control disturbances.

There are 15 paramilitary units with more than 250,000 men, housed in barracks and subject to military discipline. They fall under several ministries of the central government. The Central Reserve Police Force (CRPF), the major riot control force, assists state police whenever necessary. The Border Security Force (BSF), the largest paramilitary unit with more than 100,000 men, the Assam Rifles, the Indo-Tibetan Border Police (ITBP), and the Ladakh Scouts have as their primary mission the patrol of India's borders. Other paramilitary units include: the Defense Security Corps (DSC), which protects defense installations; the Central Industries Security Force (CISF), which guards public sector industrial facilities; and the Railway Protection Force (RPF), which does just what its name suggests.

Since 1967, paramilitary forces have been greatly expanded, both to enhance the coercive capacity of the government and to reduce the need to call in regular Army units in aid of the civil. With little regard to their primary mission, they have been called in with increasing frequency to back up state police. The Border Security Force, for example, has been used to quell disturbances far from border areas--to control communal disturbances in Moradabad and Meerut, to put down the police riots in Bombay. But paramilitary forces themselves have not been immune from indiscipline and unrest. They are often poorly trained--and, like the civil police and provincial armed constabulary, suffer low pay and poor working conditions.

The increasing centralization of decision-making with respect to law and order and the extensive use of central government paramilitary forces have tended to "nationalize" local problems. By identifying the central government with the problem and its resolution, Mrs. Gandhi in particular has weakened the buffers of the federal system which once more fully insulated local problems and absorbed much of the blame.

The expansion of paramilitary forces was, in part, to insulate the Army from law and order functions. Given the unreliability of both police and paramilitary forces, however, the Army has played an increasingly prominent role in controlling domestic unrest. The Army has long been involved in maintaining order in the Northeast, but it has been drawn increasingly over the past five years into riot control. In Moradabad, for example, the Army went in after the Central Reserve Police and the Border Security Force proved unable to cope with communal disturbances. In 1979, the Army suppressed mutiny within units of the CRPF and the CISF, and in the Bombay police riots, order was restored only by Army intervention. Once the Army enters "in aid of the civil," it assumes command over the otherwise uncoordinated police and paramilitary forces already on the scene. The Army, while it has performed well, has never been at ease with its role in controlling domestic unrest. When facing not a foreign enemy but fellow Indians, Army morale is sure to suffer, but officers also fear that frequent use of the Army in aid of the civil may diminish the respect in which it is held.

The use of the Army in controlling domestic unrest could have wider political implications. Military officers could become convinced that civil authorities--specifically the politicians, for whom in any case they have no great respect--are unable to maintain law and order and that the Army should step in to take control of the government. There is nothing at the present to suggest that the military is prepared to intervene or even that there is much sympathy among the officer corps for such a move, but growing domestic unrest and increasing reliance upon the military to control it could well invite greater military involvement in the governance of India.

Instruments of Law

The Government of India possesses a formidable array of laws for the control of domestic unrest. The President may declare a constitutional emergency in a state if, on receipt of a report from the Governor, a situation has arisen in which the government of the state cannot be carried on in accordance with the Constitution. The President may then (1) assume any or all of the state functions or may vest these functions in the Governor, (2) declare that the powers of the state assembly shall be exercised by Parliament, and (3) make other provisions necessary to fulfill the objectives of the proclamation, including the suspension in part or whole of any constitutional body or authority in the state except the judiciary. The proclamation must be approved by Parliament. Ordinarily it expires after six months, but it may be extended by Parliament for an additional six month period. President's Rule was used sparingly under prime ministers Nehru and Shastri, but since the late 1960s, the Center has intervened with increasing frequency--often for solely political reasons.[12]

The Constitution, Article 352, provides that the President may suspend political freedom and the right to constitutional remedies in situations of national emergency--"whereby the security of India or any part of the territory thereof is threatened, whether by war or external aggression or internal disturbance." Such a proclamation is made on the advice of the Prime Minister and automatically lapses if it is not approved by Parliament within two months. A national emergency has been declared three times, two in response to the threat of external aggression (the 1962 Chinese invasion and the 1971 Indo-Pakistan war) and the third, the Emergency, was imposed on June 26, 1975, in response to an alleged threat to internal security by the political opposition.

During the Emergency, India's bill of rights was, in effect, suspended and rigid press censorship imposed. But independent of emergency powers, the government already had powerful legal instruments of repressive order. The Constitution itself provides for preventive detention, and this was augmented by the Defense of India Rules (DIR), used, for example, in the arrest of striking railworkers in 1974. The majority of those arrested during the Emergency, 1975-1976, were detained under DIR. Others including leaders of the opposition--were arrested under the provisions of the Maintenance of Internal Security Act (MISA) of 1971. The DIR was also the instrument by which 26 organizations, including the RSS, the Jamaat-e-Islami, and the Naxalites, were banned during the Emergency.*

Among the first acts of the Janata Government in 1977 was the repeal of both DIR and MISA, but the Government was not prepared to relinquish its broader powers of preventive detention. With the lifting of the Emergency, several states enacted their own preventive detention measures. In 1980, perhaps at the instigation of the Center, new Congress Governments in Uttar Pradesh, Gujarat, and Maharashtra passed preventive detention laws. In 1980, giving legislative sanction to an earlier ordinance, the Parliament passed the National Security Act (NSA), permitting the government to detain people suspected of undermining national security, public order, and essential economic services. Detainees

---

* The Unlawful Activities (Prevention) Act of 1967 empowers the government to ban any organization advocating secession of Indian territory. The Dal Khalsa and the National Council of Khalistan in the Punjab and various secessionist groups in the Northeast have been outlawed under the Act.

can be imprisoned without trial initially for three months, with as many as three subsequent three-month extensions. The government must notify the detainee within ten days of the reasons for his arrest, and the detainee has the right to judicial review. In 1981, the Supreme Court upheld the National Security Act as constitutional, but warned the government that "care must be taken to restrict (its) application to as few situations as possible." In response, the government specified sixteen "essential supplies and services" whose disruption would permit NSA enforcement. The sixteen services had been previously identified in the 1981 Essential Services Maintenance (ESMA), which empowers the government to prohibit strikes and lockouts in crucial sectors of the economy.

A wave of repressive state legislation seemed in the offing in August 1982, with the passage of the Bihar Press Bill. The act was modeled after similar (though largely unenforced) legislation long on the books in Tamil Nadu and Orissa. The law, vague and probably unconstitutional, served to unite the opposition parties in Bihar against the Congress Government. Mrs. Gandhi, though perhaps using the Bihar Government as a stalking horse for new press censorship, kept her distance, and in the face of statewide agitation an and mounting national criticism, the Bihar chief minister backed down, withdrawing the unpopular measure in July 1983.

Since Mrs. Gandhi's return to power in 1980, the opposition has denounced each of these acts as a step toward reimposition of the Emergency. Another Emergency is an unlikely prospect, but the government has armed itself with the legal instruments and police power such as to make so extreme an action unnecessary. But political stability cannot be purchased through repression, as the Emergency itself bears witness.

The prospect for stability in India lies in the balance between the maintenance of order and the satisfaction of basic demands for economic improvement and social justice. It is imperative that India maintain a steady--and, if at all possible, heightened--rate of economic growth and that it expand agricultural production to ensure continued self-sufficiency in food. It is imperative that there be greater equity in the distribution of income and that the basic needs of India's poor be met. No government, however, can satisfy all of the people all of the time. Even in the best of times, the satisfaction of the demands of any one group is likely to be opposed by another. All of this is made more difficult by the entry of new groups into the political arena, by heightened expectations, and by sharpened conflict in the competition for scarce resources.

India's political stability will be measured less by the challenges of social unrest than by the strength of its institutions. Weak political institutions are less the result than the cause of unrest. It is not the pace of change but rather the capacity of institutions to cope with change that is at issue.

THE PROSPECT FOR SOCIAL UNREST IN INDIA: THREE SCENARIOS

In projecting trends over the next five years in alternative scenarios for social unrest, we make one basic assumption--that the South Asian regional strategic environment will remain stable and that India will not be involved in war. For analytical purposes, we hold the external environment stable,* while we examine domestic change and social unrest, government response, and the impact of unrest on political stability. The scenarios range from the most probable to possible best and worst cases. Change in India, as in any society, is nonlinear; there are a multitude of variables, known and unknown; and the future is often shaped by unpredictable, chance events--a natural disaster, an assassination, the rise of a charismatic leader. In a world of uncertainty, even short-term projections are risky ventures, but in projecting alternative futures, we are at least less likely to be caught unprepared by the course of events.

Most Probable: Continuing Unrest, but Basically Manageable

Over the next five years, India's population will grow by 74 million people, putting increasing pressure on housing, services, and food. Even in the most favorable conditions, employment opportunities will not be able to keep pace with the 30 million new entrants

---

* Although India's size makes it less vulnerable to the seismic effects of instability among its neighbors, it is not impervious to such influences. Ethnic conflict in Sri Lanka may stir mobs in Tamil Nadu. Domestic politics in Pakistan may affect Hindu-Muslim relations in India, or the possible breakup of Pakistan could give impetus to separatist movements in India. Famine, natural disaster, or civil war in Bangladesh would surely increase illegal immigration into India, imposing greater stress on Bengal and the Northeast.

into the labor market, let alone absorb the backlog of unemployed. Unemployment will continue to grow, and educated unemployment will grow at an even faster rate.

Economic growth will be variable, but will continue to average around 3.5 percent per year, perhaps with an upwards trend toward the end of the decade. Erratic monsoons will continue to take their toll both in agricultural and industrial production. But drought will be localized, and the probable failure of one monsoon during the period can be absorbed without serious economic setback or the need to import foodgrains beyond relatively small amounts to stabilize prices on a short-term basis. So long as drought conditions are neither prolonged nor widespread, ameliorative "Food for Work" programs can cushion their full impact. Over the next five years, foodgrains production will expand modestly, with the gradual extension of irrigation and use of fertilizers, but major areas of the country will remain beyond the green revolution. India will be able to sustain marginal self-sufficiency in food production, but agriculture will remain on a production plateau.

Industry will fare somewhat better, with improvement in coal, power, and rails, but by no means an end to the infrastructural bottlenecks that have constricted industrial growth. Foreign exchange pressure in the mid-1980s will result in import restrictions and a general belt-tightening, but the basic thrust of the more liberal economic policy, with relaxed controls, will remain intact and sustain reasonable confidence within the private sector. Both domestic and foreign markets for Indian manufactured goods will modestly expand. Overall, the economic prognosis is fair to good, with a steady, if slow, rise in GNP and in per capita consumption expenditure.

Economic disparities among states, within states, between the rich and poor of both rural and urban areas will continue to widen, even as most may experience some level of improvement. The more backward regions are unlikely to move forward, and some may suffer absolute decline. The percentage of the population below the poverty line--virtually unchanged over the past three decades--is unlikely to change appreciably, and the poorest sections will hold their own at best.

Over the next five years, expanded literacy and media consumption and electoral competition among parties will heighten political consciousness and widen the arena of political participation. With an expanding middle class increasingly challenged by those rising up from below, conflict will intensify in competition for jobs and scarce resources. Social unrest, fed by widening disparities and frustrated aspirations, will grow, but violence, agitation, and protest movements will remain essentially ad hoc, episodic, and contained by the multiplicity of social cleavages that have historically compartmentalized conflict in India.

Regional disparities, in the context of heightened political consciousness and expanding participation, will sustain the trend toward the regionalization of Indian politics. The federal relationship will come under increasing pressure as conflict between state and Center and among the states over the allocation of finances and Plan resources becomes more intense. While still holding the pursestrings, the Center will give way to a greater degree of decentralization in finance and planning. Regional identities in terms of ethnicity and language will become more sharply defined at the same time that the various regions are bound more closely together by an increasingly national market economy and by a national system of communications.

Compromise and accommodation in Assam and the Punjab will ease the current crises--although not before each situation grows even more serious; non-Congress Governments will come to power in both states; and each will secure a degree of autonomy from the Center. But unrest will not be wholly contained. Terrorist attacks by unreconciled extremists will require the continued presence of paramilitary forces and the watchful eye of the Army in maintaining domestic peace.

Ethnic/religious violence of the sort associated with regionalism in its more chauvinistic forms may be activated by elections. The next parliamentary elections, to be held no later than January 1985, carry the danger of renewed violence in Assam and perhaps in the Punjab. Given the serious miscalculation in holding elections in Assam in February 1983, the government is unlikely to hold either new assembly or parliamentary elections in those states unless fair and peaceful polling can be assured.

Continuing unrest among the tribal states of the Northeast and new ethnic unrest in Sikkim will be contained, and the government will resist intensified demands for the creation of new states--notably Jharkhand and Vidarbha--while at the same time seeking, at least symbolically, to redress the intrastate disparities that give rise to such movements. If agitation is sustained with higher levels of violence, especially in the case of the Jharkhand movement, the government may capitulate and form the new state.

In the coming five years, communal conflict will deepen as Hindu, Muslim, Christian, and Sikh consciousness is heightened by the growing spirit of revivalism. The number and intensity of the incidents of communal violence are likely to increase, and although primarily an urban phenomenon, rural areas will not be immune from the contagion of communalism. Violence, however, will be ad hoc and intermittent, and with the rapid intervention of paramilitary forces and, if necessary, regular Army units, it can be brought under control and contained.

As Harijans have managed to improve their positions in rural India, they have met violence from the vulnerable backward caste Hindus just above them on the social scale. Caste violence is likely to increase as Harijans become better organized and more assertive. The Congress party today can no longer take the Harijans for granted, and in political competition for their support, Harijans are likely to become more politically conscious and active. This, in turn, may invite further violence, and, as in the case of ethnic conflict, this may be especially serious during forthcoming parliamentary and state assembly elections.

Agrarian unrest over the next five years is most likely to be a case of more of the same. Conflict between landowners and landless laborers (manifest in caste terms most sharply in the conflict between backward castes and Harijans) will remain endemic, with intermittent violence. It will remain ad hoc, confined to local areas, and largely unorganized. But violence will increase where the landless are being organized, either on an economic class or caste/tribal basis, with southern Bihar potentially explosive.

Capitalist farmers are critically positioned as the source of agricultural surplus for cities and industry. They are organized, and while their movement is now quiescent, farmers are likely again to press their demands for higher crop prices and lower input costs. The movement, bound closely to disparate interests in agriculturally advanced districts, is not likely to coalesce on an all-India basis. While agitations in one district or state may be highly disruptive, government may use a combination of accommodation and coercion to preclude formation of a more broadly based movement.

Urbanization will continue to be low by Third World standards, but the rate of growth will increase. Major cities will continue to draw migrants from the countryside and from out of state, increasing pressure on housing and basic urban services--transportation, water, and power. The power situation may improve in most cities, but water supplies will be variable. Over the next five years, the quality of life for most urban residents is not likely to improve and for many it will decline as urban services are strained beyond capacity. Discontent will be most vocal among the middle class, but unrest--demonstrations, even rioting--is not likely to be sustained.

Students add an especially volatile ingredient to the urban mix. Their frustration will be measured in continued campus unrest and involvement in regional, cultural, communal, and ethnic movements. At any one time, a major portion of India's campuses are likely to be closed, dispersing students and denying them a base for agitation and protest.

Competition for jobs within the middle classes will become more intense, and the next five years will witness widened demands for job reservations for "sons of the soil" and increased opposition to protective discrimination policies providing reservations for Harijans in university and medical school admissions and in public service employment. There will be sharpened conflict between lower middle class "locals" and migrants with whom they compete for jobs, rising Harijans, and more confident and assertive Muslims.

Organized labor is likely to grow increasingly restless, but "indiscipline" will manifest iteself in the rise of slowdowns and one-day protest strikes rather than the prolonged strikes of the sort led by Datta Samant. Indian industry will continue to be plagued by labor unrest, with weakened productivity resulting from loss of man-hours, but workers will be held in check by the fear of job loss and the coercive power of government.

Police and paramilitary forces, so long as their pay, working conditions, and morale remain abysmally poor, will continue to engage in periodic protests and strikes. Police unrest underscores a lack of reliability that is likely to require the continued involvement of regular Army units "in aid of the civil" to control rioting and domestic disturbances. The Army does not welcome this role, and the government will use the military sparingly, both to ensure continued popular respect for the Army and to minimize the involvement of the Army in the political sphere.

Overall, looking to the next five years, India will see continuing, perhaps even growing, social unrest, but it is fundamentally manageable. There is little prospect that the many sources of discontent will flow together to form a single all-India movement. Unrest will remain localized, intermittent, and largely ad hoc--contained for the most part, within the structures of the federal system. Unrest may threaten the stability of a single state, forcing the resignation of the Government or prompting the imposition of President's Rule. But in the most probable course of events, unrest will not pose a threat to the stability of the Government at the Center and certainly not to the regime itself. For all of India's problems, the nation's leadership looks to the future with confidence and guarded optimism. It is not misplaced.

Worst Case: Growing Unrest, Out of Control

Prophesies of doom are familiar enough in South Asia, and while population growth in the longer view is the most ominous, India's more immediate problems could easily grow worse. Failure to maintain continued economic growth will sharpen competition for diminishing resources and will deepen social unrest in all arenas of conflict. Two serious successive droughts could have a catastrophic impact on the Indian economy, with a rapid drop in foodgrains production, requiring massive imports from abroad. Hunger and disease could take a staggering toll. Under such conditions, lacking both hydroelectric power and domestic markets for manufactured goods, industrial production will fall. Unemployment in both the countryside and cities will grow worse, and food scarcities will fuel inflation, squeezing the urban middle class.

The serious financial problems arising from prolonged drought would be exacerbated if India were also to face a decline in exports--whether due to weakened industrial productivity or to protectionist trade barriers abroad; losses in remittances from the Gulf as oil prices drop and Indian overseas workers return home; and failure to secure access to increased foreign loans. Any one of these, but most critically the latter, would seriously weaken India's capacity to cope with economic crisis and the social unrest it would inevitably engender.

In a situation of growing scarcity, the pressures of regionalism will grow more intense, as those states more critically affected place increasing demands on the Center and marginally better off states clamor to keep what they have. Competition for water and power will sharpen conflict and the movement of foodgrains across state boundaries or "food zones" could become explosive. Widened disparities within states, between districts, and between the countryside and the cities are likely to deepen unrest. In heightened competition and growing frustration, levels of violence will increase in both urban and rural areas. Movements for the creation of separate states of Jharkhand, carving out the tribal regions of Bihar and Orissa, and Vidarbha, formed from the eastern districts of Maharashtra, will take on greater intensity.

In a situation of crisis, political rhetoric on all sides is likely to become increasingly shrill. Political parties will unfurl their populist banners, hurl mutual recriminations, and denounce scapegoats--domestic and foreign. If the next parliamentary elections were to be held under such conditions, they would likely be the most turbulent in India's history. Assam and the Punjab would be especially ripe for renewed violence, but elections would also sharpen communal and caste conflict.

Independently of economic problems, failure by the government to resolve the crises of Assam and the Punjab will require ever greater use of force. This will almost inevitably require a declaration of emergency in the affected regions and possibly the imposition of martial law. It would likely involve the Army in the virtual occupation of the Northeast, bent increasingly toward secession and the use of terrorism and guerrilla warfare. In the Punjab, an even more dangerous situation could result in widespread rioting, if not warfare, between Sikhs and Hindus, with an extremist Akali Dal committed to an independent Khalistan and a government equally determined to resist. Major rioting in the Punjab would be difficult to contain, and it could well spread into Haryana and to Delhi. The volatility of the region is heightened by the substantial Sikh representation in the armed forces and the (albeit unlikely) potential for mutiny among Sikh regiments. But it would be hard to imagine Sikh soldiers firing without serious qualms on their religious cohorts. And given ethnic sterotyping if not animosities, deployment of Bengali or South Indian troops to maintain order in the Punjab would probably be met by Sikh contempt and even greater violence.

So extreme a situation, involving major secessionist movements in Assam and the Punjab, is an unlikely prospect even in a "worst case" scenario, but the regions will remain seriously disturbed so long as the basic issues remain unsettled.

In the next five years, communal tension may well deepen as Hindu communal organizations mount efforts to pass anti-conversion bills in the states and at the Center. The Vishwa Hindu Parishad's campaign to reconvert those lost from the Hindu fold and an increasingly active and militant RSS will heighten apprehension among Christians, Sikhs, and Muslims. The increasing communalization of ethnic conflict in Assam will fuel Hindu-Muslim animosities throughout India. With a sense of Islam in danger, Muslims will be increasingly susceptible to fundamentalist appeals.

With mounting violence and widespread communal rioting, from which few, if any, areas would be immune, authorities--even with the full use of the armed forces--could do little to contain it. Communal conflict, more than any other form of social unrest, has the greatest potential for breaking out of the "compartments" of the federal system to consume all India--and it is the most dangerous because it is the least amenable to accommodation.

In a deteriorating economic situation, with the likely erosion of police authority, Harijans will become victims of increased violence. The backward peasant castes, their own marginal position threatened, will lash out against Harijans to hold them down. But they will also find in the Harijans a vulnerable scapegoat, with little means of retaliation, upon whom they can vent their frustration and anger.

Reinforced by rural caste conflict, in a possible worst case scenario, agrarian relations will become increasingly violent. But lacking effective organization and the resources to sustain prolonged resistance, landless laborers and poor peasants have little prospect of fermenting revolutionary upheaval--or even, for that matter, of uniting in common interest among themselves. Agrarian discontent will manifest itself in higher levels of violence and in scattered uprisings--episodic, uncoordinated, and localized--of growing intensity.

Capitalist farmers, starved for power and water for irrigation, will heighten their demands for government protection from risk. Organized and with political power in the state assemblies, they will mount renewed agitation for major concessions--blocking roads and rails in the most extreme tactics to withhold food from the cities.

Cities in a worst case projection will be centers of deepening unrest. Food riots will become a daily occurrence, police firings a routine response. Hard times would likely spur migration from the countryside into the cities, placing increasing strain on urban housing and services. Urban ethnic, caste, and communal conflict will sharpen as competition for jobs becomes increasingly desperate. Students' agitations will mount in intensity, and wage demands by labor, accompanied by an increasing number of strikes, will be met by industrial lockouts which, in turn, will provoke violent worker response. By no means would India necessarily face all these problems simultaneously, but they are linked by an economy and society that, despite regional tendencies, has become increasingly integrated. The sources of national unity, ironically, are also the bridges by which the compartments that once quarantined conflict can be bridged. As the situation grows worse, opposition parties are likely to unite against the Government and attempt to weld the disparate movements of protest into a single all-India movement. But even short of a national upsurge, serious unrest throughout India would pose a major threat to stability of the Government at state and Center levels and potentially to the regime itself.

The police and paramilitary forces--already proven unreliable--will be unable to control growing unrest and widespread violence. The Government will call in the Army, perhaps declare a national emergency, and impose martial law in the most distrubed areas. If civil authorities in a context of political instability simply prove unable to cope with the situation, the President could call upon the military to assume power until such time as law and order can be restored and civilian Government reconstituted through new elections. The sheer size and complexity of India, if it does not preclude it altogether, limits the capacity of the military to assume permanent power. But increased unrest could well draw the military into a greater role in governance, perhaps like the Turkish army as a guarantor of stability, prepared to intervene as need be on its own initiative.

India, even under conditions of severe drought and economic crisis, is not likely to face so wrenching a course of events as projected in this five-year worst case scenario. But even elements of the scenario would impose enormous stress on India's institutions, and growing unrest in particular regions could well get out of control.

Best Case: Increasing Prosperity, Declining Unrest

Over the past three decades, despite relatively low rates of economic growth, India has made impressive progress. The economy remains a half-filled vessel, bemoaned by those who see only poverty, inequality, and disparity, but applauded by those who see self-sufficiency in agriculture, growth in industry and more Indians better off now than they have ever been. India has the infra-structure for a major push forward in economic growth on both agricultural and industrial fronts, and over the next five years, barring severe drought, a "best case" scenario will involve a substantially higher rate of growth. But if higher rates of growth are not to deepen unrest, they must be accompanied by a more equitable distribution of income.

In agriculture, India has great potential for increased yield per acre. The extension of the area under irrigation, expanded use of fertilizers and pesticides, and a major breakthrough in the development of new high yielding varieties will dramatically increase foodgrains production. Agricultural prosperity, with double and triple cropping, will increase rural employment opportunities. It will support the development of ancillary rural industry, as it has done in the Punjab, and widen the market for industrial goods both for agriculture and for personal consumption.

Basic infrastructural improvements in coal, steel, cement, rails, and power will sustain rapid industrial growth in response to increased domestic demand. A broad based international economic recovery and foreign government resistance to protectionism will provide a growing export market for manufactured goods. While employment will not expand as rapidly as industrial production, new jobs in industry and in services will absorb the larger number of new entrants into the urban labor force, especially from among the expanding educated middle class. Continued liberalization of industrial policy--though cautious and selective--will provide increased incentive for expansion and investment. Growth in domestic petroleum production, sustained foreign remittances, higher levels of foreign investment, and continued access to multilateral development loans will strengthen India's balance of payments and rebuild foreign currency reserves.

Higher rates of agricultural and industrial growth will tend to widen regional disparities, but development priorities and investment in more backward states and regions will take the edge off sharper conflict and involve all states in a more cooperative federalism.

The government will yield a greater degree of administrative autonomy to the states and decentralize planning. Unrest in the Northeast, Assam, and the Punjab will ease, as extremists are politically isolated by government accommodation of basic demands and compromise is affected among the principal parties involved. Constitutional and legislative provisions will ensure a greater degree of cultural, linguistic, and religious protection. Special efforts may be taken to protect tribals--economically, culturally, and politically--by the creation of restricted and autonomous areas.

Religious consciousness will rise among all communities, but with it a confidence that sustains a greater sense of security rather than mutual animosity. As part of a Hindu renaissance, the Virat Hindu Samaj, with the support of the Vishwa Hindu Parishad, the Arya Samaj, and the RSS, will mount an offensive against the continued practice of untouchability. Violence against Harijans, in the short run, is likely to increase as they become assertive, but their position will improve and their rights will be more vigorously protected by government. Their problems, however, are massive, and in the span of five years, progress can at best be incremental.

It is not through social reform but in economic change that Harijans--largely landless laborers--are most likely to find a better life. The extension of the green revolution to new regions offers the landless the possibility of greater economic opportunity and substantive improvement, even as the relative gap between landowners and laborers may widen. Rather than sharpened conflict--the spectre of the green revolution turned red--agricultural modernization will ease social unrest as it provides more jobs and a greater sense of economic security. The capitalist farmers will be the principal beneficiaries of agricultural prosperity, but bearing greater risk for increased profits, they will exert increasing power as a formidable lobby to which competing political parties will pay court.

Urban unrest will be substantially reduced, as job opportunities expand in industry and services and as housing, public transportation, and power improve. Manageable inflation will reduce the pressure on the salaried middle class. Greater university discipline and brighter employment prospects will bring a relative calm to India's troubled campuses.

Improved pay and working conditions for police and paramilitary forces, together with curtailment of political interference, will substantially improve police morale--and, with it, efficiency and reliability. While social unrest will decline, the process of change will inevitably affect groups differentially. Even if most improve their position in absolute terms, feelings of relative deprivation will still engender group conflict that will manifest itself in ad hoc and episodic violence. The level of unrest, however, should be within the capacity of the civil police, backed by paramilitary forces, to control. Except for the strategically sensitive tribal states of the Northeast, with their underground guerrilla movements, the role of the military in aid of the civil should be greatly reduced and may prove unnecessary.

NOTES

1. "Election Defeats Portend Rise in Dissidence," India Abroad, February 4, 1983.

2. The "delinking" of state assemblies and parliamentary elections has, to considerable degree, nationalized issues in the general elections--albeit the principal issue has been Indira Gandhi herself.

3. L. Natarajan, American Shadow Over India (New Delhi: People's Publishing House, 1956). PPH is the publisher for the Communist Party of Indian and the outlet for Soviet books and periodicals. It is widely assumed to operate under a subsidy from the Soviet Union.

4. Reported by Seymour Hersh, New York Times, September 13, 1974.

5. See Myron Weiner, India at the Polls, 1980: A Study of the Parliamentary Elections, Washington, D.C.: American Enterprise Institute, 1983, pp. 58-59.

6. The Politics of Scarcity (Chicago: University of Chicago Press, 1962), p. 201.

7. See the discussion in Robert L. Hardgrave, Jr., India: Government and Politics in a Developing Nation, 3rd ed. (New York: Harcourt Brace Jovanovich, 1980), pp. 114-17.

8. Michael T. Kaufman provides a brief glossary in "In India, There's a Protester to Suit Any Given Occasion," New York Times, April 23, 1981.

9. Portions of the above discussion are drawn from Robert L. Hardgrave, Jr., "India Enters the 1980s," Current History, 81 (May 1982), p. 199.

10. The survey by the Bureau of Police Research and Development covered both urban and rural areas, and the people interviewed included political leaders, professionals, educators, traders, members of panchayats, and trade union representatives. Reported by Kuldip Nayar, "Police Find That Their Image is Poor," Sunday (Calcutta), May 30-June 5, 1982, p. 7.

11. For a description of police pay and working conditions, see India Today, June 16-30, 1979, pp. 44-50, and India Today, Sept. 15, 1982, pp. 7-9.

12. Hardgrave, India: Government and Politics in a Developing Nation, pp. 58-59. Also see S. R. Maheshwari, President's Rule in India (Delhi: Macmillan, 1977). I examine the imposition of President's Rule in the next chapter, pp. 74-77.

2
The Prospects for Political Stability in India: A Five-Year Perspective

"Deinstitutionalization" is a term used in India with increasing frequency to describe the degeneration of the nation's basic governmental institutions. Of greatest concern is the condition of political parties and the bureaucracy. India's parties and party system are widely perceived to be in a state of advanced decay, seriously weakened in their capacity to absorb and order expanding participation, to represent the public interest, and to reconcile conflict. The bureaucracy, once the "steel frame" of the Raj, is increasingly seen as a cheap alloy, corroded by low morale, corruption, and political interference. The courts are under increasing pressure as the executive seeks to transform the independent judiciary into an instrument of personal power. Long overburdened, judges are now demoralized by arbitrary transfers and political interference. It is the erosion of institutions and their loss of legitimacy in the eyes of the people that constitutes the greatest threat to political stability in India today. Weak and unresponsive institutions generate social unrest--at the same time they are unable to contain it. At issue is the continued capacity of India's institutions to cope with change, to manage unrest. But though weakened and under increasing pressure, India's political institutions remain one of the nation's principal sources of strength and stability.

For more than three decades, challenged by social unrest, economic crisis, and war, India's political system has demonstrated remarkable resiliance. Almost alone among the nations of the Third World, India has retained democratic institutions and sustained basic continuity in policy. Its stability is measured by the orderly succession on the death of two prime ministers and by the peaceful transition of political power from one party to another in 1977 and in 1980. India has had seven general parliamentary elections and a host of state assembly, municipal, and village panchayat elections. Each election has served not only to raise political consciousness and to expand the arena of participation, but to reaffirm and deepen the legitimacy of democratic institutions. Support for the constitutional order of parliamentary democracy is broadly based. Democracy will not be easily displaced in India, and for all the problems it faces--the pressures of social unrest and weakened political institutions--the stability of the regime is fundamentally secure. The prospects are favorable for stability of the central Government--whether under continued Congress rule or an opposition coalition. But the next five years holds out the possibility of greater ministerial instability at the state level and perhaps the emergence of weak and unstable coalition Government at the Center.

LEVELS OF POLITICAL INSTABILITY

In India, we can usefully distinguish three levels of political instability: state Government ministerial instability; central Government ministerial instability; and regime instability.

State Government Ministerial Instability

Our concern here is with the continuity of state Government (that is, the ministry) in its capacity to serve out its full term of elected office. A state Government may collapse either from outside pressure or as a result of internal dissension. A chief minister may resign either voluntarily or be forced out by the party's "high command." Under such circumstances, if a new Government cannot be formed, the Center imposes President's Rule.

The Center may impose President's Rule under conditions of constitutional emergency or if a state Government is unable to cope with unrest and to maintain law and order. To use the words of the Indian Constitution, the Center may invoke such power "if the President on receipt of a report from the Governor of the State or otherwise, is satisfied that a situation has arisen in which the government of the State cannot be carried on in accordance with the provisions of this Constitution." The proclamation must be approved by Parliament and ordinarily expires after six months. President's Rule may be extended for an additional six months, but the total period may not exceed one year. Under President's Rule, the Governor, as agent of the central government, assumes emergency powers of administration until such time as elections are held and a new Government constituted. Under Prime Ministers Nehru and Shastri, from 1950 to 1966, President's Rule was imposed a total of 8 times. During Indira Gandhi's tenure as Prime Minister, it has been imposed more than 40 times, often with clearly partisan motivation. The dismissals of the opposition Governments in Gujarat and Tamil Nadu during the Emergency provide especially dramatic examples.

In facing pressures of social unrest with which it cannot cope, a state Government with an otherwise secure majority in the Legislative Assembly may step down. Similarly, scandal might force the resignation of a Government, as in the case of Maharashtra Chief Minister A. R. Antulay's fall in 1982. In the ensuing "crisis"--the term is used here in the European sense--there may be an attempt to form a new Government. So long as the party's legislative majority remains intact, a ministry might be reconstituted under a new chief minister of the same party. If it is unable to retain its majority, another party or coalition may seek to form a Government. If no Government can securely command the confidence of the Assembly, the state may then be brought under President's Rule.

In Uttar Pradesh in 1973, amidst economic crisis, student unrest, and police revolt (the mutiny of the Provincial Armed Constabulary), Chief Minister Kamalapati Tripathi--still commanding the support of the state's Congress legislative party--submitted his resignation, and President's Rule was imposed. In 1982, again in U.P., Chief Minister V. P. Singh, unable to cope with the deterioration of "law and order," resigned in the wake of renewed decoit violence. In this case, he was succeeded by another Congress chief minister, formally selected by the Congress party's legislative majority but, in fact, imposed from above by Indira Gandhi.

One of the most dramatic instances of a state Government falling to outside pressure involved a student movement in Gujarat in 1974. With rising prices, food scarcities, and unresolved political grievances, Gujarat had been tense for months. Student discontent was focused initially on increased hostel charges, but with the formation of the student "Society for Reconstruction," the agitation widened. Sarvodaya leader Jayaprakash Narayan, emerging from political retirement, called upon the students to assume leadership of a statewide Gujarat Bandh--a general strike--in January 1974. The unprecedented agitation that followed gave rise to widespread violence, resulting in 50 deaths. One month later, the Congress Government resigned and President's Rule was declared.

If the state Government cannot control social unrest, yet refuses to step down, the Center may intervene. In 1959, the Center used this powerful instrument in what it called a breakdown of law and order to unseat the Communist Government in Kerala. President's Rule has subsequently been used to depose state Governments that have allegedly lost popular confidence. After it took office in 1977, the Janata party secured imposition of President's Rule and dissolution of the assemblies in those states where Congress retained power but had suffered defeat in parliamentary polling. Although it denounced the action against "duly constituted" state Governments, Congress, after its return to power in 1980, followed a similar tack against those states under Janata rule.

Internal dissension and defection can also bring down a state Government. Until 1967, state Governments, with the notable exception of Kerala, typically ruled with secure legislative majorities. Nearly all were Congress ministries. In the 1967 state assembly elections, however, Congress losses enabled opposition parties to form coalition Governments in Bihar, Uttar Pradesh, the Punjab and West Bengal. But one by one, the non-Congress coalitions collapsed through defections, and the states were brought under President's Rule.

Many of these defections were engineered--typically involving payment or the promise of a ministerial berth in a new Government. In Haryana, Congress was the victim. Almost immediately after coming to power with a narrow majority, the Congress Government was brought down through defections to the opposition. The successor United Front ministry, formed from Congress defectors, lasted only eight months before its own support was eroded through floor-crossings back to Congress. (The movement back and forth has come to be described by the phrase Aya Ram Gaya Ram, referring to frequent party switching by a Harayana politician named Ram and meaning, in effect, "easy come, easy go.") President's Rule was imposed and new elections called.

Defection remains today a spectre that hangs over any state Government with a weak majority or a loose coalition. But coalitions are subject to the additional strain of inter-party dissension, and those that survive individual defections are likely to succumb, sooner or later, to the breakup of the Government as one or more constituent parties break away. The most dramatic case is Kerala. Since it was formed as a linguistic state in 1956, Kerala has had a history of unstable, shifting coalitions, with 13 Governments and 4 periods of President's Rule.

Over the past decade, state Governments under Congress (I) rule have suffered another form of instability arising out of party centralization under Indira Gandhi. Going back to the 1972 elections, when she replaced four strong chief ministers by her own nominees, Mrs. Gandhi--as we will discuss in detail later--has sought to ensure that the state chief ministers are without independent political bases and are dependent upon her alone. Playing state party factions off against one another, she has not only imposed her own choices upon the states, but she has intervened with increasing frequency to depose chief ministers who have lost her confidence. Central interference has weakened state Government, undermined party organization, discipline, and leadership, and increasingly discredited the Congress in the eyes of the people. The succession of chief ministers in Andhra Pradesh since 1980--four in three years--was a major factor contributing to the Congress party defeat in the January 1983 state assembly elections.

Looking to assembly elections over the next five years, Congress prospects are mixed, and it may well lose its majorities in other states. If Andhra and Karnataka (rather than Kerala) portend future trends, single parties, rather than coalitions, will constitute state Governments. These may be either regional parties or parties that are national in name but with concentrated regional support. No single party will offer an all India alternative to Congress, but different parties in each state will provide that challenge. Assembly majorities, however, are vulnerable to erosion, and Governments can be brought down by party splits and floor-crossings. How the Telugu Desam in Andhra and the Janata in Karnataka fare in providing stable Government will likely have a major impact on the prospects for opposition parties in other states.

Central Government Ministerial Instability

While India has seen considerable ministerial instability at the state level, the Center has been more secure. From independence in 1947 until 1969, when the party split, the Congress commanded overwhelming majorities in Parliament. From November 1969 until new elections in March 1971, the Congress was without a majority in the Lok Sabha. The Government of Indira Gandhi depended on external support--notably from the Communist Party of India (CPI) and the Tamil nationalist

DMK--and was thus vulnerable to political extortion, for any one of the segments supporting her could threaten to withdraw and potentially bring down the Government. Not surprisingly, the period was the high point of Congress party populism.

It was not until the Janata Government, 1977-1980, however, that India experienced its first--and so far its only--bout with ministerial instability at the Center. The Janata was an amalgam of five parties, disparate in ideology and social base and united only by their common opposition to Indira Gandhi and the Emergency. Dissension sapped the spirit and capacity of the Government from its inception, and by 1979, it was virtually immobilized by factional conflict. As defections eroded the Janata majority, Morarji Desai finally yielded to pressure from within the party and stepped down as Prime Minister--only a day before the parliamentary vote that almost surely would have toppled his Government.

In the second week of the Government crisis, as various contenders maneuvered for parliamentary support, the President recognized Charan Singh's claim to have marshalled the necessary majority. But unable to translate his claim into solid support and facing inevitable defeat on a vote of no-confidence, Charan Singh resigned as Prime Minister after 24 days in office. Convinced that the parliamentary situation was so fluid that no Government could command a stable majority, the President dissolved Parliament and called elections. In January 1980, the electorate returned Indira Gandhi to power on the promise to provide "a government that works."

The Congress (I) now commands a substantial majority in the Lok Sabha, the lower house of Parliament, but the next elections, to be held by January 1985, might for the first time in India bring a coalition Government to power at the Center. In the scenarios later in this paper, we will examine the possible forms such a coalition could take--either under Congress leadership or as a combination of opposition parties--and their implications for political stability. Coalition Government, however, is not inherently unstable, as the experience of Norway, the Netherlands, and other European countries indicate. During the years of one-party dominance, the Congress was, in essence, a coalition embracing an ideological span from right to left, a plurality of interests, and provincial party units with a high degree of autonomy under state "bosses." Government constituted by a combination of parties need not be less stable. Indeed, it might be more genuinely representative of India's diversity, more accommodative to varied interests. But coalition Government at the Center is vulnerable to the internecine struggles witnessed within the Janata party when it was in power and to the pressures of political extortion and power play that have undermined state coalition Governments, Kerala being the most dramatic case of chronic instability. There is then, if Congress fails to secure a majority in the next elections, a real possiblity that weak and unstable Government could emerge at the Center.

Ministerial instability may involve immobilisme, the incapacity of the Government to make decisions and to project policy. But when the Government is immobilized by dissension or in the crisis following its collapse, the day-to-day administration of government may carry on very much as usual. The bureaucracy here assumes a critical role in providing what, in the European context, has been called "the permanent government." During the many periods of immobilisme and crisis under the French Third and Fourth Republics, bureaucracy provided on-going administration and gave stability to a regime otherwise torn by political strife. Similarly, in Italy, with 44 Governments since World War II, the bureaucracy gives continuity to government (with a small "g"), as Government coalitions come and go.

Regime Instability

India came to independence in 1947 with an experience of democratic government and a commitment to democratic values. Like the United States at its founding, India was served by leaders of remarkable ability and vision. Foremost in shaping the character of modern Indian politics was Jawaharlal Nehru, who took office as Prime Minister in 1946 under the interim Government and served until his death in 1964. The new State was sustained by an institutional strength unique among nations emerging from colonial rule. Most important were the Congress party, heir to the nationalist movement; the bureaucracy, with its elite services, among the best in the world; and the Army, capable, honored, and non-political. The Constitution, adopted in 1950 and patterned after the Government of India Act of 1935, established a democratic republic: parliamentary, federal, secular, and socialist. The later, more sentiment than ideology, symbolized a commitment to economic equality and social justice. Pragmatic rather than doctrinaire, "socialism" represented essentially a conception of a mixed, regulated market economy in which the State plays a leading role.

These values and commitments were broadly shared by those who had participated in India's struggle for freedom. Even as opposition to the ruling Congress party emerged, it was largely the product of a "Congress culture," which today remains at the center of Indian political life. In the formative years after independence, India's one-party dominant system--often called "the Congress system"--gave stability to government through continuity at the Center and coherence among the states. The system had unity with the Congress as ruling party, while at the same time, with the opposition parties acting as pressure groups, it accommodated diversity. It provided the opportunity for the regime to secure its foundation during a time of change, of expanding participation and rising political consciousness. By the time the Congress system broke down in 1967, there was a fundamental and broadly-based consensus on the legitimacy of the Indian political system. Even those elements that had initially opposed the constitutional order--the Communists, the Hindu nationalists, the Dravidian separatists--had, for the most part, been "domesticated" and had reconciled themselves to a democratic, secular, and united India.

The legitimacy of the regime and the broad consensus upon basic values are the foundation of continuity in both Indian foreign and domestic policy. Whatever Government may be in power in the near future, abrupt or radical departures from present policies are unlikely. Stability of policy arises from two principal sources: first, the essentially centrist and pragmatic character of Indian politics and, second, the role of the senior civil servants and the bureaucracy--the "permanent government."

Political life in India takes place largely on the middle ground of conflict between the center-right and the center-left. While there are strident voices of dissent from the extremes of both right and left, they command little support. There is a high degree of consensus among contending political parties on foreign policy--a consensus reflected in the consistency of Indian foreign policy over the years and in the continuity of policy with changes of Government in 1977 and 1980. In domestic policy, differences are more substantial, but as among Republicans and Democrats in the United States, these are differences within a range of mutual acceptance. Thus, in domestic economic policy, for example, the differences between the Janata and Congress Governments were not fundamental. Indeed, in recent years, domestic policy issues have been subordinated to questions of personality and style.

Another factor contributing to policy stability is the prominent role played by senior civil servants in shaping foreign and domestic policy. This has become even more pronounced since 1980, as Prime Minister Gandhi has relied increasingly upon high level bureaucrats and less upon Cabinet ministers and political advisors. Ministries and ministers may come and go, but the bureaucracy remains. "If a new Government comes," a key civil servant said privately, "we'll still be here to advise them."

From the time of independence, political soothsayers have predicted India's national disintegration and the collapse of democracy. Liberal democracy, some said, was an alien form of government imposed from above, that it was not deeply rooted in foreign soil and would inevitably wither. For others, democracy was simply inappropriate to a country so burdened by poverty and social injustice, that it was a luxury that India could ill afford. The resiliance of India's institutions, however, has defied the predictions of disintegration, collapse, agrarian revolt, revolution, and military coup. In the face of enormous problems, India has demonstrated remarkable strength. It has proven itself capable of managing domestic conflict and of providing for the national defense. The regime has withstood the stress of four wars (three with Pakistan, one with China), economic crises, episodic violence, and endemic unrest, and it survived Emergency rule, a challenge from within. Overall, even under conditions of growing unrest and possible ministerial instability at the Center, the prospects for regime stability over the next five years are very good.

Emergency Rule and Constitutional Change

For nearly two years, from June 1975 until January 1977, democracy in India went into eclipse. During the Emergency, the Constitution was, in effect, suspended. Prime Minister Indira Gandhi proclaimed her continued dedication to democracy and insisted that "what has been done is not an abrogation of democracy but an effort to safeguard it." Actions taken during the Emergency--secret arrests, press censorship, political repression, and numerous "excesses"--suggest otherwise, but Mrs. Gandhi may well have believed her own rhetoric--that a shock treatment was necessary to put India back on course. Her decision to call elections in 1977 and to "relax" the Emergency was taken, no doubt, in misplaced confidence in victory. But it also reflected, at least implicitly, her recognition that some form of democracy _is_ necessary for India. The Janata victory--welcomed as a "restoration" of democracy--was a massive repudiation of the Emergency. Mrs. Gandhi accepted the electoral verdict, and there is no evidence to support the rumor that she sought military intervention to keep herself in power.

Mrs. Gandhi's return to power in 1980 was accompanied by renewed speculation that she would replace India's parliamentary form of government with a presidential system along Gaullist lines. While the Prime Minister remained aloof from such discussion, she tacitly encouraged debate to test the political winds. Some saw in presidential government greater political coherence. Others saw it as a means to enhance executive authority--although why under her highly centralized and personalized rule, Mrs. Gandhi might think that necessary is unclear, save in anticipation of a possible loss of a parliamentary majority. A presidential system would provide direct access to the voters, unmediated by parliament. Even as her charisma may wane, Mrs. Gandhi remains far and away the preferred leader among likely alternatives, as measured by public opinion polls in India. It is not to sustain her own rule, so speculation goes, that she would favor a presidential system, but to secure dynastic succession. Rajiv Gandhi, as heir apparent, would be more likely to gain and hold leadership, according to this argument, if he were able to contest the presidency in a direct national election. In a parliamentary system, representing one of 542 constituencies, Rajiv--even with a Congress majority--could lose out in the struggle among factions and would-be prime ministers.

Rajiv, perhaps to put down such speculation, has affirmed his commitment to parliamentary government. Talk of a basic change toward a presidential system has receded, but there continues to be speculation as to possible tinkering with the Constitution to reinforce Mrs. Gandhi's power and to ensure the succession of Rajiv. Prime Minister Gandhi, if she were inclined to seek basic changes in the structure of government, is restrained by lack of the two-thirds majority in the Rajya Sabha, the upper house of Parliament, necessary for a constitutional amendment. Moreover, any such effort would surely provoke widespread protest and serve as the catalyst for opposition party unity.

Another matter of speculation and concern is a possible reimposition of the Emergency. One occasion for the proclamation of an Emergency might be conditions of widespread unrest such that elections could not be conducted. Polling was not conducted in Assam in the 1980 parliamentary elections, and the violence during the February 1983 elections in Assam, continuing unrest in the Punjab, and the election violence in the June 1983 Kashmir assembly elections raise the possibility for postponement of parliamentary elections, now scheduled to held no later than January 1985. Under the Constitution, the duration of Parliament is no longer than five years, but while an Emergency proclamation is in force, ordinary legislation may extend the life of Parliament one year at a time.

Any move to extend Mrs. Gandhi's term of office by declaration of an Emergency would likely be met by violence and massive resistance. The Emergency proclamation of June 26, 1975, was received initially with a mixture of opposition, support, and ambivalence. The reception accorded to another Emergency would be very different. Although opposition leaders and intellectuals have denounced various legislative measures, such as the National Security Act and the Bihar Press Bill, as steps toward the reimposition of the Emergency, few believe that another Emergency is a likely prospect.

POLITICAL PARTIES AND THE INDIAN PARTY SYSTEM

One of the major sources of India's political stability has been the institutional strength of the Indian National Congress--the movement, founded in 1885, that led India to independence and, since 1947, the party that has held power at the Center for all but thirty-three months. That strength is today seriously weakened, and the larger party system is incoherent.

In assessing the prospects for political stability in India, the stability of the parties and of the party system is a matter of critical concern. Party stability refers to the organizational continuity of a party from election to election. Has it retained a stable leadership? Has it split? Have there been factional breakaways? Is it torn by dissidence and defection? Party-system stability refers to continuity in the basic pattern of party competition from election to election. Are the principal party contestants the same, or does each election bring forth a new range of contenders? Along what lines are parties divided--class and social base; ideology; issues; personality? Do parties merge and break only to merge again, or do they retain their separate identities? Do they contest elections on their own, or do they enter into alliances and electoral adjustments? Are patterns of alliance stable over time, or are they fluid, opportunistic, and essentially unpredictable?

Given India's federal structure, the character of parties and the party system differs between the all-India arena of parliamentary election, with its focus on the office of the Prime Minister, and the states, and it differs among the states themselves. Thus, party politics at the national level may be stable or unstable, while at the same time, conditions at the state level may cover the gamut from high levels of party and system stability to complete chaos.

Congress party dominance in the states and at the Center is no longer assured. While Congress is the only genuinely all-India party and no single opposition party offers a credible challenge to its power at the Center, it is highly vulnerable. The Congress has had solid majorities in the Lok Sabha during its time in power, save for the period immediately following the 1969 party split. But Congress has never had an absolute majority of votes in parliamentary elections. In 1980, for example, the Congress (I) secured 70 percent of the seats in the Lok Sabha, but won less than 43 percent of the vote. A similar pattern has characterized Congress power in most states.

Congress dominance has been the product of a divided opposition. That message was made clear in 1967, when in a number of states in North India, opposition party alliances--so long as they remained intact--were able to displace Congress Governments. In 1977, united by their opposition to the Emergency and to Indira Gandhi, five parties came together to defeat the Congress at the Center, but as had been the pattern of earlier United Front Governments in the states, the Janata Government collapsed as a result of internal factional struggle and defections. What many had hoped would offer India the possibility of a stable two-party system fell apart as the Janata splintered, opening the door to Mrs. Gandhi's return to power.

Congress is vulnerable not only to defeat by a united oppositon, but in a number of states, a single opposition party offers a credible alternative to Congress rule. In 1967, the regional DMK party defeated Congress and took an absolute majority of seats in the state assembly. The party and its offshoot, the AIADMK (now in power under Chief Minister M. G. Ramachandran), have since reduced Congress to a weak third party in the state. The National Conference in Jammu and Kashmir and the Communist Party (Marxist) in both West Bengal and Tripura command majorities in the state assemblies, and in 1983, the new regional Telugu Desam party formed a Government with an absolute majority in the Andhra assembly.

India's party system is highly unstable, and all parties, including the Congress, are involved in continuous processes of fission and fusion. The efforts by non-Communist opposition parties to unite or even to reach electoral understandings have been frustrated again and again by the ambitions of their various leaders. Whether they can overcome their petty feuds and continuous squabbling to form a national front against the Congress (I) in the forthcoming parliamentary elections is problematic.

The Congress (I)

The "deinstitutionalization" of the Congress party is rooted in the leadership and style of Indira Gandhi. She has sought to transform the party into an instrument of personal power and to assure that it nurtures no one who might challenge her position as Prime Minister or endanger the succession of her son--first Sanjay, now Rajiv. Organizational elections have not been held in more than a decade, the last in 1972. The All-India Congress Committee and the Working Committee, once the crucial decision-making center of the party, are moribund. State party units have no autonomy, and provincial, district, and local Congress committees, insofar as they function at all, are creatures of the central party "high command"--a euphemism for Mrs. Gandhi. The grass-roots have been cut, and the Congress is an organization with no base. Inder Malhotra of The Times of India describes the Congress as "no more than a rabble held together by one towering personality."[1]

While the state Congress party organizations are torn by dissension, in only a few states are there clearly identifiable and stable factions. The bases of dissidence and factionalism vary from state to state: region, urban-rural, caste, personality, but in no state can factionalism be said to be ideologically based. Instead of factions, in most states, there are free-floating, self-styled leaders in search of support. The Center plays each off against the other, with no claimant for power permitted to establish an independent base of support. All profess personal loyalty to Mrs. Gandhi, and all are dependent upon her. One of the principal reasons the party has not conducted organizational elections is that they would provide local and state party leaders not only the opportunity to test their strength against one another, but they would provide the victors with bases of support independent of New Delhi. Mrs. Gandhi has kept the pot boiling, and party dissension has been the inevitable product of uncertainty. But while she has assured her unrivaled position within the party, she has so weakened the organization that if Rajiv is to succeed his mother as Prime Minister, he will inherit a party that may be unable to sustain his power or its own coherence.

In those states where the Congress is in power, chief ministers dangle like puppets on strings. Rather than rise up from their own base of political strength as leaders of the state legislative parties, they are imposed from above by Mrs. Gandhi. The Congress legislative parties have, in fact, clamored for her to do so, unwilling to assume responsibility themselves. Personal loyalty, rather than competence, has been the prime qualification for office. That Mrs. Gandhi has largely limited her choices to those "faithful" who stood with her during her time out of power, rather than to include more experienced politicians who came back to the Congress fold when they sensed a change in the political winds, is understandable, but it has considerably narrowed the field. It has, moreover, put a premium on "sycophancy," a term widely used in India to describe the relationship of chief ministers and Cabinet ministers alike with Mrs. Gandhi.

There has always been corruption in state Governments, and leaving the choice of chief minister to the state legislative party is no guarantee of either honesty or competence. But because the Congress chief ministers are imposed from above, because they are perceived as the Prime Minister's minions, their venality tarnishes Mrs. Gandhi's own image. All Congress chief ministers have by no means been corrupt, incompetent, or servile, but on the whole the states have been badly served. The situation has required Mrs. Gandhi's constant intervention, and she has deposed one chief minister after the other--Andhra, with a succession of four chief ministers in three years, being the most blatant case. But central intervention in Andhra, even to depose the corrupt or inept chief minister, became a source of increasing resentment within the state and an affront to the pride of the Telugu people. It was a major factor in the January 1983 Congress defeat at the hands of the Telugu Desam party.

On the other hand, the failure of Mrs. Gandhi to depose corrupt chief ministers can also be costly, as the Congress discovered in its defeat in Karnataka. In an effort to cleanse the party in preparation for parliamentary elections, Mrs. Gandhi has begun to ease out some of her more serious liabilities in the states, but she is not wholly willing to yield to the Congress legislative parties the power to name their own state chief ministers.

Maharashtra, one of the most critical states for Congress in the next parliamentary elections, is a case in point. Former Chief Minister A. R. Antulay engaged in corruption on such a scale and so brazenly that, as a direct result of a court decision against him, he resigned in 1982 under pressure from the party's high command. Perhaps his ultimate sin, however, lay in his success in building up a personal power base among members of the state legislative assembly (largely by conferring patronage upon them for allotment of cement and liquor licenses) and in the arrogance of his belief that he was beyond Mrs. Gandhi's control.

The high command then named Babasaheb Bhosale as chief minister. Described by the press as a "non-entity," Bhosale was a source of continuing embarrassment to Mrs. Gandhi, and a year later, in the aftermath of the Congress defeats in Andhra and Karnataka, he too was out. This time Mrs. Gandhi stepped back to permit the Maharashtra Congress legislative party to elect by secret ballot Vasantrao Patil. Patil, a leader of the powerful Maratha sugar lobby, had twice previously served as chief minister. (The Marathas have 33 percent of the state's population and control the sugar cooperatives, the strongest economic interest in Maharashtra. The Congress party split in 1978 divided their loyalties between Patil and Sharad Pawar, leader of the breakaway Congress (S), and Pawar now poses the major threat to continued Congress (I) rule in Maharashtra.) The press acclaimed Patil's selection as a move toward restoring popular confidence in the Congress, and the manner by which the new chief minister was chosen was seen as part of a larger effort to revitalize the party organization. Yet Mrs. Gandhi weakened Patil's authority by forcing him to accept his arch rival, Ramrao Adik, as deputy chief minister--an action hardly calculated to rally Maratha support to the ruling Congress or to bring greater coherence to the state Government.

This continuing manipulation from above has encouraged dissidence in the party and has increased the commuter traffic between the state capitals and New Delhi, as the various groups, trading allegations of disloyalty, corruption, and favoritism, vie for the ear of the Prime Minister. In an atmosphere of court politics, chief ministers are in frequent attendance--to defend themselves, to curry favor, and to bring matters of policy and politics before the party's high command. Just as state party candidates are screened by the

Center, so chief ministers must also clear any changes in their own state cabinets with New Delhi. In the process, holding out hope to party dissidents that their turn may come, the high command ensures the continued dependence of state Congress politicians on Mrs. Gandhi.

Rajiv has been increasingly a part of this process, as he has sought, with the aid of political advisers Arun Nehru and M. L. Fotedar, to build the personal loyalties upon which he can draw to secure his succession. At the same time, Rajiv has diagnosed the politics of uncertainty, the balancing of one group by another, by which Mrs. Gandhi has sustained her domination over the Congress, as a major source of party weakness. In a March 1983 interview, Rajiv stated that "over the last...ten maybe 15 years, the party has stopped functioning as a party.... We have to restore the responsibilities of the lower office-bearers, the block presidents and district presidents and really restore a democratic functioning within the party." He described decentralization as "the only way" things work and asserted that party elections will be the first step to revitalize the Congress.[2] But for all the talk of organizational elections and reform, the party remains an institution perilously dependent upon one person.

Dissidence is ultimately held in check by the perception that the Congress remains the only game in town. To the degree that changes--and it is changing--at the state level and, looking to the next parliamentary elections, at the Center, Congress party unity will be under increasing pressure. There is no state in which Congress is invulnerable. The last two states to have been continuously under Congress rule--Andhra and Karnataka--fell to the opposition in January 1983, and political defeat brought a virtual collapse of the party organization in each state. There is hardly a state where internal party dissension has not seriously affected Congress standing, but only in one so far has it reached the point of open break. In Gujarat, in 1982, after their efforts to unseat the chief minister failed, dissidents bolted the party to form the Rashtriya Congress. At the same time, however, the Congress standard remains a powerful force, and estranged elements are drawn continuously back into the party. The return of two state units of the opposition Congress (S)--the Antony group in Kerala in 1982 and the Priya Ranjan Das Munshi group in West Bengal in 1983--underscores the continued resiliance of the Congress. The Congress remains a commodious umbrella for a plurality of interests. The strength of the Congress, like that of India itself, lies in its tolerance for ambiguity and contradiction.

The Congress today is held together largely by opportunism--by the power, patronage, and money that public office can command. No longer an organization of continuous activity, it has become an electoral machine to be activated periodically for the campaign. Mrs. Gandhi used it skillfully as the vehicle of her return to power in 1980, but its weakness has been exposed in a succession of state assembly elections and bye-elections. In only two assembly elections since its return to power at the Center has the Congress won a majority of seats--Delhi and Assam. In May 1982, Congress formed Governments in Haryana and Himachal Pradesh only after defections from the opposition strengthened its own ranks. In Kerala, it joined in coalition Government, and in West Bengal, it was roundly defeated by the Communist Party (Marxist). In January 1983, Congress lost in Tripura to the CPM, a defeat for which it was prepared, but the defeats in the critical states of Andhra and Karnataka, which earlier had resisted the Janata wave in their continued support of Mrs. Gandhi, came as a major shock. A month later, Congress did win in the Delhi election, dealing the Bharatiya Janata Party (BJP) a major blow. And against a boycott, amidst violence, and with only 20 percent of the electorate voting, the Congress won a majority of seats in the Assam assembly--a victory that can hardly be accorded legitimacy or respect. In June 1983, Congress (as expected) lost the Jammu and Kashmir assembly elections to the incumbent National Conference--although it emerged as the favored party in the Hindu-majority constituencies of Jammu. But also in June, 1983, the Congress scored major victories over the Bharatiya Janata Party in municipal elections in Madhya Pradesh, and in the Uttar Pradesh panchayat (village) elections, the Congress overwhelmed both the Lok Dal and BJP. In the West Bengal panchayat elections, the Congress made important inroads into the rural base of the ruling Communist Party (Marxist), with a substantial increase in its share of the village panchayat seats.

These elections do not reveal a pattern from which clear trends can be discerned. Local issues predominate, and even in the simultaneous defeat of Congress in Andhra and Karnataka, the party lost each state for different reasons. And the party's victory in Delhi a month later again was highly idiosyncratic. Conditions vary from state to state, both in the strength of the Congress and the unity of the opposition. The Congress retains a broad base of electoral support despite its organizational weakness. Defeats over the past two years do reveal, however, an erosion of support among Harijans (untouchables) and Muslims--two groups, accounting for some 22-25 percent of the electorate in North India, that are an essential element in sustaining Congress power. The "Rajput strategy," crafted by Sanjay in 1980 to return the Congress to power in Uttar Pradesh, Madhya Pradesh, Rajasthan, and Gujarat has begun to come apart, with Rajputs themselves politically divided and caste rivals (such as the Patidars in Gujarat) drawn increasingly toward the opposition. In all states, the Congress social base is fluid, and no group can be taken for granted.

Whether Indira Gandhi will be able to lead the Congress to victory in the next parliamentary elections is open to question. She continues to command enormous personal popularity--far greater than any other political leader in India--and a political skill that has been most effective when she is on the defensive. Her reputed sense of political timing suggests that in going into a national election, she would try to seize the initiative with a dramatic gesture--a new domestic policy thrust, a campaign (however cynical) against corruption, a foreign policy triumph--or attempt to stir fear and find scapegoats. She would, moreover, emphasize the national character of the election--that Congress alone can provide stable majority Government at the Center and that only she is a leader of all-India stature and international respect.

There are no rivals within the Congress to Mrs. Gandhi, and she has sought to ensure that there are no potential challenges to the succession of Rajiv as prime minister. Just as she has clipped the wings of state Congress leaders, she has at the Center chosen ministers for her Cabinet who have no independent bases of support or power. Like her chief ministers, they are dependent upon her and serve only at her sufferance. The Cabinet is widely regarded as the weakest since independence, and though it contains individuals of ability and technical competence--notably Foreign Minister Narasimha Rao, Finance Minister Pranab Mukherjee, Defense Minister R. Venkatraman--they have no standing in their home states and lack political clout. Industries Minister N. D. Tewari, former chief minister of U.P., is also regarded as highly capable. The Cabinet is weakened by the periodic reshuffle of portfolios--the game of musical chairs by which Mrs. Gandhi denies ministers the opportunity to build power within their spheres of authority. Mrs. Gandhi also bypasses the ministers to deal directly with the senior civil servants who head the bureaucracy of the various ministries.

In decision-making--personalized, centralized, and ad hoc--Mrs. Gandhi has turned increasingly to bureaucrats rather than politicians for counsel. She has come to rely most heavily upon the Prime Minister's Secretariat and upon its head, her Permanent Secretary, P. C. Alexander. Of the ministers, perhaps only Pranab Mukherjee commands Mrs. Gandhi's personal confidence as a political adviser. Informally, she draws upon the advice of a small circle of retired civil servants, including L. K. Jha in economic policy (though his influence has waned) and G. Parthasarathy in foreign policy. But no one outside the family today can be identified as a source of broad-ranging counsel. No one other than Rajiv commands her full trust. Over the years, various advisers have been drawn into the inner-circle only to be exiled at the height of their presumed influence. Today that circle is smaller than it has ever been before, and those favored are called upon selectively with respect to given policies and specific decisions.

With the burden of decision-making so heavily on the shoulders of Mrs. Gandhi alone, there is a tendency toward drift and non-decision that has prompted opposition leaders to throw back her election slogan of 1980 in its call for "a Government that works." But her style has also given more power to the bureaucrats, not just as advisers, but in discretion as decision-makers in the form of a civil service raj.

Mrs. Gandhi dominates the Indian political scene as no leader of independent India--including her father, Jawaharlal Nehru--has ever done. Biographies refer to her "fragile" and "indifferent" health as a girl, but at the age of 66, she is by all appearances in excellent health. There are occasional rumors of serious medical problems, but she has never been hospitalized nor has she been incapacitated by illness at any time during her long tenure as Prime Minister. If Mrs. Gandhi's energy is to be measured by the pace of her campaign activity in 1980 and more recently during the Andhra and Karnataka assembly elections, she has the stamina to wear out any who try to keep up with her. But although people sometimes speak of "if" rather than "when" Mrs. Gandhi dies, there is increasing speculation as to the succession on the possible death of Mrs. Gandhi in office. By the late 1950s, people were already asking, "After Nehru, who?" There was no heir apparent, and on the death of Nehru in 1964, at the age of 75, as upon that of his successor, Lal Bahadur Shastri, in 1966, the succession was "managed" by the Congress party bosses.

Today Rajiv is clearly being groomed for dynastic succession, but there is no Syndicate (as the Congress bosses collectively were called) to oversee the transition. Rajiv has failed to arouse enthusiasm in either party or public, and his initial attempts at party management have drawn sharp criticism. Rajiv, while he may grow into the job, has yet to demonstrate the skills necessary for his political survival once his mother is no longer physically present to protect him. Following the death of Sanjay in 1980, Rajiv made a reluctant entry into political life. From simply "helping mummy," he was drawn into party politics and in 1981 won his parliamentary seat from Amethi, Sanjay's old constituency. But in the political fire, first in the 1982 assembly elections in Haryana, Himachal Pradesh, West Bengal, and Kerala, and then in the 1983 elections in Andhra and Karnataka, Rajiv failed to demonstrate either political skill or charisma. His involvement in the planning of the fall 1982 Asian Games in New Delhi was touted as proof of his management ability, but in the major crises of Assam and the Punjab, Rajiv has been kept at a distance. Rajiv is almost universally described as a decent young man (although occasional bursts of anger reveal the potential for a more autocratic disposition), and the newspapers have dubbed him "Mr. Clean," in apparent contrast to his controversial younger brother. But there is considerable doubt, both within the Congress and outside, that Rajiv has the toughness and skill to be Prime Minister.

Within Congress--although there are many with ambition and some of real ability--there are no obvious contenders of national stature and visibility beyond Rajiv. To assure that Rajiv does succeed and retain the _gaddi_ as Prime Minister, he must command the confidence of the Lok Sabha, and the next parliamentary elections are critical--not only to maintain a Congress majority, but to bring in members who are personally loyal to Rajiv. In February 1983, Rajiv was appointed as one of five General Secretaries of the Congress party. It had been expected before the Andhra and Karnataka defeats a month earlier that Rajiv would become Congress Party President, the post held then, as now, by Mrs. Gandhi. If this had been part of the original strategy in preparing Rajiv for the succession, it was scuttled in the wake of the election defeats. But Rajiv is now positioned to assume increasing control over the Congress party organization. It is an organization that is exhausted, and its success as an electoral machine will be defined less by its own strength than by the weakness and fragmentation of the opposition.

The Opposition Parties

The political opposition to Congress is fragmented and regionally disparate. Although single opposition parties have emerged as credible alternatives to Congress rule in a number of states, no single party poses such a challenge at the Center. But the strength of the opposition parties--regional parties and national parties that are all-India in name but regional in their concentrated bases of support--is formidable at the state level, and in alliance they have the potential to displace Congress at the Center with coalition Government. Even in disunity, they could deny Congress its Lok Sabha majority.

The challenge to Congress at the Center arises out of the regionalization of politics. The weakness of the Congress, its lack of responsiveness to regional concerns, and the absence of a strong national opposition party have contributed to the emergence of regional parties and the regionalization of national parties. The opposition continues to be divided in the national arena, but politics within each state has become increasingly bipolar. A large number of party nominees and independent candidates do, in fact, contest each seat, but voter discrimination has come increasingly to eliminate all but the most serious contenders. The result is that Congress can no longer be assured of victory as a result of divided opposition. Within most states, the trend is toward the emergence of a single opposition party as an alternative to Congress rule--albeit it may be a different party from state to state. In those states where a single opposition party has yet to emerge as an alternative to Congress, the role may be played by an alliance of opposition parties, with electoral adjustments for the allocation of seats so as to place a united front candidate against the Congress in each constituency.

The opposition parties that are likely to play a role in mounting a challenge to the Congress at the Center fall into three basic categories: non-Communist national parties; regional parties; and Communist parties. The non-Communist national and regional parties together occupy a broad middle ground, from the Bharatiya Janata Party on the center right to the Democratic Socialist Party on the democratic left. The Janata Party, like the Congress, provides an umbrella for disparate ideological tendencies, but ideological labels are difficult to place on any non-Communist party. They do not fit neat categories, and though they may embody tendencies one way or another, they are all fundamentally pragmatic. None advocates policies that are radically different from the Congress, either in the domestic economic policy of a regulated market (though there are surely differences of emphasis, accentuated by the stridency of party rhetoric) or in support for India's foreign policy of non-alignment. There are policy differences among the non-Communist opposition parties (just as there are between these parties and the Congress), but were an "opposition" coalition Government to come to power at the Center, in balancing the various tendencies, there would likely be little divergence from Congress in basic policy. The essential continuity of policy which is both a source and a product of India's political stability will be preserved.

I. The Non-Communist National Parties

The Bharatiya Janata Party. The BJP is the reincarnation of the Jana Sangh and the only former constituent of the Janata Party that was not the product of the "Congress culture." The party's close association with the Hindu nationalist Rashtriya Swayamsevak Sangh (RSS) has led to its denunciation as "reactionary" and "communal" by Congress and opposition critics alike. The party's leadership--notably Atal Bihari Vajpayee and L. K. Advani--is neither reactionary nor communal, but in taking the party on a more secular course, it has alienated the RSS cadre who form the core of the party's organizational strength and deepened dissension within the party.

The role of the RSS within the BJP has long been a matter of dispute, and the apparent RSS "noncooperation" with the BJP in the Delhi and Jammu elections in 1983 may well have been designed to demonstrate to the BJP's more secular leadership the party's continuing dependence on RSS cadre. In Jammu, the RSS may also have sought to strengthen Congress against the predominantly Muslim National Conference. Indeed, since 1980, there have been periodic reports of contact between RSS leaders and the Congress (I)--and the RSS is clearly unsympathetic to the decentralizing thrust of the opposition parties.

In the fall, 1981, at the time of the BJP's strategy conference at Vrindavan, the party seemed to be gaining momentum--perhaps destined even to emerge as the major force of a non-Communist opposition alliance. The BJP saw itself (in an assessment shared by many political analysts) as the "alternative party" in Himachal Pradesh, Madhya Pradesh, Rajasthan, and Delhi, as a "major force" in Maharashtra and Gujarat, and as a "complementary force" in Kashmir (with strength in the Jammu region), Haryana, and the Punjab. The BJP remained a factor in Bihar and Uttar Pradesh, although by its own judgment, the Janata Government debacle had seriously hurt its standing in the two states. The party's base of support in North India has been concentrated among the urban Hindu lower middle class--small traders and civil servants. But by the early 1980s, the BJP was expanding its social base--gaining rural support, making inroads among Harijans and tribals, and seeking to carve out a niche for itself in the southern states of Andhra, Karnataka, and Kerala. And, although burdened by its RSS connection, it was even courting Muslims. The BJP, however, did not project itself as a national alternative to Congress.

Looking to the next parliamentary elections, the BJP seeks to become the leading force of a national front against the Congress at the Center--a prospect seriously challenged by recent poll results. (Such a front would exclude the Muslim League and the CPI; the CPM, apparently, is at least potentially acceptable as an alliance partner.) The BJP's position was to be strengthened by a major thrust in state assembly elections. According to its 1981 strategy, the BJP would go it alone in those states where it was an alternative to Congress; in other states, it would enter into electoral adjustments where possible; and it would seek to establish a political understanding with regional parties. The prospects for the BJP, however, have dimmed over the past two years. In the May 1982 elections, the party made a major advance in Himachal Pradesh, but fell just short of the seats needed to displace the Congress. It suffered a decline in Haryana (where it was allied with the Lok Dal) and in West Bengal, and it failed to take a single seat in Kerala. In the January 1983 assembly elections in Andhra, a non-aligned BJP fared poorly, and it did only somewhat better in Karnataka. A month later, in its Delhi stronghold, with the disaffected RSS on the sidelines, the BJP suffered a major defeat at the hands of the Congress. In June, in Jammu and Kashmir--the last state assembly election scheduled before general parliamentary elections--the BJP, again with an unresponsive RSS, fell to the Congress in Jammu, a region once considered a base of BJP strength. Also in June, Congress victories in the Madhya Pradesh municipal elections dealt BJP credibility another blow. The lesson to be drawn is, first, that for all the weakness of its organization, the Congress is not to be underestimated, and, second, that as the BJP changes from a cadre party built around the RSS to a mass party, it risks the alienation of its base of support at the same time that it becomes a more acceptable partner to other opposition parties. Despite recent electoral losses, the BJP remains a powerful force in North India, and an opposition alliance that does not include the BJP will be unlikely to displace Mrs. Gandhi.

In August 1983, the BJP joined the Lok Dal in the formation of the National Democratic Alliance. With strength largely in North India, the Alliance combines the BJP's predominatly urban support with the rural base of the Lok Dal.

The Lok Dal. Led by Charan Singh, 81, the caretaker Prime Minister after the collapse of the Janata Government in 1979, the Lok Dal commands support among the Jat, Ahir, and Gujar peasantry of Uttar Pradesh, Haryana, Bihar, and parts of Rajasthan. Substantially reduced in strength and geographic reach by factional splits, it is today largely a personal party and is unlikely to survive its aging leader. But in his home base, Charan Singh remains a powerful force and is courted by various parties in hope of breaking the National Democratic Alliance, isolating the BJP, and drawing the Lok Dal into the Janata-led United Front.

The Janata Party. The Janata Party has grown since 1980 as it has reabsorbed breakaway elements of the Lok Dal and the Congress (S), and, following its victory in Karnataka, merger with its regional ally, the Kranti Ranga. The Janata now governs Karnataka and is the major opposition party in Gujarat, Bihar, and Orissa, with extensive support in Maharashtra and Haryana. The party's leadership includes those with strong state bases, such as Ramakrishna Hedge (now chief minister of Karnataka), Biju Patnaik (Orissa), Kapoori Thakur (Bihar), and Devi Lal (Haryana), in addition to former Prime Minister Morarji Desai and free-floaters as disparate as Subramaniam Swamy (closely associated with Desai) on the right and socialists George Fernandes, Madhu Lamaye, and Raj Narain on the left.

The United Front (to be examined more closely in the context of opposition unity efforts) was formed in September 1983 and is composed of five parties--the Janata Party, the Democratic Socialist Party, the Congress (S), the Rashtriya Congress, and the Janwadi Party. The Front, while augmenting Janata Party strength, imposes increased strain on Janata coherence. The Front strengthens the socialist faction within the party, and the prominence assumed by H. N. Bahuguna, leader of the Democratic Socialist Party, gives discomfort to Desai, Subramaniam Swamy, and the more conservative Janata elements.

Attempting to hold the party's various factions and feuding leaders together is Janata president Chandra Shekhar, a Gandhian socialist who was one of the few to emerge from the shambles of the Janata Government relatively untarnished. In 1983, Chandra Shekhar walked the length of India, from Cape Camorin to New Delhi, 2,700 miles in six months, to dramatize the Janata Party's concern for the rural poor and to call for a restoration of moral values to national life. As the fortunes of the Janata Party have risen over the past year, so too has Chandra Shekhar's star. He is considered by many observers to be the probable leader of the opposition United Front in the next parliamentary elections and, if it is victorious, the next Prime Minister of India.

The Democratic Socialist Party. The DSP was formed in 1981 by H. N. Bahuguna, a former Congress chief minister of Uttar Pradesh and itinerant politician who broke with Mrs. Gandhi in 1977, joined the Janata Party, went back to Congress, and then came out again to organize his own party. Bahuguna is viewed with considerable suspicion and unease by other opposition leaders, and he is anathema to Mrs. Gandhi. He sees himself as the rightful heir of Congress socialism and denounces Indira Gandhi as an apostate. Bahuguna wears a white "Gandhi cap" and emphasizes his Congress experience from the grassroots to party general secretary, and there is little doubt that after Mrs. Gandhi passes from the scene, he would try to seize the mantle of Congress leadership. The DSP projects itself as a socialist, secular, and left-of-center party, and Bahuguna hopes to make it the core of a "left and democratic front," which would include both Communist parties and exclude the BJP. In his foreign policy stance, Bahuguna is clearly pro-Soviet, and during the Janata Government, in a fit of pique, Charan Singh publicly accused him of being a KGB agent--an accusation now conveniently forgotten by each as they engage in discussions toward a political understanding.

The DSP is limited largely to Uttar Pradesh, where Bahuguna (a Brahmin) has considerable following among Muslims. Having failed in efforts to merge various parties under his leadership, Bahuguna brought the DSP into the United Front and serves as its spokesman in Parliament.

The Rashtriya Congress. A breakaway from the Congress (I) in Gujarat, the Rashtriya Congress has no pretense to the status of a national party. Its leader, Ratubhai Adani, is respected, but the party is largely confined to the Saurashtra region of the state. As a partner in the United Front, however, the Rashtriya

Congress bolsters the Janata Party in challenging the Congress (I) in Gujarat.

The Janwadi Party. Led by Chandrajit Yadav, the Janwadi Party has virtually no support outside Yadav's home constituency in eastern Uttar Pradesh and is based on a personal following among the Backward Castes. Yadav leaves a trail of party affiliations--the CPI, Congress, Janata, and Lok Dal. He is, like Bahuguna, generally pro-Soviet, but is viewed as a pragmatic and able politician.

The Congress remnants. Over the past four years, the opposition Congress, most recently identified as (S) for party president Sharad Pawar, has been weakened by attrition. There has been a steady movement of leaders--most notably Y. B. Chevan--back to the Congress (I); the Kerala and West Bengal units of the party formally merged with the Congress (I); the Orissa unit joined the Janata Party in early 1983. The Congress (S) has been reduced virtually to the status of a regional party in Maharashtra, where under Sharad Pawar, it poses a powerful challenge to the ruling Congress (I). Also bearing the Congress name, Jagjivan Ram's Congress (J) lacks a geographic base in any state. But Ram, once a contender for the Prime Ministership during the Janata phase, has a following among his fellow Harijans, primarily in Bihar and Uttar Pradesh, and remains an attractive constituent of any opposition alliance.

Rashtriya Sanjay Manch. In 1983, Maneka Gandhi, Sanjay's young widow, transformed her movement for the propagation of Sanjay's views, the Sanjay Vichar Manch, into a full-fledged opposition party. In April, at the first meeting of the Rashtriya Sanjay Manch, a year after she dramatically left her mother-in-law's household, Maneka attacked the Congress party as "reeking with corruption," and, though she did not mention Indira by name, denounced the rulers who had "lost touch with the people."

Though her party, with the support of the Telugu Desam, won three seats in the Andhra assembly elections and took one assembly seat in Uttar Pradesh in the December 1983 bye-elections, the Rashtriya Sanjay Manch is unlikely to become a major opposition, and Maneka in her own right does not pose a threat to Mrs. Gandhi. But Indira Gandhi could overplay her hand, and a martyred Maneka could be used most effectively by the opposition. At this point, Maneka is primarily a nuisance, but she could prove a formidable obstacle to Rajiv's succession--and this, surely, is Mrs. Gandhi's greatest fear. Maneka has announced her intention to contest the Amethi constituency against Rajiv in the next parliamentary elections. A united opposition would likely rally to her candidacy, and even short of victory, Maneka could seriously embarrass Rajiv if she gained substantial support.

II. Regional Parties

The DMK and AIADMK. Rooted in Tamil nationalism going back to the turn of the century, the DMK and its AIADMK offshoot have dominated politics in Tamil Nadu since taking power in 1967. The two parties, distinguished by leadership rivalry, have essentially identical policies--support for the Tamil language, greater administrative autonomy for the states, more favorable financial allocation for Tamil Nadu, and a vaguely populist economic policy. Each party has, at one time or another, allied itself with Mrs. Gandhi, and Chief Minister M. G. Ramachandran's reluctance to identify the AIADMK with an anti-Congress opposition alliance suggests that he is keeping his options open.

The Telugu Desam. Formed in 1982 by film star T. N. Rama Rao, the party, in an assertion of "Telugu pride," defeated the Congress in the January 1983 Andhra elections. As chief minister, Rama Rao joined non-Congress chief ministers of Tamil Nadu, Pondicherry, and Karnataka in the formation of a Southern Council directed toward a new balance in Center-State relations. In May, grooming himself for a more national role, Rama Rao took center stage in hosting a conference of leaders of 14 opposition parties, a step toward opposition unity out of which came a call for the redress of the federal balance and devolution of power to the states.

The National Conference. The ruling party of Jammu and Kashmir, with its base primarily among the Muslim majority of the state, the National Conference guards the unique autonomy of Kashmir granted by the Constitution.

The Akali Dal. Both a regional and communal party, the Akali Dal is confined to the Punjab and open only to Sikhs. While opposing the creation of an independent Sikh nation of Khalistan, the Akalis demand greater autonomy for the Punjab and protection of Sikh religious values.

III. The Communist Parties

The Communist movement in India is divided and regionally concentrated, with two major parties, the Communist Party of India (Marxist) (CPM) and the Communist Party of India (CPI); a pro-Congress CPI splinter, the All-India Communist Party (the Dange group), of no consequence; and more than a dozen tiny Naxalite (Maoist) parties and factions once associated with the Communist Party of India (Marxist-Leninist). The Communists have been unable to break out of their regional bases of strength in West Bengal (and by Bengali ethnic extension, Tripura) and Kerala; they have bogged down in Bihar; and they have lost support in Andhra and the Punjab. Communist trade unions in Bombay have also declined in influence. Overall, Communism in India is stagnant, and there is no state where support for either the CPM or CPI is growing.

The Communist Party of India (Marxist) is the larger of the two major Communist parties. It is the ruling party in West Bengal and Tripura and is the largest single party in Kerala. Beyond this concentration of strength, the CPM has a smattering of support in Andhra, Assam, Bihar, Maharashtra, the Punjab, and Tamil Nadu, but its overall weakness nationally has transformed the CPM into what is, in effect, a regional party--and, increasingly, a Bengali party.

In Kerala, the CPM--now in the opposition--has been in and out of office since 1957 (the united Communist Party of India split in 1964), but has stagnated, unable to expand its base of support. In West Bengal, the CPM is on the defensive against a resurgent, although factionally divided, Congress. The party's once unsullied reputation has been tarnished by corruption. The death of state party boss Promode Das Gupta in 1982 was a major loss to the organization, and the domineering stance of the CPM has led to a deepening with its allies--the Revolutionary Socialist Party, the Forward Bloc, and the CPI, each of which potentially could be lured into an electoral understanding with Congress.

Politics in India is not highly polarized in class terms, and even the two Communist parties draw support from a diverse social base. While they favor more radical policies than pursued by Congress at the Center, each has been restrained in its own policies by participation in electoral politics and the responsibility of Government. The parties have become more reformist than revolutionary, and it is for this reason that more radical elements of the CPM advocate withdrawal from the electoral arena and abandonment of Government under the

Constitution and central authority. There is some attrition from the CPM to Naxalite factions, but there is little prospect that the party will trade political power--even if regional--for the revolutionary underground.

The CPM leadership is aging (the average age of the politburo is 72), and its revolutionary fervor has been leavened by electoral politics and the responsibility of Government. The party, independent of Moscow, has assumed a more favorable stance toward the Soviet Union, facilitating closer cooperation with the CPI--but the merger of the two Indian Communist parties, seen by some to be on the horizon two years ago, is an unlikely prospect.

The Communist Party of India (CPI) has more evenly distributed national support than the CPM, but it is everywhere weak, and only in Bihar does it have a concentrated base of support. The CPI is officially recognized by Moscow, and even Mrs. Gandhi views it as subject to Soviet direction--as implied by her reported request while visiting Moscow in September 1982 that Brezhnev rein in the CPI and curtail its criticism of the Congress. The CPI has at various times supported the Congress, and it did so during the Emergency, but in 1977, the party broke with Mrs. Gandhi and has since moved closer to the CPM. CPI General Secretary Rejeshwara Rao supports links with the CPM and joins the Marxists in a willingness to enter into a united opposition alliance against the Congress--even exploring at one point the possible inclusion of the BJP.

The CPM is prepared to cooperate with the BJP in order to unseat Mrs. Gandhi, but the CPI officially regards the BJP as a reactionary and communal party and thus unacceptable as a political partner. There is a faction within the CPI that sees the BJP and "the forces or Right reaction" as a far greater danger than the Congress. In its view, only the Congress, supported by left and democratic elements, can block the emergence of these forces. This group, believed to be closely connected to Moscow, favors CPI cooperation with the Congress, and the highly publicized article by Soviet India specialist Rostislav Ulvanosky[3] suggests that Moscow is exerting some pressure in that direction.

Opposition Unity Efforts

The strength and character of the opposition parties are highly fluid, and election outcomes tend to be highly specific to the conditions of each state, making patterns and national trends difficult to discern.

Since 1980, in following assembly and bye-election returns, the press has alternatively declared the opposition prostrate and ascendant. The demonstrated capacity of the opposition to deny Congress political power remains a compelling incentive for unity, but, given the experience of the once-united Janata Party and the increasing regionalization of party strength, the merger of the non-Communist opposition into a single party is an unlikely prospect. Since the breakup of the Janata Party and Mrs. Gandhi's return to power, periodic unity efforts have run aground on questions of leadership, allocation of seats in elections, and (more a smokescreen than a matter of substance) the allegedly communal character of the BJP. Initial efforts toward unity were frustrated by the continued bickering of Morarji Desai, Charan Singh, and Jagjivan Ram, in a replay of the dissension that had brought the collapse of the Janata Government. While still physically on the political scene, Desai, Singh, and Ram (who at 75 is the youngest of the three) no longer command center stage. They have been effectively displaced by the next generation, the product of post-independence politics. The opposition embraces many who nurture ambition to become Prime Minister, but the leadership issue may decline as an impediment to unity as the various opposition parties test their relative strength and credibility in electoral competition with the Congress and with each other. Who does emerge as leader will be more a broker of interests than one who imposes his will from above. Similarly, as the parties establish regional bases of strength, the question of allocation of seats may be less contentious, save in those states and constituencies where a single opposition has yet to emerge as a clear alternative to Congress. To the degree that competition between opposition parties declines relative to competition between Congress and a single opposition party in a given state, the chances for opposition unity will be enhanced.

What form is opposition unity, if it can be forged, likely to take?

There is little chance of the non-Communist opposition merging into a single party, nor is there much support for the effort. Regional parties--the DMK and AIADMK in Tamil Nadu, the Telugu Desam in Andhra, the Akali Dal in the Punjab, the National Conference in Kashmir, and the tribal parties in the Northeast--have no interest in submerging their separate identities in an all-India party, and those in power are not prepared to share the bounty of office. A second impediment to grand merger is the Bharatiya Janata Party, which opposes merger in principle, although it now supports the formation of a national democratic front. But the BJP--and the role of the RSS within it--also remains a source of contention among other opposition parties, and even among leaders who favor electoral cooperation with the BJP, there is little inclination to draw the party within the embrace of a more inclusive all-India opposition party.

Short of a grand merger of the non-Communist opposition, however, there are continuing efforts to merge the remaining constitutents of the once-united Janata party. These parties and their progeny--principally the Janata, the Lok Dal, the Democratic Socialist Party, the Congress (S), and the Congress (J)--are divided heirs of the "Congress culture." In grappling for unity, elements of each have split, merged, and split again. Complete merger of the parties is unlikely if only because of the personalities involved. The Janata Party, even as it is divided factionally, is likely to grow in strength, and the Democratic Socialist Party, fed by mergers, could become increasingly visible in its efforts to forge a "left and democratic front."

Opposition unity capable of challenging Congress power at the Center will not be the product of merger but of the alliance of parties with regional bases of power and electoral adjustments among potentially contending opposition parties. Rather than making common cause on a national platform, the opposition parties--separately or in combination--may enter into adjustments by state and constituency. Such arrangements may vary in composition: what is achieved in one state may be unacceptable in another. Accommodation will not be easy to achieve, and the record of unity talks preceding state assembly elections since 1980 hardly enhances opposition credibility.

In May 1983, at the initiative of Andhra Chief Minister T. N. Rama Rao (leader of the regional Telegu Desam and aspirant for a starring role on the national stage), 24 leaders of 14 opposition parties met at Vijayawada to discuss their common interests. Although the Communists and the BJP used the occasion to take jabs at each other, that the gathering took place at all was remarkable. Setting aside ideological differences, the parties unanimously adopted a statement sharply critical of Mrs. Gandhi and, in an expression favorable to regional sentiment, called for greater autonomy for the states--a likely theme for opposition unity. Pursuant to their agreement at the Vijayawada conclave, opposition party leaders again met in June at Delhi and in October at Srinagar. A fourth conclave, hosted by the CPM's Jyoti Basu, chief minister of West Bengal, met in January 1984 in Calcutta. But the difficulties of achieving opposition unity were underscored by the failure of the BJP to attend the Delhi meeting and by the absence of both the BJP and the Lok Dal from Srinagar and Calcutta.

In August 1983, the Lok Dal and the BJP--together a major force in North India--formed the National Democratic Alliance. A month later, four parties came together to form a United Front: the Congress (S), with strength in Maharashtra; the Democratic Socialist Party, with a Muslim following and a base in Uttar Pradesh; the Rashtriya Congress, the Gujarat splinter; and, at the helm, the Janata Party. They were soon joined by the tiny Janwadi Party. Remaining outside, the Telegu Desam, the National Conference, and the two Communist parties indicated their support for the Front. United Front leaders continued to court the Lok Dal, hoping to split the National Democratic Alliance and isolate the BJP. But the Bharatiya Janata Party, despite its electoral losses in 1983, remains the strongest non-Communist opposition party, and an opposition alliance that does not include the BJP will be unlikely to displace Indira Gandhi.

THE BUREAUCRACY[4]

In an assessment of the prospects for political stability in India, political parties, as they organize power, are inevitably the central concern of analysis, but bureaucracy plays a vital role in sustaining stability, and it assumes increased responsibility to the degree that party Government is weak or unstable. Bureaucracy constitutes the "permanent government": It provides continuity between Governments at both the central and state levels, and in the federal system, it links the states, ruled by an array of parties, within a centralized structure of administration. The bureaucracy, in short, provides the framework of governance and national unity.

Indian bureaucracy, once the "steel frame" of the Raj, has corroded over the past decade and a half. It has been weakened by pervasive corruption, by political interference, arbitrary transfers and promotions, and by low pay. The services continue to attract men and women of impressive ability, and at the highest levels India is well served. But top salaries have been frozen for 30 years, and senior officers in the Indian Administrative Service (IAS) earn a fraction of the salaries of the counterparts in the private sector. The result has been an unprecedented hermorrhaging of the IAS. Many of India's most competent government servants take early retirement or simply resign to make a lateral shift to high-level management positions in business and industry.

In recruitment, the elite all-India services can still be highly selective: Of some 40,000 applicants each year, only about 400 are selected. The IAS, however has lost much of its attractiveness for India's brightest youth, who may now find business offering both greater prestige and financial reward. The service continues to be dominated by the urban, westernized, and wealthy classes, but the social background of recruits has begun to change. Some 25-30 percent of new entrants come from the scheduled castes (untouchables) and tribes and from the depressed classes, and an increasingly large portion is drawn from more backward states, such as Bihar and Orissa. The result is that the services are no longer as socially homogeneous as they once were nor are recruits as westernized and "sophisticated" as their predecessors. The services are being "Indianized," but if often less polished by European standards, they are not necessarily less competent.

While the highest levels of the Indian bureaucracy continue to command respect, that respect has diminished in recent years as cases of corruption have tarnished the image of the elite services. Corruption has long been endemic in the lower and middle levels of bureaucracy, but it has begun to reach higher, especially in those states where there has been considerable political interference in administration. All generalizations about India are subject to qualification in terms of regional variation, and this is especially evident in judging the character of state governments. Within the Indian federal system, states range from the reasonably well administered to those that are in virtual collapse. Most states are served by senior officers of capability and integrity, but every state administration is under pressure. In some state ministries, corruption is widespread and cynically accepted as a fact of life.

The courts, in the British tradition of an independent judiciary, occupy a unique position within India's "permanent government." They are the guardians of individual liberty and provide an important mechanism for coping with change and managing unrest. Although long overburdened, the courts are now being weakened by the same pressures that have eroded the bureaucracy in general--low pay, arbitrary transfers, and political interference. The courts are increasingly less capable of checking the excesses of local, state, or national officials and of providing a forum for the redress of grievances. At the state level--and Bihar is an archetype--the courts are increasingly corrupt and ineffective. There are throughout India and at every level courageous judges who have stood up for judicial integrity against political interference and who have battled for the protection of individual rights, but the larger number are demoralized. As Indians lose confidence in the judicial system, disputes once litigated in the courtroom may be fought out in the streets.

Political interference is present to some degree in the administration of most states and at the Center. Politicians (normally ministers) have gained leverage over judges and bureaucrats by the threat of transfer to the mofussil (the "boondocks") and by control over the avenues of promotion. In Madhya Pradesh, a particularly dramatic case, legislators as well as ministers have been able to transfer civil servants in order to bring in political cronies, to oblige relatives, or to extort favors. The result has been a decline in bureaucratic morale and efficiency. In the most extreme cases, such as Bihar, ministerial incompetence and venality have gutted effective administration.

At the same time that the bureaucracy in many states has been eroded by political interference, corruption, and low morale, its power at the Center (and in some states) has grown--so much so that it has been described as "civil service raj." Bureaucrats were subjected to enormous political pressures during the Emergency; most acquiesced in whatever orders came down from above: some were overzealous in their exercise of new-found power. Following the change of political power to the Janata Party in 1977 and back to the Congress in 1980, punitive transfers took their toll on bureaucratic morale, but by 1982, Mrs. Gandhi--in part to restore morale, but primarily to further centralize executive authority--began to insulate senior civil servants at the Center from ministerial interference. Indeed, she increasingly bypassed ministers to deal directly with the highest echelons of the bureaucracy within each ministry. Most ministers are reshuffled so frequently that they have little knowledge of their spheres of authority, and, in any case, many function primarily as political trouble-shooters in Congress party affairs. The secretaries of each ministry have come to play increasingly important decision-making roles and are linked to the Prime Minister through her Principal Secretary, P. C. Alexander, and Cabinet Secretary Krishnaswamy Rao Sabib. The Prime Minister's Secretariat has also opened channels to the state chief secretaries, strengthening the civil service tie between the Center and the states.

During the transitions from Congress to Janata and back again, the bureaucracy provided continuity in administration, as it did in 1947 with the transfer of power from the British to an independent India. During the last months of the Janata Government and under the caretaker Government of Charan Singh, the bureaucracy provided stability in a period of political crisis. Ministries and ministers may come and go, as we have said, but the bureaucrats remain. During periods of political instability in the states or at the Center, the bureaucracy and senior civil servants in particular can be expected to play an increasingly important role.

Coalition Government, to the degree that it is unstable or involves shifting partners and exchange of ministerial portfolios, makes a strong and capable bureaucracy all the more vital. Bureaucracy in France under the Third and Fourth Republics, as it has (though without French efficiency) in Italy since World War II, provided "government as usual" during almost continuous ministerial crises. Indian bureaucracy--among the most capable in the world, for all its red tape and labyrinthian character--can fulfill that role.

But political instability or weak party Government does not in itself enhance the power of the bureaucracy nor is there any guarantee that bureaucracy will be able to sustain its greater responsibility. Political interference has already weakened Indian bureaucracy, and insecure ministers, as political buccaneers, may be all the more inclined to penetrate the bureaucracy, both in an effort to demonstrate their power and to secure what spoils they can. If Government at the Center is chronically unstable and if the bureaucracy has been politically penetrated to so weaken efficiency and morale that it is unable to provide effective administration and, through civil authorities, to maintain law and order, the military will in all probability take a more active role in the governance of India.

THE MILITARY

The military is the ultimate guarantor of stability in India. The Indian army, with nearly one million volunteers, is the world's fourth largest standing army, and its officer corps is respected, highly professional, and, by tradition, non-political. But pressure within the military, potential political instability, and the inability of civil authorities to cope with social unrest could draw the army into a more active role in government.

The social character of the Indian military is changing. Officers are increasingly recruited from a broader social base and from more humble backgrounds than the affluent families of martial tradition that were once the principal source of military leadership. As the culture of the officer corps changes, as it loses its Sandhurst character, it may also lose something of its non-political tradition.

The military has long been an effective lobbyist for defense expenditure, but officers more recently have been drawn into the political arena over the issues of pay, promotion, and retirement. Low pay is a source of discontent among officers, but it has also taken its toll in recruitment. A Lieutenant Colonel, for example, receives today approximately $270 per month, less than a third of what he took home in real income in 1947. At these levels, the military has been unable to compete with private sector employment opportunities, and, unwilling to lower its recruitment standards, the military now faces an officer shortage which is especially serious in those areas requiring engineering and technical skills.

But while there is a shortage of junior officers, there is enormous pressure at the upper levels for promotion to command rank. The bottleneck was widened somewhat recently by increasing the number of brigadiers, and a step up in pay grade is now possible without promotion in rank. But limited prospects for promotion, like pay, affects the military's ability to attract the best recruits, and it is also a potential source of unrest among junior officers. One of the classic patterns of military coups in the Third World--though not in South Asia--is the seizure of power by colonels. This has typically involved junior officers of more humble origins who are frustrated in promotion, while the senior ranks remain the preserve of officers from affluent and socially prominant backgrounds. Such a social distinction is not now evident in the Indian officer corps, but the changing base of recruitment together with limited promotion to command ranks could bring it about.

Promotions also raise the sensitive issue of political interference. The military has been highly protective of its internal affairs, and for the most part this has been respected by civil authorities. The Government, however, has the right to choose the Army chief of staff from among the senior generals. This has, with two notable exceptions, followed the principle of seniority. In 1975, in an appointment with political overtones, Mrs. Gandhi named Lieutenant General T. N. Raina to the top post, superseding the senior officer. In June 1983, she again stirred controversy by selecting Lieutenant General A. S. Vaidya over his senior, Lieutenant General S. K. Sinha. While both generals have distinguished records, Sinha was widely judged in military circles to be the more qualified and, as the senior officer, the one properly to have been chosen. Sinha, in protest against being passed over, submitted his resignation. Politics, in fact, may have played no part in the selection, but the process must be above suspicion. The barriers to political involvement by the military are weakened to the degree that there is political interference in military.

Officers are also concerned about retirement benefits, and those without independent sources of income face the prospect of considerably diminished standards of living. Relatively low pay during active service is at least augmented by various perquisites, most critically housing, but few such perqs are sustained in retirement.

The military officers' worry about pay and retirement may turn to anger in the context of widespread corruption in government, as they contrast their own integrity with an image of venality among petty bureaucrats and politicians. Many officers openly express contempt for politicians, but, as noted in the previous chapter, there is nothing at the present to suggest that the military is prepared to intervene in government or that there is much sympathy among the officer corps for such a move. Even if the army were to overcome its tradition of restraint, a coup would require the concerted action of the five regional commands--no easy task.

A number of factors beyond the structure of the army itself make a military coup d'etat in India an unlikely prospect. First, the sheer size and complexity of India would impose an enormous burden on the army. Second, more than thirty years experience with democratic politics has awakened a level of political consciousness that will not be easily suppressed, as Mrs. Gandhi found during her authoritarian venture with Emergency rule. Third, the Indian military commands widespread popular respect that it will not lightly sacrifice to the expedience of political intervention. The Pakistan military's sullied reputation among the people and the corruption that has accompanied its involvement in politics bear witness to the costs of military rule.

The Indian Army, however, would not remain passive in the face of the breakdown of law and order, political chaos, or national disintegration. In the past four years, the military has been called in with increasing frequency "in aid of the civil" to control domestic unrest, such as police strikes and communal rioting. If civil authorities are unable to control unrest, the army may one day simply refuse to return to the barracks. The most likely scenario for greater military involvement, however, is not a seizure of power, but the gradual expansion of the army's participation in domestic affairs. This might come through the imposition of martial law in regions or states where domestic security is threatened by social unrest. It could come, perhaps by invitation of the President, in the event of chronic political instability at the Center and prolonged Government crises.

Of the three major institutional sources of India's strength at the time of independence (the Congress party, the bureaucracy, and the Indian Army), only the army has retained its elan. But for all their weaknesses, India's political parties and the bureaucracy continue to display remarkable resilience. The prospects for ministerial stability at the Center--whether under continued Congress rule or under a non-Congress coalition--are reasonably good, and the stability of the regime, the constitutional order, is fundamentally secure. The strength of the system should, in fact, provide a capacity to sustain a considerable degree of political instability at both state and central levels. If India does experience rounds of ministerial instability at the Center, perhaps along Italian lines, the bureaucracy is capable of carrying on normal administrative functions and maintaining law and order. If, however, in the face of instability at the Center and growing social unrest, the bureaucracy is unable to bear its responsibility, if it is so politically penetrated as seriously to undermine administration and the maintenance of law and order, the army will assume a greater role--but not without caution and considerable restraint.

THE NEXT FIVE YEARS: SCENARIOS FOR POLITICAL STABILITY

In projecting the course of probable and possible political developments over the next five years, we begin by assuming conditions of continuing, but basically manageable, social unrest--the "most probable" scenario laid out in the first chapter. Under such conditions, we project no fundamental change in the character of the Indian political system or in the nature of India's domestic or foreign policies. We can, however, expect to see considerable political turbulence in the struggle for power and leadership, the possible emergence of coalition Government at the Center, and the continued regionalization of politics, with increasing pressure for greater state autonomy.

Before turning to the parliamentary elections and their political aftermath, we first consider what might happen on the sudden death of Prime Minister Indira Gandhi.

Succession on the Death of Indira Gandhi

If Mrs. Gandhi were to die in office, what possible course of events might follow? Who would likely succeed? Would the Congress party remain intact? How would her death affect the prospects for political stability?

Rajiv's chances for succession will improve over time if he is able to demonstrate political skill and build a body of personal support in the Lok Sabha. If Mrs. Gandhi were to die suddenly before the next parliamentary elections, Rajiv's prospects would be considerably more difficult. President Zail Singh would call upon Pranab Mukherjee, Finance Minister and ranking member of the Cabinet, to take control of Government as Acting Prime Minister. (Gulzari Lal Nanda played this role after the deaths of both Nehru and Shastri.) The process of electing a new leader of the Congress Parliamentary Party (CPP)--the next Prime Minister--would then begin.

In the earlier successions, the state chief ministers and the Congress party high command, notably the Congress President and the Working Committee, played a decisive role in shaping the consensus on the selection of Shastri after the death of Nehru and in bringing a majority of the CPP behind Indira Gandhi after the death of Shastri. The second succession involved the first contested election for Congress party leadership. After eight days struggle behind the scenes, the party bosses marshalled their forces and, by secret ballot, the Congress Parliamentary party elected Indira Gandhi as leader. Each succession took place during the period of the "Congress system" of one party dominance. Opposition parties posed no threat.

Today, the Congress party is politically on the defensive. With the party organization weak and the chief ministers dependent upon Mrs. Gandhi for their power, neither the Working Committee nor the chief ministers is likely to play a significant role in the succession. The critical actors will be within the Lok Sabha, as Congress MPs scramble to protect themselves and salvage their political futures. Unlike the earlier successions, where there were a number of potential contenders of national stature and visibility, there are today few obvious candidates beyond Rajiv. Mrs. Gandhi, far more than her father, has been the banyan tree under which nothing grows.

In the grief--and political panic--that will follow upon Mrs. Gandhi's death, the initial reaction of Congress MPs is likely to be to rally behind Rajiv. He does not at this point, however, command wide confidence in Parliament, and there will be a strong preference among many to bypass Rajiv in favor of another. Some observers suggest that the party might seek someone around whom a consensus might be built, someone with the demonstrated qualities of a Prime Minister, but who is without a base of personal power and who would likely function as a broker of interests in holding the Congress together. Foreign Minister Narasimha Rao, from Andhra, would surely be an attractive choice for such a role. He might be expected to govern in a Shastri-like manner, with a consensual style and collective Cabinet leadership, in which ministers represent various party factions and states. Strong state chief ministers would probably again emerge, as would more autonomous state party organizations.

Some Congress MPs would favor a "caretaker" Prime Minister, someone unlikely to secure himself too firmly and who can be displaced once the factional struggle for party control throws up a new leader. Defense Minister Venkataraman--without a political base in his home state of Tamil Nadu, respected, and old--has been mentioned in this context. Pranab Mukherjee, believed to harbor ambition for higher office, might offer himself as a contender, and as Acting Prime Minister and keeper of the party purse, he would command powerful resources for the exertion of influence. Another contender could be Industries Minister N. D. Tewari, former chief minister of Uttar Pradesh.

The critical factor in choosing the next Prime Minister is the election of someone who can lead the Congress party to victory in the next parliamentary elections--to be held by January 1985. Here the choice of a "technocrat" for Prime Minister loses its luster, although Rao might hold his own under such considerations. It is this concern, however, that is most likely to draw the party together behind Rajiv. As the surrogate for his mother, Rajiv, in dynastic succession, would provide continuity in leadership. At a time of unease that follows the loss of a leader, the selection of Rajiv as Prime Minister would respond to concern for national unity and political stability--the probable Congress party themes for the election campaign. Moreover, in elections following relatively soon after the death of Mrs. Gandhi, Rajiv would inevitably draw a sympathy vote from a nation in mourning.

The Congress Parliamentary Party, however, could reach beyond Rajiv to select someone from the reduced ranks of the older Congress generation--specifically Y. B. Chavan, aged 70 and currently Chairman of the Finance Commission. Chavan, once thought to be the probable successor to Nehru, broke with Mrs. Gandhi after her defeat in 1977. He returned to the Congress (I) in 1981, but was denied access to its inner circle. Chavan would bring to the Congress and to the Prime Ministership a background in the nationalist movement, continuity of leadership by his association with Nehru, experience as chief minister of Maharashtra and Cabinet minister with a wide range of portfolios over time, and national visibility and respect--although Chavan's image has been weakened by his opportunism in moving with the political winds. Most importantly, Chavan could be the unifying force of the Congress culture, drawing back to the party those alienated by Mrs. Gandhi over the course of her rule.

During the two earlier successions, the President of India played an essentially passive role awaiting the choice of the Congress Parliamentary Party. But if the party is unable to resolve its conflict over the leadership, or even to preempt its free choice, President Zail Singh--handpicked by Mrs. Gandhi and beholden to the Nehru family--could invite Rajiv to form a Government. There would surely be an outcry against the violation of parliamentary convention, but given the nod, Rajiv would have little difficulty, at least initially, in sustaining a majority in the Lok Sabha.

Rajiv could, of course, take himself out of the running, saying that he was not yet sufficiently experienced, and, playing king-maker, give his support to someone like Chavan, Rao, Venkataraman, or Tewari. Perhaps a safer choice, however, would be Kamalapati Tripathi, 79, former U.P. chief minister and "working president" of the Congress party, a position to which Mrs. Gandhi appointed him in February 1983 and for which there is no precedent. Rajiv might subsequently, when he judged himself ready, take the mantle of office--with the honor of not having pursued it too soon. But to forego the opportunity to lead the party in the parliamentary elections is to risk political oblivion.

Forthcoming elections would be a powerful force to hold the party together--at least until the tickets are handed out. Then there will be a likely attrition of disappointed claimants from the Congress to the opposition. If Rajiv (or whoever may be Prime Minister) can lead the Congress to a solid victory, he will be securely in control of a stable Government. Indeed, Congress success at the polls would likely bring a post-election expansion of the party's majority in the Lok Sabha, as dissident parties--the Congress (S), the Congress (J), the Rashtriya Congress, for example, return to the fold.

A narrow majority or a minority Government would render the Prime Minister and the Government vulnerable to challenge--not just from factions within Congress, but from elements outside the party who seek to force a split and claim the Congress banner under new leadership. H. N. Bahuguna can be expected to make such a bid in the name of Congress socialism. Chandra Sekhar would surely try to wed sympathetic Congress factions to the Janata under a Gandhian umbrella. The Congress Government could fall, followed by a Janata-led coalition containing Congress dissidents. But such a coalition would itself be vulnerable to dissension and breakup. India might then enter a period of prolonged instability at the Center, while the bureaucracy maintains law and order and carries on administration as usual. This is a situation that India could probably sustain for some time, as Italy has since World War II, but if ministerial instability so undermines order as to ferment social unrest that threatens the stability of the regime, the military will intervene and send the politicians packing.

If Congress were to lose the elections, Rajiv (or whoever led the party to defeat) would almost surely be forced to step down as leader of the Congress Parliamentary Party, and in all probability, the party would split. Gradually, out of a process of shifting alliances, splits and mergers, a party realignment would begin to take shape. Its most probable form would be at the national level--a broad centrist party representing the vestiges of the Congress culture, a right of center party (the BJP), and an alliance of the left (CPM, CPI, and smaller Marxist parties). At the state level, regional parties (some, as now, national in name) will increase in number and power.

We have thus far explored a range of possibilities following on the death of Mrs. Gandhi <u>before</u> the next parliamentary elections. If she were to die in office <u>after</u> the elections, Rajiv's prospects for succession will be considerably more secure, and, depending on the Congress margin of seats in the Lok Sabha, the possibilities of a party split will be substantially diminished.

We turn back to the prospects for political stability over the next five years with the assumption that Mrs. Gandhi will continue to be a vigorous force in Indian public life.

Calling Elections

General parliamentary elections must be held by January 1985, and there is wide speculation as to whether Prime Minister Gandhi will call early elections. Her decision will be based on political intelligence--an assessment of Congress party strength on a state-by-state basis and the prospects for opposition unity--and an analysis of economic trends, so as to choose the most propitious time to enter into electoral battle. With good monsoons in 1983, and prospects for bumper crops and a resurgence of industrial activity, the economy would augur well for Congress in early elections. The economy, given India's vulnerability to the monsoons, carries considerable political risk, and there is a strong incentive to seize a favorable situation, as against an unknown future, for contesting elections. Even in a favorable economic situation, however, the assessment of relative political strength between the ruling party and the opposition is the decisive factor in calling elections--and unless the Congress is reasonably confident of victory, of relative advantage now rather than later, Mrs. Gandhi is unlikely to go for early elections.

The position of the Congress party today is problematic, and the results of recent state assembly and bye-elections, however mixed they may be, are not favorable to Congress. The party is still reeling from its losses in Andhra and Karnataka, and, if the Congress is to refurbish its image--to replace corrupt chief ministers and to quell dissension--it needs more time. With more time, the Congress might be able to draw back splinters like the Congress (S) and the Rashtriya Congress and to welcome the return of such individuals as Karan Singh, leader of the Virat Hindu Samaj. Time would also enable Mrs. Gandhi to build up Rae Bareli, her constituency in Uttar Pradesh, with new projects and investments, and it would give Rajiv the opportunity to devote more time to his neighboring Amethi constituency, where he is likely to be opposed by his brother's widow, Maneka.

Mrs. Gandhi may also choose to bide her time in hope that Andhra Chief Minister T. N. Rama Rao may stumble or that the Janata Government in Karnataka may fall apart. Neither, at this point, appears to be a likely prospect. Rama Rao, despite his autocratic style, has proven his political skill to be more than celluloid, and in Karnataka, the Janata Government has weathered a major test in the withdrawal of a dissident faction and is firmly in place.

Waiting to call elections, however, carries risks for Mrs. Gandhi. Time may enhance the image of the non-Congress state Governments, and it may also provide the opposition parties the opportunity to forge an electoral alliance. While a call for early elections could rally the opposition behind a united front, the differences now--particularly over the role of the BJP--are deep and not easily resolved. In a call for early elections, Mrs. Gandhi could undermine opposition unity efforts and at the same time exploit differences among the parties and their factional constitutents.

Events in the Punjab could also play a role in the timing of the elections. A settlement would be hailed as a triumph of Mrs. Gandhi's leadership and would be high ground indeed from which to contest an election, but the Akali Dal is in no mood to come to terms with New Delhi. One factor in the Akalis' intransigence may be a calculation that by holding out they may one day be able to deal with a more sympathetic Government at the Center--but moderate Akalis, under increasing pressure form Sikh extremists, would probably benefit from an early resolution of the crisis. In any case, Mrs. Gandhi will surely use continued turmoil in the Punjab in projecting herself as the defender of Indian national unity.

Serious violence in Assam during the February 1983 elections and current political unrest in the Punjab raise the probability that elections will be postponed in the two states unless there is a commitment from all parties to support the conduct of elections and by the Akali Dal in the Punjab to suspend the agitation if a settlement has not been reached by the time the election is scheduled. There should be a strong incentive for the opposition parties to cooperate, given probable electoral results in each state, but the risk of violence remains, especially in the Punjab, where the volatile situation could end in communal conflagration.*

In a fluid situation, the Prime Minister will keep her options open. On balance, however, unless she can score a dramatic political success, Mrs. Gandhi is likely to hold off elections until January 1985 as she attempts to rebuild the Congress party and to postpone as long as possible the risk of being turned form office once again.

Elections

Whenever elections are held, the Congress will face serious opposition--not from a single national alternative, but from an array of regional parties and regionally-concentrated parties that are "national" in name only. Separately, these parties will surely reduce the number of Congress seats in the Lok Sabha, and they may be able to deny Mrs. Gandhi her parliamentary majority. In alliance, they may be able to displace the Congress and form a coalition Government.

The regionalization of politics poses a major threat to Mrs. Gandhi, but it also provides her with fuel for what will surely be her major campaign theme--that the Congress party alone can ensure continued national unity and political stability. Mrs. Gandhi will seek to nationalize the election, stressing the weak and divisive character of coalition Government in Indian experience. She will portray--as she has done with increasing frequency--the opposition parties as

---

* In the unlikely prospect of national unrest growing out of control, depicted as the "worst case" scenario in "Social Change and Political Stability" (pp. 65-68), elections, if they could be held at all, would sharpen tension and provoke further violence. Under such conditions, the Government might be compelled to proclaim a national Emergency and postpone elections. Unless the Government were to secure the concurrence of the opposition parties in taking such action--perhaps even seeking to form a "national Government" of all parties to deal with the crisis--imposition of Emergency rule would likely be met with opposition resistance, by deepening unrest, and widespread violence. Civil authorites having proven themselves unable to control the situation, martial law would be imposed over extensive areas, with the military perhaps assuming a major role in the central government.

"anti-national" malcontents, without a program and united only by their common opposition to her.

She can be expected to hold up the violence in Assam and continued agitation in the Punjab as the spectre of national disintegration, at the same time that the opposition denounces the Center's inept and insensitive handling of the situation in each state. In an appeal that will likely find favorable response in North India, especially among the urban middle class, she will emphasize her resistance to separatist forces and will project herself as the only leader capable of holding India together.

Mrs. Gandhi is also likely to pick up the danger of the "foreign hand." Here Pakistan (without evidence, alleged to be supporting Punjab secessionists) is a convenient scapegoat. (The United States will probably be spared direct attack, at least by Mrs. Gandhi, although references to foreign powers seeking to destabilize India are widely assumed to point to the CIA.) Anti-Pakistan rhetoric is again on the rise, and in the course of an election campaign, the Prime Minister is likely to play on fears of a nuclear Pakistan armed with American F-16 aircraft.

The Congress will pursue different strategies in each state, reflecting not only regional differences but the fact that the party is really a federation of state units with one person--Mrs Gandhi--at the top.

In shaping the campaign strategy to the peculiarities of each state, Mrs. Gandhi faces a dilemma with respect to the sensitive communal question. If she appeals to awakening Hindu consciousness or if (as the Congress has done in Jammu and the Punjab) she panders to Hindu fears, she may be able to weaken the BJP by neutralizing the RSS, if not winning its cadre over to active Congress support. There is a reservoir of Hindu sentiment that can be tapped politically, but it carries serious dangers, not just to the nation in sharpened communal conflict, but to the Congress by alienating the minorities--the Muslims, most critically--that have long formed a vital component of the party's social base. Mrs. Gandhi is likely to tread carefully, for the Muslim vote will be decisive in a number of U.P. and Bihar constituencies--two states where the Congress must do well if it is to have any chance of retaining power at the Center.

Economic issues are unlikely to play a major role in the next elections. The Congress populist rhetoric of the late 1960s and early 1970s has been notably absent from recent campaigns, and the party's 1980 election manifesto did not even mention the word socialism. The opposition alliance, whatever its final form, is likely to take a Gandhian socialist orientation to economic policy, with a call for emphasis on rural development and the poor--a theme of Chandra Sekhar's padayatra (political trek).

The major issue of the alliance, however, as already seen at Vijayawada and subsequent opposition party conclaves, is likely to be the federal Center-state relationship. Just as Mrs. Gandhi will seek to nationalize the election, the opposition will seek to regionalize it, playing upon regional sentiment and local concerns. The thrust of the attack will be against the distortions of the federal system brought about by Mrs. Gandhi's centralization, and there will be a call to redress the balance in some sort of "new federalism," with decentralization of planning and greater administrative autonomy for the states. The question of financial allocation among the states is likely to be avoided or soft-pedaled, as are other potentially divisive issues relating concretely to regionalism. The point is that in the federal relationship, conflict exists not only between the Center and the states, but among the states themselves.

So long as her health remains good and her energy high, Mrs. Gandhi will wage a vigorous and extensive national campaign, as she did so impressively in 1980. This time, Rajiv will be at her side--on the dais and in the posters that have so closely identified mother and son in recent state elections. The Congress campaign may also gain glamour with the candidacy of Bombay film star Amitabh Bachchan. There is likely to be enormous pressure on Bachchan to enter politics. He is India's highest paid film star; the son of a nationalist poet from Uttar Pradesh and an intimate of the Nehru family; a close childhood friend and schoolmate of Rajiv; and a Muslim. In July 1983, Bachchan underwent emergency surgery, and as his life hung in the balance, all India waited. Rajiv cut short his trip to the United States (he accompanied Mrs. Gandhi on her official visit to Washington) to be at Bachchan's bedside. Upon her return to India, Mrs. Gandhi also went to Bombay to visit the stricken star.

The cinema has long been a political force in Tamil Nadu, and the Tamil film was the vehicle for the rise of the regional DMK and its offshoot AIADMK, led by film star and chief minister M. G. Ramachandran. In Andhra, Telugu film star T. N. Rama Rao has the state's leading role as chief minister. The Hindi film, with nationwide popularity, is one of the major unifying forces of India, and the potential role of Bachchan in the Congress campaign and in enhancing Rajiv's image for the succession should not be underestimated.

Mrs. Gandhi and her apparent commitment to dynastic succession will be issues on which the opposition can unite most easily--although the CPI is divided, and the AIADMK is waffling. Mrs. Gandhi enjoys considerable popularity, however, and she is less vulnerable as a personal target now than in 1977 when she carried the burden of the Emergency. But public opinion polls also register considerable dissatisfaction on a wide range of questions, and voting trends have increasingly gone against the party in power. Mrs. Gandhi will surely remind the voters of the Janata Government's sorry performance, but the verdict on election day will be on Mrs. Gandhi and her Government.

The election results will turn on the capacity of the opposition to forge a united front and to present to the voters a credible alternative to Congress rule. If the opposition parties--the Janata-led United Front, the National Democratic Alliance, the two Communist parties, and the major regional parties--can come together under a single banner, they stand at this point a better than even chance of defeating the Congress. If they are divided, Mrs. Gandhi will return with reduced seats--perhaps even without a majority, forcing her into a dependence on outside support (as in 1969-1971) or even a Congress-led coalition Government. The vulnerability of the Congress is revealed in its 1980 "resurgence." With only 43 percent of the vote, facing a divided and discredited opposition, Congress won 351 (67 percent) of the 525 contested seats in the Lok Sabha. In only 203 cases did the Congress win its seat by an absolute majority. In 267 cases (just under a majority of the seats in the Lok Sabha), it won by a margin of more than 10 percent, but 62 of these were in Andhra and Karnataka, where the Congress will be unable to repeat its 1980 performance.

The table below is a projection of results by state for the next parliamentary election if the major opposition parties, incuding the BJP, stand together in alliance against the Congress. The tabulation combines seats for all opposition parties, but a few will remain outside any opposition alliance. The AIADMK will, in all probability, support the Congress, and some of the regional parties in smaller states and union territories (e.g., the Northeastern tribal states, Sikkim, Goa, and Lakshadweep) may, as they have before, give parliamentary support to Congress.

The projection, admittedly impressionistic, is an estimate of likely electoral performance, using the 1980 results as the base and factoring in recent political developments; the results of recent assembly and local elections; and 1980 margins of victory above 10% for Congress--probably the minimum cushion Congress will need in most constituencies to face a united opposition. The figures may err on the high side for Congress, as the projection does not incorporate the potential for further attrition from party ranks. There is serious dissension in a number of states, and efforts to impose discipline may splinter the party. Moreover, the selection of candidates will put great strain on the Congress, and those aspirants denied tickets may contest as independents (as they did with considerable success in Haryana in 1982) or join forces with the opposition alliance.

The projection totals give the opposition 308 seats (57%) against 234 seats for Congress. If a united opposition can perform no better, these figures underscore the critical role of the BJP to opposition victory. If the BJP were to stand alone, it would pick up a few seats, but by creating three-cornered contests in a number of constituencies, it would substantially reduce the number of opposition victories--potentially denying the opposition parties the coalition Government that might have been theirs.

Post-Election Scenario I: Congress Returns

A Congress return to power in the next parliamentary elections is likely to entail a diminished number of seats in the Lok Sabha. The Government will sustain its current, more liberalized economic policy, selectively limiting imports at the same time that it continues to relax controls in other areas. In foreign relations, India will continue to follow a policy of non-alignment, of balance between the superpowers, and of preponderance within the region. Mrs. Gandhi's leadership and style is unlikely to change, and senior civil servants within the Prime Minister's Secretariat and in the ministries will retain a dominant role in decision-making under her watchful authority. As Prime Minister and Congress Party President, Mrs. Gandhi can be expected to continue her efforts to pave the way for Rajiv's succession.

Without a Majority. If the Congress fails to win an absolute majority of seats but, against a divided opposition, emerges (as it surely will) as the largest single party, President Zail Singh will invite Mrs. Gandhi, as leader of the Congress Parliamentary Party,

PROJECTIONS FOR 1984/1985 LOK SABHA ELECTION BY STATE WITH UNITED OPPOSITION FRONT

States & Union Territories	1980 Seats		1984/85 Seats Projections		Basis for Projection
	Congress (I)	Opposition	Congress (I)	Opposition	
Andhra Pradesh	41	1	8	34	Same proportion of seats as in 1983 assembly election
Assam	2*	0	1	13	Assam agitation; 1980 margin of victory above 10% for Congress
Bihar	30	24	19	35	Based on 1980 margin of victory above 10% for Congress
Gujarat	25	1	15	11	Factoring in effect of party split and dissidence
Haryana	5	5	5	5	The 1982 assembly results, dissidents in Congress, and the 1980 margin of victory above 10% for Congress would likely entail a decline to 2 seats for Congress. But Congress standing in Haryana may be sustained because of Mrs. Gandhi's firm position on the Punjab agitation.
Himachal Pradesh	3	0	2	2	1980 margin of victory above 10% for Congress; 1982 assembly election results

* Elections not held in 12 of the 14 Assam constituencies

Jammu and Kashmir	1	4	2	4	1980 margin of victory above 10% for Congress; 1983 assembly election results
Karnataka	27	1	5	23	Proportion of seats as in 1983 assembly election plus added opposition strength through alliance of BJP, CPI, and CPM with Janata
Kerala	5	15	5	15	Congress (I) strengthened by merger with Congress (S); holds its own, with continued alliance partners
Madhya Pradesh	35	5	28	12	1980 margin of victory above 10% for Congress
Maharashtra	39	9	35	13	1980 margin of victory above 10% for Congress; assumes the party will resist dissidence.
Manipur	1	1	0	2	1980 margin of victory above 10% for Congress
Meghalay	1	0	1	1	
Nagaland	0	1	0	1	
Orissa	19	1	19	2	1980 margin of victory above 10% for Congress; assumes the party will resist dissidence.
Punjab	12	1	6	7	Punjab Sikh agitation; for Congress, the 3 Hindu-majority seats and (optomistically) 3 of the 10 Sikh-majority seats (6 less than it won in 1980)
Rajasthan	18	7	12	13	1980 margin of victory above 10%
Sikkim	0	1	0	1	
Tamil Nadu	20	19	18	21	Assuming that the Congress will be in alliance with the AIADMK
Tripura	0	2	0	2	

(table continues)

(cont.)

States & Union Territories	1980 Seats		1984/85 Seats Projections		Basis for Projection
	Congress (I)	Opposition	Congress (I)	Opposition	
Uttar Pradesh	51	34	30	55	1980 margin of victory above 10% for Congress
West Bengal	4	37	13	29	Merger of Congress (S) with Congress (I); improved Congress position in panchayat elections
Andaman & Nicobar Is.	1	0	1	0	
Arunachal Pradesh	2	0	0	2	1980 margins of victory above 10% for Congress
Chandigarh	1	0	1	0	
Dadra & Nagar Haveli	1	0	1	0	
Delhi	6	1	6	1	Congress holds its own, reflecting 1983 assembly elections
Goa, Damon & Diu	0	2	0	2	
Lakshadweep	0	1	0	1	
Mizoram	0	1	0	1	
Pondicherry	1	0	1	0	Assuming alliance with the AIADMK and retention of the seat for the Congress candidate
TOTAL	351	174	234	308	

to try to form a Government. As has occurred so many times at the state level, the promise of power, patronage, and money can lure members of the opposition across the floor into the Congress fold. If a post-election realignment does not provide Congress its majority, Mrs. Gandhi can seek outside support for a minority Government. She may already have allies in the AIADMK and in a scattering of regional parties from smaller states and union territories. She may also succeed in splitting the CPI by bringing its pro-Congress faction to the support of her Government. In going after parties with strong regional bases, Mrs. Gandhi opens herself to the pressure of their influence--not just in forming the Government, but in retaining the confidence of the Lok Sabha so long as withdrawal of their support could bring down the Congress Government.

If such support is necessary to form a Government, the first demand on Congress by its potential partners could well be participation in a coalition Government. Congress now heads a coalition Government in Kerala, but if Kerala is the model, the coalition will remain vulnerable to the continued threat of withdrawal, thus keeping Mrs. Gandhi on a short leash as a broker of competing and often contradictory interests. But coalition Government with a dominant partner under a single powerful leader is likely to be fairly stable--at least at the core. Control of Government is a powerful resource both in imposing discipline and in attracting new support, and Mrs. Gandhi can hold her weaker allies in check by the threat of dropping them in favor of more compliant partners.

If a united opposition front wins the greater number of seats, even with the Congress as the largest single party, the President by convention would be expected to call upon the leader of the alliance to form a Government. If the President were not to do so, if he were instead to invite the Congress to form a Government, India would face a major political crisis and serious national unrest. The potential for such action is not without precedent at the state level. In the 1982 Haryana assembly elections, the Congress won 36 seats, while the Lok Dal-BJP alliance won 37 and claimed the additional support of 3 Congress (J), 1 Janata, and 6 of the 12 Independent assembly members for a narrow majority in the 90-seat assembly. The Governor, however, called upon the Congress, as the largest single party, to form a Government--and, with the promise of ministerial posts and the bounty of office, the Congress weaned away the Independents and secured its majority to loud national protest by the opposition and almost universal condemnation by the press. Any attempt by the

President to replay the Haryana maneuver at the Center would be widely perceived as a presidential coup d'etat and would seriously threaten political stability.

With a Majority: Prospects for the Succession and After. With a secure Congress majority in the Lok Sabha, Mrs. Gandhi will be able to move Rajiv into position for the succession. Rajiv will play a major role in the selection of Congress candidates for the parliamentary elections, building the personal support base that will be decisive in the succession--especially if it were to come in the wake of Mrs. Gandhi's death. Rajiv will assume a prominent and highly visible role in the campaign and is likely to likely to display increasing self-assurance at the hustings. Unless the opposition unites behind Maneka's challenge to him in Amethi, Rajiv should take the constituency. A substantial victory will enhance his prestige and move him along more quickly toward national leadership. A narrow win, however, would be embarrassing and slow his momentum. A defeat would, in effect, take Rajiv out of the running as a serious contender for succession, even if he were to be brought into the Lok Sabha through a bye-election and given a ministerial portfolio.

Prime Minister Gandhi will likely bring Rajiv into the new Cabinet, most probably as Minister of Information and Broadcasting, the post held by Mrs. Gandhi under Prime Minister Shastri. Rajiv should also move up fairly soon after the elections to succeed his mother as President of the Congress party. This will be an important vantage point from which Rajiv may extend his power over state party units--trouble-shooting, screening candidates, and cultivating (if not choosing) chief ministers. All of this will take time, and if Rajiv is to succeed his mother as Prime Minister, he must prove himself politically skilled and capable of leading the party to victory.

Rajiv has no guarantee that Mrs. Gandhi will step down (or up) to make way for his ascension to the gaddi. She may, like Queen Victoria, simply stay on as the heir apparent grows old. But if Rajiv is to succeed and to secure his position as Prime Minister, he needs Mrs. Gandhi's physical presence--at least initially--to protect him from the political wolves that are already nipping at his heels. The five-year term of President Zail Singh will be up in 1987. Indira Gandhi will be nearly 70 years old and might choose to offer herself as a candidate for the presidency, with Rajiv stepping in as Prime Minister in a family duumvirate.

Post-Election Scenario II: A Non-Congress Coalition

If the major opposition parties can form a united front against the Congress, they are likely to emerge in the parliamentary elections with a majority of seats. Janata Party President Chandra Sekhar, although perceived as weak by many of his colleagues, is for this very reason the likely choice of the alliance for leadership. Rather than imposing his will on the coalition, he would function as a broker of interests, and arbiter of conflicts, at the same time his Gandhian image would lend moral legitimacy to the Government.

Called upon by the President to form a Government, Chandra Sekhar will face his first challenge in the allocation of ministerial portfolios among the alliance partners. The greater the number of alliance seats in the Lok Sabha, the stronger his hand will be, but a relatively narrow margin could give to one or more parties decisive power in making or breaking a Government. This would substantially weaken Chandra Sekhar's leverage in shaping the coalition Government and, if a disaffected party were to withdraw its support, could deny the alliance the majority necessary to form a Government, or, if a Government is formed, to retain power. The Congress could seek to undermine the alliance by offering a more attractive deal for one of its party constituents--a greater number of ministries in a Congress-led coalition, for example--in a bidding game for political power. A relatively narrow margin in the Lok Sabha will render the non-Congress coalition continuously vulnerable to political extortion from within and subversion from without and thus potentially unstable. A substantial margin will give greater stability to the Government by reducing the leverage of any single coalition partner.

The very nature of the coalition, an amalgam of national and regional parties, with a span of the ideological spectrum from the BJP on the center right to the Communists on the left, will reduce the capacity of any party to pull the coalition too far in any direction. It will necessarily be a centrist coalition based on a middle ground of common understanding. In domestic policy, it will likely emphasize rural development and the uplift of the poor, although a radical change in Plan investment allocation is unlikely. There will probably be a selective pullback from Mrs. Gandhi's more liberalized economic policy, with greater emphasis on achieving economic self-sufficiency in terms of "appropriate" technology. There is a shared sentiment among the opposition parties that might be described as autarkic (reflected, for example, in their general opposition to the 1981 IMF loan to India), but India's involvement in the international economy and, most critically, its continuing dependence on petroleum imports will limit the degree to which any Government can dramatically shift Indian economic policy.

In giving new balance to the federal relationship, the coalition Government will yield to the states greater autonomy in administration and planning, but in an increasingly interdependent nation, the Center will retain overarching authority. Regionalism and the regionalization of politics will continue to reflect awakening political consciousness and expanding participation. But Center-state conflict will be balanced and held in check by conflict of interests among the states. In both Center-state and state-state relations, conflict will be mediated by the compelling need for cooperation that will ensure India's national unity.

The coalition Government will sustain continuity in foreign policy in its commitment to non-alignment and to good relations with both the United States and the Soviet Union. The one major change that should accompany a new Government is improved relations between India and its neighbors in the South Asian region--notably Pakistan, which has long seen Mrs. Gandhi (and the Nehru family) as an impediment to rapprochement.

A Capsule Perspective

The projection of political trends is inevitably subject to a wide range of contingencies. But looking to the next five years, the critical event is likely to be the forthcoming parliamentary elections, to be held by January 1985. The results will be formative in shaping the course of subsequent events.

1. If the Congress party faces a divided opposition, as it did in 1980, it will be returned to power, although with a reduced majority in the Lok Sabha. The prospect would be for continued political stability at the Center, even in the event of the sudden death of Prime Minister Indira Gandhi.

2. If the Congress fails to gain a majority in the Lok Sabha but is the largest single party against a divided opposition, it would possibly form a minority Government with outside support. More likely, it would be compelled to take its partners into a coalition Government. In either case, the Government would be vulnerable to the withdrawal of support and potentially unstable.

3. If a united opposition front wins a greater number of seats than the Congress, but the President calls upon Congress, as the largest single party, to form a Government, India would face a major political crisis and serious national unrest. The events arising out of widespread violence could involve the reimposition of Emergency rule--likely to deepen unrest--and possible military intervention.

4. If the major opposition parties can form a united front against Congress, they are likely to emerge with a parliamentary majority and the capacity to form a coalition Government, most probably with Janata Party President Chandra Sekhar as Prime Minister.

4a. If the majority is sufficiently great that no single coalition partner can bring down the Government by its withdrawal, the prospects for stable Government are reasonably good.

4b. If any single party can by its withdrawal from the coalition deny the Government its majority in the Lok Sabha, the chances of the Government surviving its full term of office are considerably diminished.

If either a Congress minority/coalition Government or a non-Congress coalition Government were to fall, there would likely follow--at least until new elections--a period of shifting coalitions, punctuated by Government "crises" as parties split, merge, and negotiate in efforts to form a new ministry. The image is that of France under the Fourth Republic. Under such conditions of _immobilisme_, the bureaucracy, as the "permanent government," will assume greater responsibility. For all its loss of morale, the Indian bureaucracy, with highly competent senior civil servants, should be able to carry on administration and maintain law and order. If, however, ministerial instability at the Center, together with serious social unrest, threatens national unity or the stability of the regime itself, such that civil authorities are unable to cope with the situation, the Army--probably at the invitation of the President--will assume an active role in governance and in the maintenance of domestic order. Under conditions of clear and present danger, the Army would be prepared to intervene as the ultimate guarantor of the nation's stability.

If India were to face the prospect of chronic Government instability at the Center, it is not military rule so much as constitutional change--probably to a presidential system, perhaps along Gaullist lines--that would be most likely. At most, military rule would be transitional, but the Army could assume a Turkish role, perhaps even by constitutional provision, as the guardian of political order.

Looking to the next five years, the question of succession must be considered. If Mrs. Gandhi were to die in office <u>before</u> the next parliamentary elections, Rajiv would be the Congress Parliamentary Party's probable choice as the next Prime Minister. But, given his lack of strong personal support in the Lok Sabha, his succession is by no means secure. Even with a struggle for Congress party leadership, however, the Congress is likely to remain reasonably intact as it goes into the parliamentary elections. If Rajiv (or whoever emerges as Prime Minister) is able to lead the party to a solid victory, a stable Congress Government is a good prospect. If it is a marginal victory, the Government will be vulnerable to defection and collapse and the party to split. If the Congress is defeated, a split would be inevitable, with subsequent party realignment in a period of political flux.

If Mrs. Gandhi were to die in office <u>after</u> parliamentary elections, the prospects for Rajiv's succession would be greatly enhanced--assuming that he performed well in his own constituency of Amethi against the probable challenge from Maneka Gandhi and that he was able to use the selection of candidates to bring in personally loyal Congress MPs prepared to support him.

Assuming Mrs. Gandhi's continued good health, the question arises as to whether--and at what point--Mrs. Gandhi would step aside to allow Rajiv to assume the prime ministership. Mrs. Gandhi will not easily relinquish power, but if she is to ensure dynastic succession, she must be physically and politically present to protect Rajiv. The most probable avenue would be for her to step up to the presidency--perhaps in 1987 at the end of President Zail Singh's tenure--passing the prime ministership to her son.

Whatever its mode or circumstance, the succession--if it is to occur in the next five years--will likely be conducted with order, posing no threat to the stability of either the Government or the constitutional order. The Indian political system remains highly institutionalized, despite the weakness of the Congress party organization and the erosion of the bureaucracy. Even under increased stress, the prospects for India's political stability are among the best for any nation in the Third World.

NOTES

1. Times of India, April 29, 1982.

2. Sunday (Calcutta), 13-19 March 1983, p. 27.

3. "Indian National Congress: Lessons of Revolution," Asia and Africa Today (Moscow), November 9, 1982. Reprinted in Mainstream (New Delhi), December 18, 1982.

4. Portions of the paragraphs below are adapted from Robert L. Hardgrave, Jr., "India Enters the 1980s," Current History, May 1982, pp. 198-99.

3
Continuity and Change in India's Foreign Policy: The Next Five Years

Indian foreign policy is rooted in two traditions. One is that of British India, with a concern for the territorial integrity and security of South Asia. The other is that of the Indian National Congress, evolved from the 1920s, almost wholly under the directive of Jawaharlal Nehru and focusing on the problems of world peace, anticolonialism, and antiracism. Often enunciated in lofty and moralistic terms, it reflects a mixture of idealism and Indian self-interest. Its central concept is non-alignment--neither a policy of neutralism nor of isolation, but of independent action taken on the merits and circumstances of each case.

In the United States, non-alignment was once viewed as "immoral" and, more recently, as a euphemism for the "pro-Soviet" policy that many Americans believed India to pursue. During her 1982 visit to the United States, Prime Minister Indira Gandhi was asked at the National Press Club whether her presence in Washington suggested that India was now leaning toward the United States rather than toward the Soviet Union. "India does not lean," she replied. "It stands up straight." It was a masterly response and one that fairly describes the difficult course India has set for itself between the world's two superpowers.

Under Indira Gandhi, the practice of Indian foreign policy has shifted from the more visionary globalism of Nehru to a more pragmatic and explicit concern for India's national interests and for the region of South Asia, the arena of India's immediate security concerns. But for whatever shifts in style, the substance of India's foreign policy has shown remarkable continuity over the past thirty-six years. It bears the indelible imprint of Nehru and commands a national consensus reflected in press and public opinion and across the political spectrum. The measure of that stability is revealed in the constancy of India's foreign policy during the period of the Janata Government, 1977-1980. The notable distinction of Janata policy was improved relations with India's neighbors--especially Pakistan and Bangladesh. There was some improvement as well in relations with the United States. But Janata's foreign policy did not mark a sharp break with the past, and its essential character reflected the broad consensus upon which Indian policy before and since has been based.

Indian foreign policy embodies three basic goals: First, India seeks to guarantee its national security against invasion from without and subversion from within, against external support for secessionist and insurgent movements and foreign interference in its internal affairs. Indian security is fundamentally regional in its scope of concern. For India, successor state to the Raj, its defense perimeters are those of South Asia itself, which for India constitutes a strategic entity. As a nation of 700 million people, with the fourth largest standing army in the world, India is the preeminent power of the subcontinent. Viewed by its neighbors, as having hegemonic ambition, India seeks recognition of its status in the region it regards as its natural and rightful sphere of influence. India has opposed external intervention and great power presence in the region both as a threat to regional security and as a challenge to its own preeminent position.

Second, India seeks independence and self-reliance. While maintaining its close and traditional friendship with the Soviet Union, India strives also to improve relations with the United States and the West. It seeks to gain greater diplomatic flexibility and to widen its options. This involves not so much a "distancing" from the U.S.S.R. as an effort to reduce dependence and to achieve greater balance. Through a conscious policy of diversifying arms sources and in pursuing Western high technology, India seeks self-reliance and enhanced security in defense and economic development.

Third, India, already a "rising middle power," aspires to great power status--to be at least regarded as China's equal in world affairs. By virtue of its size, political stability, economic strength, and military power, India can be expected to play an increasingly important role in international politics. In the next three years, in chairing the Non-Aligned Movement, India will assume special prominence in promoting South-South cooperation and in articulating the views of the Third World in the North-South dialogue. In asserting its leadership, India has eschewed stridency and spoken with a voice of moderation for cooperation not confrontation. But whether words and aspiration will be translated into the deeds of a more active foreign policy is yet to be seen. Domestic concerns impose constraints on India's role in the world arena, and economic crisis or a deterioration in the law and order situation would likely turn India inward. India today is reluctant--as Nehru was not--to venture outside South Asia. It is beginning to project its power within the Indian Ocean, but India has taken no initiative to mediate or resolve the political conflicts within the non-aligned world that threaten the unity of the movement--the Iran-Iraq war, the Kampuchea imbroglio, and the Soviet occupation of Afghanistan. Perhaps it is better judgment, but it reflects a certain passivity in Indian foreign policy that arises out of the way in which decisions are today made in India.

FOREIGN POLICY DECISION-MAKING

Decision-making in Indian foreign policy tends to be informal, ad hoc, and reactive. It involves no grand design or long-range strategy, but a framework for tactical maneuver. The process varies with the character of the decision and with the Prime Minister's interest in the issue.

There is a hierarchy of decision-making levels culminating in the office of the Prime Minister. Within the Ministry of External Affairs (MEA), most routine decisions--those for which policy guidelines are available--are taken at the Under Secretary (Branch Officer) level. On matters of somewhat greater importance, the Joint Secretary (in the territorial divisions of MEA) might take the initiative, passing it then to the Secretary for final decision. If sufficiently important, it goes to the Foreign Minister or Prime Minister. In all of this, the role of the ambassadors at foreign posts is advisory, largely through periodic reports, and they are rarely involved directly in policy decisions.

On major issues commanding the Prime Minister's attention, she may, in consultation with her advisers, take the initiative. A note is then routed to MEA by the Foreign Minister or, more typically, through the Prime Minister's Principal Private Secretary to the Foreign Secretary. MEA then responds with a position paper, sending it up through the same channels.

When an initiative comes from within MEA, it may be brought to the Prime Minister by the Foreign Minister or by the Foreign Secretary directly or through the PM's Principal Secretary. In the case of direct contact with the Foreign Minister or Foreign Secretary, the Prime Minister normally refers the note to her Secretariat. The Principal Secretary reviews the material, calling attention to certain points or paragraphs and may attach his own comments in helping to shape the options available to the Prime Minister.

The whole process, however, is much more informal than any "flow chart" would suggest. For the most important decisions, formal institutions give way to personalism. Mrs. Gandhi, as did her father, Jawaharlal Nehru, has made foreign policy her special field of interest. But Mrs. Gandhi is over-burdened and only when an important matter demands immediate response is it likely to be brought to her. Less pressing issues may be deferred or handled as routine within the existing framework of ongoing policy. Decisions taken by the Prime Minister, however, may involve little or no consultation with the Ministry of External Affairs. In some instances, the Ministry has learned of a decision only when it was announced to the press. Sometimes it is simply informed of a decision taken. In the case of India's recognition of Kampuchea, for example, the Ministry learned of the decision only a few days before recognition was formally announced. Often Mrs. Gandhi will make a snap decision while MEA is still formulating a position or the available options, as she did in support of Mrs. Thatcher on the Falkland Islands.

With increasing frequency, the Ministry may be involved in decision-making to the exclusion of the Minister of External Affairs. The Foreign Minister is the Prime Minister's spokesman in Parliament and in the international forum, but his actual role in decision-making is variable. Indeed, the Foreign Minister may be bypassed in the direct contact between the Prime Minister or her Secretariat and the Foreign Secretary. Narasimha Rao is highly respected and has performed well as Foreign Minister, but it is widely believed that he has been excluded from many high level decisions. The nature of these relationships, however, depends more on personal confidence than institutionalized linkage. When T. N. Kaul, an intimate of the Nehru family, served as Foreign Secretary, Mrs. Gandhi relied heavily upon him. Similarly, the current Foreign Secretary, M. K. Rasgotra, has a close relationship with the Prime Minister, as does MEA Secretary Natwar Singh. But their predecessors, R. D. Sathe and Eric Gonsalves, were not so favored.

In decision-making, Mrs. Gandhi makes extensive use of the Prime Minister's Secretariat. She perhaps relies less on Principal Secretary P. C. Alexander than she did on P. N. Haksar, who preceded him from 1969 to 1973 and exercised a major role in making foreign policy, but Alexander, as head of the Secretariat, occupies a key position in the decision-making process. Virtually all papers pass through his hands and, even if he offers no independent advice, by shaping the options open to the Prime Minister and drawing out the implications of decision alternatives, the Principal Secretary plays a critical--often decisive--role. Alexander, a member of the Indian Administrative Service and a specialist in international trade, is highly capable and judged by observers to be without foreign policy biases.

Mrs. Gandhi turns to advisers within the Secretariat and the Ministry of External Affairs and to personal confidants on an ad hoc basis. Within the Secretariat, R. N. Kao, former director of the Research and Analysis Wing (RAW)--India's C.I.A.--serves as the Prime Minister's national security adviser, although without the broad-ranging responsibilities of his American equivalent. Reaching outside official circles into the informal group of retired senior civil servants she has gathered around herself, Mrs. Gandhi relies on her trusted adviser G. Parthasarathy--"G.P.", as he is widely known. A retired journalist and diplomat, G. P. has great influence with the Prime Minister but acts as something of an alter ego rather than as a source of decision-making initiative. He is called in for consultation on particular issues and does not serve as a general foreign policy adviser on a continuing basis. Parthasarathy also serves as a frequent emissary for the Prime Minister--most recently to Sri Lanka on the issue of the status of that nation's Tamil minority.

Mrs. Gandhi also turns from time to time for advice to B. K. Nehru, her cousin and former ambassador to the United States, as well as to another former ambassador to the U. S., L. K. Jha, although his influence is more economic and may, in any case, be waning. T. N. Kaul, typically described as pro-Soviet, continued to be very close to Mrs. Gandhi after his retirement as Foreign Secretary, but in the past four years he has fallen from favor. The break--and most observers in New Delhi believe that Kaul no longer has Madam's ear--may have come as a result of the January 11, 1980, speech by India's Ambassador to the United Nations. The speech, accepting the Soviet justification for the invasion of Afghanistan at face value, was drafted by Kaul and proved an embarrassment from which India has sought to extricate itself. Two other advisers once close to Mrs. Gandhi and regarded as pro-Soviet are also gone: D. P. Dhar, who played a critical role in Indo-Soviet relations in the early 1970s, died in 1975; and P. N.

Haksar, who as Mrs. Gandhi's Principal Secretary from 1969 to 1973 functioned as "*de facto* Foreign Minister,"[1] was exiled from influence *after* he locked horns with Sanjay.

Historically, Indian foreign policy has been centered within the office of the Prime Minister. Nehru, who served as his own Foreign Minister, dominated foreign policy and shaped the Ministry of External Affairs in his own image. While other ministries were expected to place before the Cabinet matters affecting other ministerial spheres and policy initiatives that involved a significant departure from the past, MEA did not do so. It saw itself as answerable only to the Prime Minister, and this relationship has been perpetuated by Mrs. Gandhi, as it was for the most part during the Janata interregnum.

The Political Affairs Committee of the Cabinet, chaired by the Prime Minister, is formally the highest decision-making authority of the Indian Government. In the early 1970s and especially during the course of the Bangladesh crisis, Mrs. Gandhi regularly consulted the Committee--albeit, most typically *after* a decision had been made within the Prime Minister's inner circle. By 1973, with increasing centralization of authority in the hands of the Prime Minister, the Committee lost any significant role in foreign policy decision-making, as the Cabinet itself ceased to be a deliberative body. The importance of the Committee and Cabinet alike was restored under the Janata Government by Morarji Desai, but since 1980, Mrs. Gandhi has again drawn the decision-making process into her Secretariat.

Like the Cabinet, the Parliament plays no active role in foreign policy. The Congress Parliamentary Party's Standing Committee on External Affairs seldom meets and then only at the call of the Foreign Minister to inform MPs of decisions already taken by the Government. Parliament's Consultative Committee on Foreign Affairs, with a membership reflecting the relative strength of the parties in the Lok Sabha, is also largely a channel of one-way communication used by the Government to garner support and mute criticism. But that the Government is sensitive to parliamentary opinion and potential attack underscores the importance of Parliament in holding foreign policy within bounds of the consensus shaped by Nehru.

Indian foreign policy is based on a broad consensus. It has never been a central issue in an election campaign, and while the press devotes considerable attention to foreign policy issues, it is a fundamentally supportive and reinforcing influence. But the Prime Minister is not unlimited in his or her exercise of authority in foreign relations. Public opinion, as expressed in the press and voiced in Parliament, can exert influence and impose restraint, seen most dramatically in the pressure on Nehru from 1959 to 1962 to toughen Indian policy towards China and, most recently, in Indian press criticism of Mrs. Gandhi's initial (negative) response to the Pakistani proposal for a no-war pact. But "public opinion" is less a source of influence in creating foreign policy than it is a limit on the decision-makers' range of options. The major constraints on Indian foreign policy are imposed by the consensus itself. Within that consensus, the Prime Minister has considerable freedom and support, but a break from "policy as usual", a movement too far one way or the other, is likely to meet considerable resistance from both government and public. But in giving continuity to Indian foreign policy, the consensus also minimizes initiative and reinforces the essentially reactive character of Indian policy.

Coordination

There is little coordination among the various ministries concerned with India's international relations--notably External Affairs, Defence, Commerce, and Finance. Frequently ministries other than MEA will make important decisions on sensitive issues affecting the conduct of Indian foreign policy. Sometimes even state governments have been involved, as West Bengal in relations upon Bangladesh. There are periodic and ad hoc meetings between officials of different ministries, though these are judged generally ineffective. These contacts are usually at the level of Secretary and rarely involve junior officers. The problem is most critical in the lack of coordinated strategic policy between MEA and the Ministry of Defence. Each guards its sphere of authority, diplomatic and military, with MEA having primary responsibility for national security policy. MEA, however, does not have a separate functional division on military affairs or national security--nor does the Foreign Service training program include a specialized course of strategic studies. Similarly, the Ministry of Defence has no specialized unit on foreign policy issues.

The proposal for a National Security Council, with G. Parthasarathy as chairman, has encountered resistance from senior secretaries, and the Foreign Secretary can be expected to oppose the creation of any body that may diminish the role of MEA. The increasing prominence of the Prime Minister's Secretariat in making foreign policy has already created some of the conflict that characterizes the relationship between the U.S. Department of State and the National Security Council.

There has been some effort to coordinate intelligence. The Research and Analysis Wing (RAW), established in 1968, is in charge of external intelligence. It is located within the Cabinet Secretariat, with direct responsibility to the Prime Minister. The Joint Intelligence Committee (JIC) coordinates intelligence activities. Its membership represents MEA, Defence, Home, RAW, IB (Intelligence Bureau of the Home Ministry, which is responsible for domestic intelligence and counterintelligence), and the three military intelligence units. Under the chairmanship of an Additional Secretary of the Cabinet Secretariat, the JIC meets regularly to prepare a weekly report on national security and periodic papers on special issues. The JIC, however, with only a small secretariat, has little capacity for long-range assessment. It reports to a Steering Committee under the Cabinet Secretary. The Committee is composed of the Foreign Secretary, the Defence Secretary, the Home Secretary, the Director of RAW, Chairman of the Chiefs of Staff, and the Chairman of the JIC. They in turn formally report to the Political Affairs Committee of the Cabinet--but in practice, the linkage is from the Cabinet Secretary directly to the Prime Minister.

Research and Policy Planning

The daily flow of information from missions abroad into the Ministry of External Affairs is voluminous: daily telegrams; more detailed and less urgent dispatches; intelligence reports from RAW and military attaches; an array of regular and ad hoc reports; and foreign press clippings and news summaries. MEA's capacity to process and analyze this vast amount of material and to conduct research is limited. The Historical Department prepares background papers (largely historical, as the name suggests), but nothing comparable to the analyses of the Research Department of the British Foreign Office or of the U.S. Department of State's Bureau of Intelligence and Research. In India, the burden of assimilating and evaluating the inflow of information falls almost wholly on MEA's territorial and functional divisions, where the daily desk traffic of cables requiring immediate response gives officers little chance to take a broader, long-range, or more considered perspective. Moreover, many Foreign Service

Officers, however capable they may be, often lack specialized knowledge of the problems they confront. FSOs in India are in the classic generalist tradition, and while some have developed expertise in particular nations or regions, there are few "area specialists." Nor does MEA draw such specialists onto its staff as consultants.

In 1966, the Ministry of External Affairs established the Policy Planning and Review Division (PPRD). At the time of its creation, its functions were defined as follows:

> The Policy Planning Division undertakes the study in depth of important problems pertaining to our external relations; it collects factual data based on historical research and analyses, and reports from our Representatives abroad, and endeavors, in the light of developing trends and after weighing the political, economic and security aspects of a question, to evaluate the adequacy of the current policies, and anticipates the short-and long-term problems which may arise, and seeks the promotion of our relations with the outside world in the future. The studies and recommendations, after scrutiny by the Policy Planning and Review Committee, are submitted to Government for approval and form the guidelines and directives for our future policy.[2]

From the beginning, PPRD faced problems of coordination within the Ministry, as the various divisions, unwilling to cede policy planning to others, guarded their turf. Though it has been served by able officers, PPRD has, in fact, produced few policy papers, and there is little to suggest that it has any impact in the making of Indian foreign policy. With a small staff, PPRD devotes much of its effort to writing speeches for the Foreign Minister and Prime Minister, an important task surely but some measure of the relatively low priority given policy planning.

Journalist Inder Malhotra, of the Times of India, states flatly, "India has no policy planning,"[3] and off the record, this judgment is confirmed by any number of Indian diplomats. As is the case with so many countries, including the United States, long-range planning in India has fallen victim to the immediate demands of day-to-day decisions, to the "ad hocism" that characterizes the policy process. Justified in terms of making each decision "on merit," the approach is a response to the demands--and the expediences--of the moment. But the point should not be lost that for all the ad hocism in Indian foreign policy, decisions are made within the context of a broad consensus on national interests and policy goals--a consensus shaped by Nehru. And if Indian policy is essentially reactive, with little long-range planning, it operates in terms of a basic position. All of this has given stability and continuity to Indian foreign policy since 1947, and it reduces the prospects for any significant departures from established policy over the next five years.

If a non-Congress coalition Government were to come to power in the next parliamentary elections, the Foreign Minister and the Political Affairs Committee of the Cabinet will likely assume a greater role in making foreign policy. Similarly, if Rajiv succeeds Mrs. Gandhi as Prime Minister, he can be expected to be far less involved in foreign policy than his mother has been. In either case, foreign policy decision-making is likely to become more concentrated in the hands of senior civil servants -whether in the Prime Minister's Secretariat or in the Ministry of External Affairs.

INDIA, PAKISTAN, AND THE STRATEGIC ENVIRONMENT OF SOUTHWEST ASIA

India's strategic concerns are regional, and Pakistan is the lens through which India tends to view most other relationships. India regards itself as the successor state to the British Raj and as such heir to the historic strategic concerns of South Asia. For India, the subcontinent is a strategic entity, its outer boundary forming India's own "natural" defense perimeter. As the preeminent power of the region, India sees the subcontinent as its sphere of influence. India's South Asian neighbors see in its power a domineering stance and hegemonic ambition. During the Janata phase, India's relations with its neighbors improved markedly. Mrs. Gandhi, since her return to power in 1980, has not been so generous, but neither has she assumed an overbearing role. Yet Pakistan--truncated in size and constituting no realistic threat to India--remains an obsession, and India's smaller neighbors are like so many thorns in its side.

Other states of the region, not surprisingly, have sought to resist Indian hegemony and have done so principally by turning outward. From its inception, spawned by the two-nation theory, until the creation of Bangladesh in 1971, Pakistan regarded itself as India's rightful equal and sought military parity with its larger neighbor. Pakistan found in the United States and later China willing partners. For the United States,

Pakistan--the eastern flank of the northern tier bordering the U.S.S.R.--was an ally in the containment of the Soviet Union and, through its SEATO membership, of China. But, while there was divergence in Pakistani perceptions of Soviet intentions, Pakistan saw little threat to itself from the Soviet Union and even less from China. India was its enemy, and the United States its source of arms and support. By the early 1960s, as Sino-Indian relations deteriorated, Pakistan drew closer to China, reinforcing its security shield against India.

India saw in Pakistan's call for the liberation of Kashmir, its build-up of arms, and, most critically, in its involvement of external powers--the United States and China--in the subcontinent a major threat to Indian security. The linkage between India's two main adversaries, Pakistan and China, was of special concern. As a counter-weight, from the early 1960s, India strengthened its ties with the Soviet Union, forging a security relationship symbolized by the 1971 Indo-Soviet Treaty of Peace, Friendship and Cooperation.

The dismemberment of Pakistan and the creation of Bangladesh in 1971 changed the character of the South Asian strategic environment. India emerged as the undisputed power of the region. Pakistan, albeit reluctantly, accepted the reality of India's superiority, and from 1972, in the "spirit" of the Simla Agreement, the two nations moved with fits, starts, and reversals toward detente. This was possible, in part, because of the lower profile assumed by the United States in the region and by Pakistan's movement toward non-alignment. But the 1970s also witnessed a relaxation in India's relations with China, beginning with the exchange of ambassadors in 1976. Tensions within the region arising out of India's sometimes domineering stance toward its neighbors were eased under the Janata Government, as India reached accords with Bangladesh and Nepal over long-standing disputes and took the initiative toward improved relations with Pakistan.

Pakistan, however, if prepared to accept the reality of India's preeminence within the region was not prepared to accept India's political, economic, or cultural hegemony. After the loss of East Bengal, to shore up the two-nation theory upon which it was founded, Pakistan turned increasingly toward the Islamic world as a source of identity and away from South Asia--in effect rejecting the concept of South Asia as a strategic entity and the Indian paramountcy that it implied.

The Soviet invasion of Afghanistan in December 1979, however, made clear that South Asia is a strategic entity, and that if Pakistan is now a "frontline" state, its capacity to withstand Soviet pressure depends in large degree on India. India-Pakistan rapprochement is the key to regional security and is essential to resisting the expansion of Soviet influence in the area.

The Afghan invasion not only brought the Russians to the gates of South Asia--in reality making the Soviet Union itself a South Asian power--but Indian fears were awakened by America's response in a major arms commitment to Pakistan and in the buildup of naval forces in the Indian Ocean. As reports of the Soviet invasion came in, the major voices of the Indian press--*The Times of India*, *The Hindustan Times*, *The Statesman*, *The Hindu*, and *The Indian Express*--unaminously condemned the Soviet action, but at the same time expressed alarm over United States intentions to renew military assistance to Pakistan, which they saw as a direct and immediate threat to Indian security. They warned that the arms the U.S. might supply to Pakistan would constitute no credible deterrent to the Soviet Union. But American arms, whatever their intended purpose, had been used in the past against India, and an emboldened Pakistan could again employ them--perhaps in a new adventure in Kashmir. In the face of a rearmed Pakistan, India would have to respond in kind, with a resulting arms race in the subcontinent that could only deepen tensions, set back the progress toward Indo-Pakistan detente, and thwart the emergence of a common regional response to the Soviet invasion of Afghanistan.* Above all, by bringing the superpowers into confrontation in South Asia, the security of India--and of Pakistan--would be threatened. Implicit, but unstated, was the understanding that India's influence within the region would be accordingly diminished with enhanced Soviet and American presence.

Even before formally taking the oath as Prime Minister in January 1980, Mrs. Gandhi assumed control of Indian foreign policy, but it was a time of frantic political activity in the formation of the new Government. A draft of a United Nations speech on Afghanistan (widely believed to have been prepared by T. N. Kaul)

---

* It should be noted that during the late 1970s, India had already embarked on a major arms modernization program. Negotiations with the French for the Mirage 2000, for example, began before any suggestion that the F-16 might go to Pakistan.

was cleared with Mrs. Gandhi. Some say it was no more than passed before her eyes, but whether or not it got her close scrutiny, the speech, delivered on January 11, was soon regretted--not so much for its basic policy perspective as its apparent acceptance of Soviet justifications at face-value. In the vote on the UN resolution calling for the immediate withdrawal of Soviet troops from Afghanistan, India was one of the few non-aligned nations to abstain.

In refusing to join the chorus of condemnation, India believed that, based on its traditional friendship with the Soviet Union, it would be in a position to apply pressure privately--although the failure of the Soviets to advise India of its intentions in Afghanistan, despite the consultation provisions of the 1971 Indo-Soviet Treaty, was hardly a good omen for any influence India might be able to exert. But India also believed that isolating the U.S.S.R. would only make the Soviets more intransigent and that Soviet withdrawal could be affected only by means of a political solution.

India has sought to "defuse" the situation. Viewing the Soviet presence in Afghanistan in part as a consequence of growing superpower rivalry in the region, India publicly calls for an end to all foreign interference, careful to balance its disapproval of Soviet troops in Afghanistan with criticism of outside support for the mujahideen. In the first months after the Soviet invasion, there was some hope that India might play a constructive role in securing a Soviet withdrawal, but whatever private pressure India may have exerted came to nought. (There is disagreement about the vigor with which India pursued the issue with the Soviets, but if India was unwilling to use the full measure of its leverage, its disapproval of the Soviet presence in Afghanistan was abundantly clear.) India chose not to take the initiative in formulating a political solution, but has lent its support to the Geneva negotiations under UN auspices. Over time, however, India has grown increasingly frustated over the prospects for a political solution. Privately, Indian officials express deep concern about the implications of a permanent Soviet presence in Afghanistan.

India would ideally prefer a Finlandized solution to the Afghan situation--a return to a government along the lines of that before the 1978 Saur revolution, perhaps with the king as a rallying point for Afghan nationalism. The questionable stability of the government, however, would be a major impediment to Soviet acceptance of such a political settlement. India is prepared to accept a non-aligned Karmal Government--but how Karmal could survive without Soviet troops is another matter. What India would find even less acceptable than Soviet troops in Afghanistan, however, would be an Islamic fundamentalist regime in Kabul--an unlikely prospect in any case given Soviet concerns about the spread of Islamic revivalism into the adjoining Muslim regions of the U.S.S.R. itself.

Indian concern about a permanent Soviet presence in Afghanistan arises out of its objective to insulate South Asia from external influence and intervention. A Soviet-controlled Afghanistan would likely result in a deepened and more awesome American presence in the region. This is already measured in the commitment of sophisticated weapons for Pakistan, the build-up of naval forces in the Indian Ocean, and the establishment of the Rapid Deployment Force. India fears, as well, the establishment of American bases and surveillance facilities in Pakistan--a presence, which from Indian perspective, can only embolden Pakistan vis-a-vis India and, at the same time, provoke the Soviet Union to strengthen its own military capabilities within the region. The prospect of American bases in Pakistan is a source of particular unease in New Delhi, and some officials express the fear that were the United States to pursue such a course, it could drive India into greater dependence upon the Soviet Union at a time when India is seeking to lessen that dependence and widen its options.

The American balance to the Soviet presence in Afghanistan and the Indian Ocean provides the nations of South Asia room for maneuver that would be difficult if one Great Power alone had predominant influence within the region. But so long as India and Pakistan are at odds, a superpower "balance" carries not only the danger of armed confrontation between the Great Powers but deepened regional insecurity in the polarization of the United States-Pakistan-China on one side and the Soviet Union-Afghanistan-India on the other. Nothing could be more threatening to Indian security or the peace of the region. For this reason, India seeks to minimize American military involvement in South Asia at the same time that it seeks to neutralize Afghanistan and secure the withdrawal of Soviet troops. A permanent presence by both the United States and the Soviet Union in South Asia would, moreover, diminish Indian influence within the region and undermine its role in the larger international arena.

For all their mutual suspicion, there is an increasing recognition in India and Pakistan that the security of each and of South Asia more generally depends upon regional cooperation and specifically on Indo-Pakistan detente. Although the F-16s are symbolic of America's commitment to Pakistan, few Pakistanis are confident that the United States would be prepared to go to war in the possible event of a Soviet attack. Such an attack is regarded as unlikely, although the Soviets could put enormous pressure on Pakistan--through support for Baluch and Sindi separatism and by raids in "hot pursuit" of Afghan guerrillas behind Pakistani lines and in refugee camps. Such raids (accompanied by the work of agents provocateurs among the Afghan refugees themselves) might be designed to stir domestic hostility against the refugees, as the Lebanese came to resent the Palestinians in their midst as they drew Israeli fire. Pakistan has a pressing desire for a political solution to the Afghan situation and, foremost, to secure the return of the refugees.

India has a vital interest in Pakistan's strength and stability--although few Pakistanis are yet convinced that this is so. As once Afghanistan was the buffer against Czarist Russia, so today Pakistan is India's buffer against Soviet power and disturbances in Iran. A breakup of Pakistan could not only involve the extension of Soviet influence, if not control, to the Indian Ocean, but it could have a contagious destabilizing effect on India itself. India is wary too of Pakistan succumbing to Soviet pressure. India wants a strong and secure Pakistan--but not one so strong as to threaten Indian security. Here India is fundamentally ambivalent. India has stated that it has no objection to Pakistan's acquisition of arms from foreign suppliers, including the United States, so long as those arms are appropriate to Pakistan's defense. India judges the F-16s, with their deep penetration capability, to be inappropriate, but more than the F-16 itself, it is the American commitment it symbolizes that worries India. India's concern about the transfer of arms to Pakistan is fundamentally a concern about external security ties with the United States, not Pakistani military power. At what point will India be secure vis-a-vis Pakistan? Absolute security, to paraphrase Kissinger in a South Asian context, can be achieved only by the absolute insecurity of India's neighbors.

For Pakistan, India remains the primary security threat, and the performance capabilities of such weapons as the F-16 give to Pakistan, so they believe, a deterrent to Indian attack. To use them in a first strike against India, however, would be to invite Indian retaliation against which Pakistan could not defend itself. Today, in contrast to the blusterous days before 1971, most Pakistanis admit that they could not win a war against India, and General Zia has said so explicitly. Pakistan--although its armed forces are greater today than in 1971--no longer seeks parity of military strength with India nor can it realistically. Pakistan has, however, proposed negotiations for an established ratio of forces, conceding in advance India's military superiority. Pakistan's security lies in deterrence and, ultimately, detente.

The Indians are not so sure. They speak often of an "irrational" element in Pakistani behavior that could lead them into yet another adventure in Kashmir. Although given little credence by India's foreign policy elite, various scenarios depict a Pakistani attack on India. One scenario projects Pakistani F-16 air strikes against the off-shore oil rigs of the Bombay High or the nuclear reactors at Trombay, together with a blitzkrieg movement into Kashmir. In this dark vision, an international call for a cease-fire--backed by American support for Pakistan--would give to Pakistan the initial advantage of time. But it would be hard to imagine India accepting a cease-fire in the face of territorial losses in Kashmir, knowing that with overwhelming military superiority it has the capacity to secure victory over Pakistan in the Punjab. Moreover, the Soviet Union could be expected to play its role in the United Nations, as it did in 1971, to give India more time. The United States would not be a guarantor of Pakistani aggression against India nor, given the continuing security ties between India and the Soviet Union, would China likely intervene. An alternate--and equally unlikely--scenario envisages a Pakistani strike against Kashmir, with F-16s held as a threat against an Indian counter-thrust across the Punjab and Rajasthan borders.[4]

However implausible these scenarios may be, perceptions shape reality. If most Indians in responsible positions reject such scenarios as farfetched, others take them seriously. The possibility of another war between India and Pakistan--whatever its origin--cannot be dismissed, and if there is a fourth round of armed conflict, it is unlikely to be limited to engagements along the border. In past wars, neither India nor Pakistan attacked strategic targets--although each had the capacity to do so. As perceived vital interests are threatened, that restraint can no longer be taken for granted. Targets of critical importance--hydroelectric dams, nuclear reactors, etc.--will be vulnerable to attack.

Indian fears are deepened by social unrest in the Punjab, complicating India's security on the western border. Indeed, some Indians are convinced that there is a Pakistani hand in the Sikh agitations and that this is part of a larger design to weaken and destabilize India. Many Pakistanis, no doubt, still seek revenge on India for the breakup of Pakistan in 1971, but an unstable India could hardly enhance Pakistan's security, particularly if India was convinced of Pakistan's involvement. But beyond heightened international tension and the possibility of war which Pakistani intervention in Indian domestic politics would surely entail, regional unrest in India might well have a contagious effect on ethnic nationalism in Pakistan.

If the scenarios played out in India's fears are unrealistic, they underscore nevertheless the profound lack of trust between the two nations. The mutual suspicion between India and Pakistan is rooted in the historical legacy of partition, three wars since independence, and centuries of Hindu-Muslim enmity. Most Pakistanis are convinced that India has never reconciled itself to partition and the existence of Pakistan. Many believe that India nurtures dreams of conquest. Indians generally believe partition to have been a tragic mistake (where they lay the blame varies), but few indeed would want to see India burdened with the absorption of 90 million Pakistani Muslims. India has no territorial claims against Pakistan--save in the special case of Kashmir, the conflict that remains after 36 years the major bilateral issue between the two countries. India has let it be known (though not yet formally proposed) that it is prepared to settle the dispute by recognizing the line of control as the de jure boundary. Pakistan has declared any legitimation of Kashmir's division unacceptable. While Kashmir remains for some an intensely emotional issue, one hears with increasing frequency in Pakistan the suggestion that the Kashmir issue be "set aside" and the matter be left to future generations to settle. There is, in effect, a willingness to accept the status quo but not yet to give it the legitimacy of formal recognition.

Against the voice of reason heard in both New Delhi and Islamabad, however, mutual suspicion and fear nourish paranoia. Many Pakistanis express the belief that India will at some point try to take Azad Kashmir by force. Some are convinced that India will attempt a preemptive strike--possibly with Israeli collaboration--against Pakistan's nuclear facilities. Some see India, acting as a Soviet proxy, mounting a full-scale attack upon Pakistan or joining the Soviets in a two-front war to dismember Pakistan and divide the spoils. This view may not be widely shared, but most Pakistanis are convinced that India seeks hegemony over South Asia, with a weak and subservient Pakistan. Many Pakistanis believe that India is exploiting ethnic discontent in Sind and Baluchistan and that there is real danger of Indian intervention in the event of serious unrest. Mrs. Gandhi is viewed with particular suspicion. Pakistani analysts feel that if Mrs. Gandhi comes under political pressure or faces social unrest in India, she will use Pakistan as a scapegoat for her own problems and for India's domestic troubles. Under extreme pressure, some believe, she might pursue diversionary military action against Pakistan. And it is widely believed that Mrs. Gandhi herself is a major impediment to improved Indo-Pakistan relations and that rapprochement will be possible only after she is gone.

The gap between India and Pakistan will not be easily bridged, but the "war clouds" that some saw on the horizon in 1980 and 1981 have receded. While rhetoric and accusations continue to rise and fall, tensions between India and Pakistan have eased. India has responded to the Pakistani proposal for a no-war pact with a counter-offer for a treaty of friendship and cooperation; Mrs. Gandhi and General Zia have met for discussions; and a joint commission has been established to promote economic and cultural cooperation. The joint commission is an important breakthrough because Pakistan, to secure its separate identity, has long sought to minimize economic and cultural relations in fear of Indian domination. The no-war pact, proposed by General Zia in 1981, reflects that concern at the same time that it is a direct response to changes in Pakistan's strategic environment. But that Pakistan made the offer at all, having repeatedly rejected similar proposals made by India since 1949, aroused Indian suspicion. Mrs. Gandhi initially rejected the offer as a subterfuge. Under pressure from Indian domestic and international public opinion, Mrs. Gandhi responded to the Pakistani overture and offered a treaty of friendship--its purpose more comprehensive in seeking to forge closer social, economic, and cultural links between India and Pakistan. The two proposals serve different purposes, though each strikes a point of mutual interest in common security. The no-war pact is designed to secure Pakistan's backdoor to India. The treaty of friendship and cooperation is designed to open that door to greater Indo-Pakistan contact and to reinforce the concept of South Asia as a strategic and cultural entity.

The two proposals, now on the table for discussion, provide a basis for meeting on common ground. Pakistan has opposed the "no foreign bases" provision in the treaty of friendship as a compromise of its sovereignty, but it would be no less a limitation on India than Pakistan--and there is within Pakistan, in any case, strong popular oppositon to any provision of bases to the United States, as there is to the use of Pakistan for operations of the U.S. Rapid Deployment Force. In serious negotiations on an Indo-Pakistan security treaty, Pakistan may yield on the basing provision, but it will not easily give way. Another sticking point is "strict bilateralism"--the provision that neither party raise bilateral issues (here referring specifically to Kashmir) in international forum. While Pakistan is not prepared to accept the status quo in Kashmir, it is prepared to "set it aside"--a phrase currently in vogue in Pakistan government circles--and to tone down the rhetoric. An Indo-Pakistan treaty could reach a compromise by invoking both the spirit and phraseology of the Simla Agreement, with its commitment to the settlement of differences through peaceful bilateral negotiations.

There are powerful incentives for both India and Pakistan to reach an accord, for it is in Indo-Pakistan detente that the region can most effectively be insulated from foreign interference--be it the expansion of Soviet influence or the greater involvement of the U.S. in the region as a counter-weight to Soviet presence. This is recognized by officials in both New Delhi and Islamabad, yet each remains distrustful of the other: Pakistan fears domination under Pax Indica, while India remains suspicious of Pakistani efforts to secure external support to balance Indian predominance with the region. China has encouraged Pakistan to patch up its differences with India, as has the United States in recognition that America's strategic interests within the larger region depend in large degree on the capacity of India and Pakistan to provide for their common security through cooperation.

India-Pakistan Relations: The Next Five Years

Given conflicting signals, the movement forward followed by sudden reversal, discerning trends in India's relationship with Pakistan is rather like reading the entrails of a sheep. Any projection of trends is all the more difficult because of the changing character of the strategic environment, potential political instability in Pakistan, the impact of events in Afghanistan, and the role of external actors--the Soviet Union, China, and the United States.

The most probable course of events for Indo-Pakistan relations over the next five years will involve alternating periods of tension and progress toward detente, but without dramatic change in the basic character of the relationship. Barring a major setback--an increase in U.S. arms commitments to Pakistan; establishment of U.S. bases, reconnaissance facilities, or RDF supply depots in Pakistan; or a Pakistani nuclear explosion--there should be a gradual improvement in relations. Out of the efforts of the joint commission, communications and visits across the border should become easier; trade is likely to increase, although it will continue to be constrained by Pakistani protectionism; and there will be a likely relaxation in cultural exchange, cinema, and publications. Movement in the political and security areas is likely to proceed with considerable caution. If a non-Congress coalition Government comes to power in India in the next election, the prospects for detente are likely to improve, but nearly four decades of mutual suspicion and hostility will not be displaced by new Governments in either New Delhi or Islamabad.

Discussions on an Indo-Pakistan treaty are likely to be protracted, while progress toward cooperation proceeds on other fronts. The caution on India's part is not solely a product of suspicion of Pakistani intentions, but comes out of a reluctance to extend "legitimacy" to military government in Pakistan.* Indian newspapers report that the Pakistan People's Party (PPP), once led by Bhutto, urges India not to sign an accord with General Zia and that the mood in Karachi is against the treaty. The reports, no doubt, express popular opposition in Pakistan to the military government and anything that might extend Zia's rule; they may also be something of a smokescreen for India's

---

* There is a certain irony in India's opposition to military rule in Pakistan and to the current romanticization of Bhutto in India. Bhutto was hardly a "friend" of India, and there is no reason to assume that a civilian government in Pakistan would be easier to deal with than a military regime. In fact, there has probably been no government in Islamabad more genuinely prepared to reach an accommodation with India than that of General Zia. The danger in military rule in Pakistan lies less in the direct threat it poses to India than in the potentially explosive political situation it has generated domestically. The prospect of political chaos and instability in Pakistan is not viewed with equanimity in New Delhi.

own suspicions of Islamabad; and they could well involve Soviet amplification to impede progress toward Indo-Pakistan detente. As India and Pakistan move toward improved relations, it should be expected that those who have little to gain--notably the Soviet Union and its stalwarts in India--will engage in a campaign against Pakistan. And if Pakistan persists in its apparent determination to "go nuclear," Islamabad will provide plenty of fuel.

India's own rigid stance, however, does not ease Pakistan's suspicions and security fears--as, for example, on the question of Pakistan's re-entry into the Commonwealth. Although Pakistan has not formally requested re-entry, India has made its opposition clear. India's argument is that Pakistan opted out of the Commonwealth under Bhutto, and only a duly-elected government, acting in the name of the people, can opt back in. (Given the character of the Commonwealth today, with its many African military dictatorships, India's position carries little credibility.) The second point in India's case against Pakistan's re-entry is that while in the Commonwealth, Pakistan continually brought up bilateral issues (that is, Kashmir) in violation of Commonwealth custom. In November 1983, India for the first time hosted the Commonwealth Conference. At the New Delhi meeting, India lost a significant opportunity for a bold and imaginative step in advancing India-Pakistan rapprochement by not proposing Pakistan's readmission to the Commonwealth.

One factor that should encourage improved relations between India and Pakistan is India's chairmanship of the Non-Aligned Movement, a three-year term that commenced in March, 1983. The responsibility for leadership of the movement, of which Pakistan is a member, should give to India added incentive to make peace with its neighbors and to exercise its preeminence within the subcontinent in such a way as to encourage regional cooperation.

The most serious impediment to Indo-Pakistan detente--and to Indo-U.S. relations--lies in the character of Pakistan's security relationship with the United States. India can be expected to oppose any significant increase in the quantity or quality of arms transfers to Pakistan (e.g., an increase in the number of F-16s or a major advance in the avionics supplied). India would be particularly concerned if the United States were to acquire bases in Pakistan (for prepositioning RDF equipment, for electronic surveillance, etc.). The stationing of troops or U.S. aircraft operations from Pakistan, even for submarine surveillance, would be a matter of grave concern to India, as would be the development of U.S. naval facilities at Gwadar or Pasni in Baluchistan.

Whatever short-term tactical advantage the United States might gain in Southwest Asia by such action would surely be offset by the far greater costs to America's long-range interests in the stability and security of the region. The costs would entail an unnecessary alienation of India; an almost inevitably closer security tie between India and the Soviet Union; and a deterioration in Indo-Pakistan relations that could possibly lead to a fourth war. There is never a guarantee that war can be regionally contained. As Kissinger writes in his White House Years, for example, the U.S. feared in 1971 that the Indo-Pakistan war could lead to Chinese intervention and Soviet response. In the uncertainty of the new strategic environment of the region, though both the United States and the Soviet Union would surely resist being drawn in, another Indo-Pakistan war carries the added danger of widened conflict and the Indian nightmare of superpower confrontation in the subcontinent.

Political instability in Pakistan, particularly regional/ethnic unrest, could play a major factor in shaping Indo-Pakistan relations. The breakup of Pakistan is not in India's interest. It would result in the creation of petty states vulnerable to penetration by foreign powers. Indian influence would by no means be guaranteed--save initially in Sind, where animosity against Punjabi domination is so intense that some might welcome the Indian Army as liberators. But even in Sind, as in Bangladesh after 1971, Indians would soon wear out their welcome. Baluchistan would probably come under Soviet influence, providing the Russians their access to the Indian Ocean, and a Paktunistan, the long-sought dream of Pathan nationalists in the Northwest Frontier Province, could survive only at Soviet sufferance.

Any attempt by the Soviet Union to destabilize Pakistan or to aid and abet in its dismemberment would be seen in New Delhi as a threat to Indian security. India has no desire to share a boundary with the U.S.S.R., or to relinquish its position as the preeminent power of the subcontinent.

NUCLEAR PROLIFERATION

The major source of tension in Indo-Pakistan relations over the next five years is likely to be Pakistan's nuclear program. Despite Pakistan's repeated denials, available evidence points to a clandestine program directed toward nuclear weapons capability. The questions are how long will it be before Pakistan attains that capability and, once it has it, whether it will opt for the testing, production, and deployment of "the Bomb." Most observers now believe that Pakistan is not as close to nuclear capability as once thought, but barring major technological problems, Pakistan should reach capability within the next five years--a time frame, Indians note, that dovetails with the delivery schedule of the last of the F-16 aircraft.

But if American arms are a restraint on Pakistan's decision to "go nuclear," the leash will not be cut with the delivery of the last F-16. Pakistan is almost wholly dependent on external sources of arms, and in access to spares, it has a thin cushion to sustain any cutoff. China cannot supply technologically advanced weapons, and third party transfers (through Saudi Arabia, Egypt, or Turkey, for example) would be a necessarily limited and insecure source. If taking the nuclear option would cut Pakistan off from the sources of advanced conventional weapons--and it surely would from the United States and probably, if only in response to U.S. pressure, from Western European suppliers as well--the bomb would make Pakistan all the more vulnerable.

A nuclear deterrent--if that is Pakistan's goal--would not displace the need for conventional arms. Without a conventional deterrent, Pakistan would be compelled to respond to any attack or incursion with "massive retalliation" or to acquiesce to aggression. Moreover, in the South Asian context, unless Pakistan faced nuclear weapons across the border in India--and it does not at this time--its own bomb would not necessarily provide greater deterrence to an Indian attack than effective conventional weapons, although it would surely raise Indian perception of risk. In its deep-penetration air strike capability, Pakistan already has sufficient strength to inflict serious damage on India and thus to deter possible (though unlikely) Indian attack. Pakistan does not, however, have the strength to defeat India militarily--nor would nuclear weapons give it that strength, for a nuclear Pakistan would be soon checked by a nuclear India with second-strike capability.

One of the principal aims of the United States in supplying weapons to Pakistan is to give Pakistan sufficient confidence in its own security that it will find the nuclear option less attractive and unnecessary. Pakistan today no longer seeks parity of military strength with India, but the challenge is to find the balance that will give Pakistan the capacity to deter an Indian attack without at the same time constituting a threat to Indian security. Security does not rest on weapons alone. The challenge is as much in modifying perceptions, in building trust on both sides, for India does not view itself as a threat to any nation and sees in Pakistani armament aggressive intent. The U.S. role here is critical, and it involves recognition of South Asia as a strategic entity. Any provision of weapons to Pakistan that upsets the ratio of military strength in the subcontinent or which introduces a new level of sophistication in arms (as did the F-16) will fuel the arms race and may increase the danger of nuclear proliferation in South Asia. Pakistan's security is inextricably bound to that of India and of the subcontinent as a whole. In providing arms to Pakistan, the United States (without giving a "veto" to New Delhi) should consult India and at least seek to assuage India of any danger to its own security. India's trust of Pakistan or of the U.S. is not likely to be enhanced when it learns of a major American offer of arms to Pakistan on the front page of the New York Times or in a television interview on "Meet the Press."

Whether or not Pakistan takes the nuclear option, it seems determined to have that option--and this, in itself, is potentially destabilizing. Nuclear technology is today sufficiently advanced that a test may not be necessary. (Israel, for example, is believed to have developed a nuclear weapon without actually testing it. An untested Pakistani device, however, cannot be assumed to have the same credibility.) But to give the signals that the capacity has been reached but the test option not taken, if credible, will surely arouse Indian fear that Pakistan has chosen the covert weapons option. A wholly covert program could serve no deterrent purpose. (It would be most unlikely, moreover, that such a program could be hidden from India.) There must be at least an element of uncertainty, but that would be sufficient to propel India toward its own "covert" program. We would thus face a situation of mutual uncertainty.

If Pakistan conducts a nuclear test (and Bhutto, who initiated the Pakistan program, insisted there was no such thing as a "peaceful nuclear explosion"), India would be compelled to respond in some way. There would be enormous political pressure for India, having already demonstrated its nuclear capability at Pokhran in 1974, to take the weapons option and move toward production and deployment. Most well-informed observers in India, however, believe that the Government of India would continue to resist the weapons option. In these circumstances, India would likely resume tests, probably with a series, to demonstrate both its resolve as well as its technological superiority to Pakistan. We would then face a situation where both India and Pakistan would have demonstrated nuclear capability through tests, each publicly denying that it had developed a nuclear weapon but retaining the option to do so. The situation is inherently unstable, for in the capacity to choose the weapons option is the capacity to develop a bomb covertly. India today can have the demonstrated capacity to manufacture a nuclear weapon and forego the decision to do so--either overtly or covertly--because Pakistan does not yet have the capacity. When both India and Pakistan have the capacity, the fear that one might have already taken the covert option may be sufficient to impel the other to do likewise. Indeed, despite the American consensus that India does not have "a bomb in the basement," many Pakistanis are convinced that India has a modest nuclear weapons stockpile. This perception, a justification by some for Pakistan's nuclear program, could lead to dangerous miscalculation.

Nuclear testing by Pakistan and India would, under the terms of the Non-Proliferation Act of 1978, trigger the suspension of U.S. assistance to each nation. The United States would thereby lose whatever leverage it may have had with each in restraining further movement toward the acquisition of nuclear weapons. The U.S., as well, would in effect have opted out of the region as a strategic counterweight to the Soviet Union.

If India were to take the nuclear weapons option in response to Pakistani tests (or if it were to pursue a weapons program on its own initiative), there would likely be a call, especially in the United States, for the imposition of severe international sanctions against India--closed loan windows, trade restrictions, and denied access to high technology. But once India and Pakistan go nuclear, sanctions may do little more than to drive them more deeply into dependence upon the Soviet Union and China respectively.

If in response to a Pakistani test, India were to take the weapons option, Pakistan would surely follow with its own program. Each with their own nuclear weapons, even with initially limited delivery capabilities (e.g., a free-fall weapon mounted on a deep penetration aircraft--an F-16 or Mirage 2000), they would achieve mutual deterrence in a regional "balance of terror." Indeed, K. Surbrahmanyam, Director of India's Institute for Defence Studies and Analyses, sees in this a new level of stability for South Asia. Few are so sanguine. Nevertheless, we should not assume that India and Pakistan would be any less responsible than the U.S. and U.S.S.R. in their policy with regard to the use of nuclear weapons, but the fallibility of command, control, and communication in South Asia enormously raises the risk of nuclear war by miscalculation.

South Asia, while a strategic entity, is not an isolate that can be quarantined. A decision by India and Pakistan to go nuclear would have wide impact, not only in stimulating further proliferation, but in upsetting the strategic balance. India's decision to test a nuclear device in 1974 was, at least in part, a response to China's nuclear status and capability, as China's weapon, in turn, was a response to the Soviet Union. How the nuclearization of South Asia will fit into Soviet and Chinese security remains uncertain and, therefore, an added element of risk.

The asymmetry of nuclear power is one of the major impediments to the control of nuclear proliferation in South Asia. In 1974, after India's Pokhran explosion, Pakistan proposed that South Asia be declared a nuclear weapons-free zone. Pakistan has also proposed that both India and Pakistan sign the Nuclear Non-Proliferation Treaty and open all nuclear facilities to international inspection. The proposals are unacceptable to India. First, and most critically, Pakistan and India do not share the same threat perception of China, and India is not prepared to deny itself the weapons option so long as China remains a nuclear power. Second, a South Asian nuclear weapons-free zone under security guarantees from the U.S., the U.S.S.R., and China is viewed in New Delhi as a design to contain India's power and influence. It would, in effect, be yet another instance of Pakistan seeking external support as a counterweight to India's predominance in South Asia. Third, India rejects the concept of a nuclear weapons-free zone, as it does the Nuclear Non-Proliferation Treaty, as a legitimation of nuclear weapons in the hands of those who already have possess them and as a means by which those powers seek to retain their nuclear weapons monopoly.

The Soviet Union opposes proliferation and has given India no encouragement in taking the nuclear weapons option. China's position is that it is the sovereign right of any nation to develop its own nuclear weapons--although China has not itself offered the bomb as "just another weapon." There have, however, been various reports of Chinese technical assistance to Pakistan in its nuclear program. There has also been speculation that China would test a Pakistani bomb at its own grounds in the Takala Makan desert. The reports, not surprisingly, are of special concern to India. That China would assist Pakistan in fabricating a nuclear weapon seems unlikely and at odds with Chinese interests. China has sought to improve relations with India and to encourage Indo-Pakistani detente, both calculated to check the expansion of Soviet influence in South Asia. Chinese nuclear assistance to Pakistan would surely undermine these efforts--deepening tension between India and Pakistan and forcing India into greater security dependence upon the Soviet Union.

Given Indian apprehension about Pakistan's nuclear program, there has been speculation as to a possible preemptive strike by India against Pakistan. There are five principal facilities in the Pakistani program: (1) Kahuta uranium centrifuge, (2) Chasma reprocessing, (3) Islamabad reprocessing, (4) Multan heavy water plant, and (5) Karachi nuclear power plant. Kahuta would probably be the most critical single target in destroying Pakistani capacity to develop a nuclear weapon. Kahuta, however, is underground and well-protected. An Indian airstrike or commando raid would have no guarantee of success. Pakistani newspapers, however, have carried reports of India-Israeli collusion for a planned Israeli strike from an Indian base--a highly improbable connection.

A preemptive strike, either directly by India or by a third power with Indian collaboration, would carry high costs for India and is most unlikely. It would almost inevitably mean war with Pakistan. It would draw international sanctions and possible embargo of Middle Eastern oil and expulsion of Indian workers from the Gulf. But beyond the risks of failure and the costs even of success, a strike against Pakistani nuclear facilities involves the danger of released plutonium and the deadly effects of radiation poisoning over a wide area--including northern India. A preemptive strike against Pakistan would also likely bring Pakistani retaliation against Indian nuclear reactors. India is not likely to bring such destruction upon itself.

There is in India a "pro-bomb" lobby that has long argued that India should produce and deploy nuclear weapons independently of what Pakistan may do. And, with a nuclear mystique of power, prestige, and technological achievement, there is in India, as there is in Pakistan, wide popular support for the bomb. Advocates argue that simply retaining the "option," given the indeterminate time required to produce and deploy nuclear weapons, is insufficient to meet possible challenge and to deter attack. They warn of Pakistan's clandestine nuclear program and of the continuing danger of China to Indian security. They call for nuclear weapons as enhancing and ensuring India's self-reliance in a time of crisis.

The Government of India has resisted the various arguments for exercising the option and will likely continue to do so, whatever the leadership in New Delhi, over the next five years--unless there is a major change in India's security situation. Testing of a Pakistani nuclear device would surely raise the question, but so too would a serious deterioration in Sino-Indian relations or Sino-Soviet rapprochement. Although India's relations with China have improved and China is not perceived as an imminent threat, India relies on the Soviet Union as a deterrent to China. A relaxation of tension between the U.S.S.R. and China might provide the opportunity for closer Sino-Indian relations and a settlement of the border dispute, but it might also be a source of considerable unease in New Delhi. If Sino-Soviet detente raises any doubt as to to Soviet reliability, India might feel that its security vis-a-vis China requires development of an Indian nuclear deterrent.

That India has not already taken the nuclear weapons option is at least partly the result of the lack of technology to sustain a full-scale nuclear weapons program--from research and development through deployment in modern delivery systems. With time, this will be more within India's reach, but unless India is prepared to remain a permanently second-class nuclear power (and thus potentially vulnerable), the costs will be staggering, as the continuing arms race between the U.S. and the U.S.S.R. bears witness.

The nuclear debate continues in Indian government, scientific, and intellectual circles at a high level of sophistication. Some early advocates of the bomb, such as Subramaniam Swamy, have had second thoughts, but even those who are generally regarded as opponents (former Prime Minister Morarji Desai, for example) are not prepared to forswear the option. There is no antinuclear movement in South Asia, although some serious doubts are now beginning to be raised about nuclear power as the answer to India's energy needs.

Nuclear proliferation in South Asia is not inevitable. Indo-Pakistani detente will surely reduce the danger, but it does not wholly solve the problem of doubt. Given India's security concerns vis-a-vis China and its position with regard to the "legitimacy" accorded the nuclear weapons powers by the NPT, there is little prospect for the declaration of South Asia as a nuclear weapons-free zone or for opening all nuclear facilities in the region to international inspection. But there is within the framework of Indo-Pakistani detente the possibility for a nuclear accord between the two states. An Indian proposal, for example, to extend the scope of the joint commission to cooperation in the field of nuclear energy might be an important first step toward mutual inspection and the development of a South Asian equivalent of Euratom.

THE REGION: SOUTH ASIA AND THE INDIAN OCEAN

Within South Asia, India's relationships with its smaller neighbors have been that of a big brother, protective but often domineering. India's preeminence has led the other states of the region to seek external support as counterweights to secure whatever degree of autonomy from India as might be possible. Some have looked beyond the region for sources of identity--Pakistan to West Asia, Bangladesh and Sri Lanka to Southeast Asia.

Regional Cooperation

Regional cooperation has been undermined by the unequal distribution of power in South Asia and by the conflict between India and Pakistan. New Delhi has in the past tended to view regionalism as a design to enable the other states to "gang up" against India. India has thus sought to deal with each country bilaterally and to discourage communication and contact among the nations on its periphery. For their part, the smaller countries have been reluctant to enter into regional cooperation for fear that India would inevitably dominate any association and that it would, in effect, institutionalize Indian hegemony.

This has begun to change. In 1980, President Ziaur Rahman of Bangladesh, not long before his assassination, proposed that there be a greater degree of regional cooperation among the seven South Asian nations--India, Pakistan, Bangladesh, Nepal, Bhutan, Sri Lanka, and the Maldives--in facing their common problems. India and Pakistan were initially reluctant, but over four sessions of discussion at the foreign secretary level, the groundwork was laid for limited multilateral cooperation in a "South Asia Forum," or, as it came to be known, South Asian Regional Cooperation (SARC). In August 1983, the foreign ministers of the seven nations met in New Delhi to give their formal assent to the promotion of "collective self-reliance" in nine fields: agriculture, rural development, planning, health, education, transport, telecommunications, sports, and culture. Emphasizing the equality of association, each nation is charged with responsibility for at least one field of cooperation. The declaration proclaimed the goal as one of mutual assistance "to accelerate economic growth, social progress and cultural development in the region." All decisions are to be unaminous and "bilateral and contentious issues shall be excluded from the deliberations."

The move toward South Asian cooperation clearly comes within the framework of the Non-Aligned Movement's new emphasis on South-South cooperation. If India, in chairing the Movement, is unable to participate in promoting cooperation of NAM members in its own neighborhood, its credibility as a leader in the movement as a whole is likely to be weakened. South Asian Regional Cooperation will keep its distance from political and strategic questions, and many essentially multilateral problems, such as water resource development in the region embracing India, Nepal, and Bangladesh, are unlikely to be moved from the bilateral level upon which India has insisted. Nevertheless, SARC provides a major step toward regional cooperation that can only enhance the security of the subcontinent and reduce the opportunities for foreign interference. The next five years are likely to see a gradual and selective extension of cooperation, but the scope and success of regional cooperation depends fundamentally on the capacity of India and Pakistan to settle their differences and India's ability to win the confidence of its weaker neighbors.

Nepal

India's strategic perimeter embraces Nepal, and in the defense of its northern borders against China, Nepal is vital to India' interests. Relations between the two nations have long been characterized by friction. Nepal, landlocked and dependent upon India for aid, trade, and transit, seeks to resist Indian domination and political interference. In the past five years, there has been significant progress in improved relations on matters of trade and on water and hydroelectric cooperation, but looking to the next five years, these areas, along with the political and strategic, remain subjects of continued and sometimes strained discussion.

In 1978, under the Janata Government, India signed a new seven-year trade and transit treaty with Nepal. Some 70 percent of Nepal's trade is with India and the rest passes through Indian territory. India's generosity in the terms of the 1978 treaty led Mrs. Gandhi, then out of power, to attack it as a capitulation to Nepal, and renegotiation in 1985 is likely to again raise rancorous issues--transit points for goods into Nepal, especially from Bangladesh; smuggling of luxury goods into India imported into Nepal from third countries; and preference for Nepali products in the Indian market.

Another area of tension is Nepali resentment against the prominent role of Indians in the kingdom's economy, but again it is a resentment arising from dependency--both on Indian investment and technical-managerial skill.

Population movement is a source of potential conflict. An estimated 500,000 Nepalis cross the border into India every year in search of work, and as many as half are believed to settle permanently. This has led to increasing ethnic tension in the northern districts of Uttar Pradesh and Bihar, in Sikkim, and in India's Northeastern states. Remittances by Nepali workers in India are important to Nepal's economy and underscores its vulnerability to Indian influence.

Nepal has tried to reduce its dependency on India by diversifying its economic relations (with little success) and sources of aid (the U.S., China, and India being major contributors), but India remains Nepal's dominant trading partner and a principal benefactor. Nepal is, in effect, on a short leash. In return for its assistance, India expects Nepal to do nothing that would undermine Indian interests, especially in the vital area of security.

The "bedrock" of Indo-Nepalese relations is the 1950 treaty of peace and friendship and the accompanying protocol that requires the two countries to consult with each other and to devise effective counter-measures to meet any threat to the security of either nation. In 1973, King Birendra proposed that Nepal be neutralized as a "zone of peace." India viewed the proposal as an attempt by Nepal to modify the special relationship under the 1950 treaty and to equate India and China--which, given India's strategic concerns in the

Himalayan kingdom, is unacceptable. Nepal has continued to push the proposal and has received support for the plan from 26 nations, including China and all of the South Asian states other than India. In 1982, India agreed to take the proposal under study but remains unenthusiastic.

Bhutan

India's "special relationship" with Bhutan is based on the 1949 treaty by which Bhutan agrees "to be guided" by India in its foreign relations. In 1978, the Bhutanese National Assembly called for renegotiation of the treaty, and the king has urged that it be "updated." But, especially in the light of China's 1982 criticism of the "unequal treaty," India is reluctant to change the terms of its relationship with this isolated but strategically vital nation. Any changes are likely to be more of form than substance and the treaty's security component will reaffirm Bhutan's position within India's defense perimeter.

With India's sponsorship, Bhutan became a member of the United Nations, and though its entry was criticized by some as giving a second vote in the UN to India, Bhutan has sought to exercise a degree of independence--even to the extent of incurring Indian displeasure by its vote on the seating of Kampuchea. But Bhutan is heavily dependent upon India--with its economic development almost wholly financed by India--and it is careful not to step too far out of line. For its part, India has not interfered in Bhutan's domestic affairs nor is it likely to do so--so long as Bhutan does not seek external support. India's concern is most critically China, with whom Bhutan shares a border but has no direct relations.

Bangladesh

Relations between India and Bangladesh have been strained since the assassination of Sheikh Mujibur Rahman in 1975. Most of the problems between the two nations, however, go back before the creation of Bangladesh in 1971 and have been the subject of intermittent negotiation. Tensions relaxed during the Janata phase, with the signing of an interim agreement in 1977 on the Ganges waters-Farakka barrage problem. The issue, relating to the flow of water into Bangladesh, is the major dispute among a number of outstanding bilateral issues.

Mrs. Gandhi's return to power in 1980 cooled relations. There was a flareup in the dispute over New Moore/South Talpatty Island, a sand spit that emerged in the Bay of Bengal in the early 1970s. The issue (now on a backburner) is heated because the maritime boundary between the two countries has never been delimited, and ownership of the island could affect oil and natural gas rights in the Bay of Bengal. Relations have also been ruffled by mutual suspicion of interference in insurgencies within each country. India has accused Bangladesh of harboring Mizo rebels, while Bangladesh has charged India with stirring tribal discontent in the Chittagong Hill Tract and with giving sanctuary to anti-Bangladeshi dissidents.

But while tempers sometimes flared, India and Bangladesh have moved forward in a number of areas: a trade agreement in 1980, a telecommunications agreement and a memorandum of understanding on technical cooperation in 1981, and a protocol on inland water transport and trade in 1982. In October 1982, Bangladesh's military ruler, Lt. General H. M. Ershad, went to New Delhi for the first talks between leaders of Bangladesh and India in eight years. The summit had been well-prepared. Ershad and Mrs. Gandhi agreed to extend the Ganges waters interim agreement for 18 months, with a slight modification in the schedule for water distribution during the dry season. The final agreement, to be reached by April 1984, awaits technical reports now in preparation, but failure to reach an understanding on the issue will seriously affect relations.

The 1982 Ershad-Gandhi summit also brought a resolution of the dispute over two tiny Bangladeshi enclaves in India. India agreed to lease in perpetuity a corridor to connect the enclaves to the rest of Bangladesh. A third achievement of the summit was an agreement to establish a joint economic commission at the ministerial level to promote cooperation in commercial, scientific, technological, transport, and communications fields.

The most serious problem in Indo-Bangladesh relations, however, is the least susceptable to diplomatic effort--the illegal movement of people across the border from Bangladesh into India. The flow of migrants seeking work in India has been especially destabilizing in Assam and Tripura, and while the February 1983 election violence in Assam, together with renewed efforts to control the border, has stemmed the tide, a deterioration of economic or political conditions in

Bangladesh could again accelerate movement across the porous border. The proposed $500 million fence--which has brought vehement protest from General Ershad--is no more likely to stop determined migrants than the fenced portions of the U.S.-Mexico border.

The weakness of Bangladesh, one of the world's poorest and most populous nations, constitutes a security threat to India. Crop failure, natural disaster, or political chaos in Bangladesh could send millions of people into India, deepening social unrest and, recalling the 11 million refugees in 1971, imposing an unacceptable burden on India. Bangladesh's weakness also poses two other security threats to India. First is the potential involvement of a foreign power, such as the United States or China, in Bangadesh. Bangladesh is non-aligned, and there is no reason to expect any change in that status. Dhaka has given India no basis for fear that it might, for example, extend basing rights to any other nation, but the weakness and instability of Bangladesh renders it potentially vulnerable to foreign interference, and New Delhi can be expected to keep a close watch. The second threat posed by the weakness of Bangladesh is the danger that at some future time political unrest could spill over into India or that Bangladesh could be used as a guerrilla base for Indian insurgents. In any of these situations, insofar as India feels its security threatened, there is a potential for Indian intervention.

Sri Lanka

Problems in India's relations with Sri Lanka relate principally to the status of the island's Tamils, who constitute some 20 percent of the population. The "Ceylon Tamils" (11 percent) trace their origin to invaders from South India more than 1000 years ago; the "Indian Tamils" (9 percent) came to Sri Lanka from South India as plantation laborers between 50 and 100 years ago. The Government of India, with special concern for the political sensitivity of Tamil Nadu, has taken a proprietary interest in the welfare and security of Tamils in Sri Lanka, and periodic ethnic conflict on the island has strained relations between the two nations. Closely related to India's interest in Sri Lanka's Tamil minority is the Indian fear of a large-scale flow of Tamil refugees from Sri Lanka if ethnic relations there seriously deteriorate. A second area of concern in India-Sri Lanka relations (as in India's relations with each of its neighbors) is the potential for foreign involvement. In the case of Sri Lanka, India's concern has most recently focused on the possible use of Trincomalee as a U.S. naval base or fueling station.

The two areas of concern came together in July-August 1983 and could have transformed a major outbreak of domestic ethnic violence in Sri Lanka into an international crisis. United Press International reported that President Junius Jayewardene feared armed Indian intervention to protect the Tamils and had appealed to the United States, Britain, Pakistan, and Bangladesh for military assistance in the event of an invasion. Pakistan and Bangladesh were said to have responded positively, while the western embassies were consulting their governments. Nothing could have been more calculated to raise Indian alarm. Jayewardene denied any threat of invasion and informed Prime Minister Indira Gandhi that Sri Lanka had appealed to no one for military assistance. Though suspicion remained, the Indian government publicly accepted his assurances. But the report itself--and that it was widely believed--underscores the volatility of the international relations of the region and the fears and insecurities underlying them.

New Delhi's response to the situation in Sri Lanka involved the enunciation of what foreign policy analyst Bhabani Sen Gupta calls "an Indian doctrine of regional security."[5] India will not intervene in the internal conflicts of a South Asian nation and strongly opposes such intervention by any other country. India will not tolerate intervention in a South Asian nation if there is any anti-Indian implication. If external assistance is required to deal with serious internal conflict, help should be sought from a number of countries within the region, including India. Exclusion of India in such circumstances will be considered an anti-Indian move.

The Indian Ocean

No area within the scope of India's strategic concern is potentially more volatile than the northwestern sector of the Indian Ocean. Conflicts between the littoral states (e.g., the Iran-Iraq war), the potential for political instability in the Gulf states and Saudi Arabia, and the growing presence of the U.S. and U.S.S.R. combine to create an uncertain and highly dangerous situation.

India, in continuity with the Raj, has always regarded the Indian Ocean as vital to its security, but facing no imminent military threat from the sea, it was not until the late 1960s, after the British withdrawal east of Suez, that India directed its concerns to the Indian Ocean. It did so principally through the proposal to make the Indian Ocean a "zone of peace," secure from external military presence. The proposal was first raised by Sri Lanka, perhaps at India's initiative and certainly with India's active support, and was brought before the United Nations in 1971. It is a triumph of Indian diplomacy that New Delhi has succeeded in drawing support for the "zone of peace" from most littoral states, for public postures do not always reflect private judgments nor do they accord with actions. The proposal was perhaps doomed from the beginning. Some states viewed the "zone of peace" as an attempt by New Delhi to transform the Indian Ocean into an Indian lake. Some, like the Shah of Iran, found in alignment support for their own quest for regional power. Others, in regional rivalries (like Somalia and Ethiopia), sought external military support for protection. And India's own enthusiasm for the "zone of peace" is not without qualification. India is well aware that other littoral states would soon demand limits on navies of the region as well as a nuclear-free zone of peace--both unacceptable to India.

By the late 1960s, both the United States and the Soviet Union had established a presence in the Indian Ocean, the U.S. with the communications facility at Diego Garcia, 1500 miles to the south of India. During the 1970s, the superpowers gradually expanded their naval forces in the region, and each began the search among the littoral states and island nations for port facilities. As the U.S. strengthened its installations at Diego Garcia, the Soviet Union acquired bases at Berbera in Somalia (from which it was expelled in 1977), then in Southern Yemen and Ethiopia. In 1978, the Soviets (to the unvoiced alarm of India) tried to obtain a base on Gan, the southernmost island of the Maldives chain, 500 miles north of Diego Garcia. The Maldives rejected the offer.

The events of the late 1970s, with the fall of the Shah and the Soviet invasion of Afghanistan, radically altered the situation in the Indian Ocean region. The U.S. saw its vital strategic interests in the Persian Gulf and the oil routes to Japan and Western Europe threatened by an expansion of Soviet power that brought the U.S.S.R. within a striking distance of 300 miles of the Strait of Hormuz. To balance the preponderance of Soviet ground forces in Afghanistan and in Soviet territory bordering Iran, the U.S. rapidly built up its naval forces in the Indian Ocean and established the Rapid Deployment Force.

Over the previous decade, India had been sharply critical of the U.S. naval buildup in the Indian Ocean and particularly of the growing importance of Diego Garcia. New Delhi remained seemingly unconcerned about the Soviet naval presence and tended to regard it as a response to American provocation. After the Soviet invasion of Afghanistan in December 1979, however, Indian apprehension deepened that the Indian Ocean would become the focal point of the new cold war--and it carried the danger of nuclear confrontation. India began to temper its criticism of the United States by expressions of concern that the "superpower" buildup in the Indian Ocean could only be destabilizing to the littoral states--thus equating the U.S. and U.S.S.R. by naming neither--and that the security of the region depended upon a withdrawal of foreign forces. Many Indians also realized that short of the very unlikely declaration of the Indian Ocean as a "zone of peace," India's own interests, in open sea lanes and access to Gulf oil might be best served by a "balanced presence" of foreign powers. But that balanced presence carries the danger of confrontation as the powers compete for influence among the littoral states. Moreover, ties with foreign powers could deepen domestic tensions and heighten regional rivalries. U.S. bases, for example, could exacerbate political unrest in the host state, even providing the catalyst for the overthrow of the regime with which the U.S. was identified. As each superpower sees its interests in a particular state threatened, there is the temptation to intervene. From India's perspective, the U.S. Rapid Deployment Force is essentially a means by which the U.S. can intervene to prop up a friendly regime threatened from within or to depose a Government seen to threaten its interests. India sees the island republics of the Indian Ocean as especially vulnerable to pressure and intervention--whether from the United States or the Soviet Union. Here the Government of India expresses special concern that the U.S. might seek to remove the leftist Government in Mauritius, which is now engaged in a campaign (with Indian support) for the "return" of Diego Garcia to Mauritius sovereignty.

In the coming years, India can be expected to project its power over an increasingly wide area of the Indian Ocean. It is now building a blue water navy and, though its capacity will be a long time coming, will likely offer assistance and "protection" to the island republics of Mauritius, Seychelles, and the Maldives. As Indian interests are not wholly in the western Indian Ocean, it will probably move toward a two-fleet navy, each with its complement of frigates, aircraft carriers, and submarines. India's concern in the northeastern sector of the Indian Ocean is the extension of Chinese influence. India expects China to deploy nuclear submarines in the Indian Ocean--although realistically, such a prospect does not lie on the near horizon. A Chinese second-strike capability based on submarine-launched ballistic missiles would introduce yet another element of uncertainty and instability into the strategic context of the Indian Ocean.

American interests in securing its friends within the region against external attack, in bolstering the capacity of non-aligned nations to resist Soviet pressure, and in maintaining open sea lanes to the Gulf mean that the United States will almost inevitably maintain a permanent presence in the Indian Ocean as a counterforce to Soviet power within the region and on the periphery. The Soviet Union also has interests that are likely to establish a permanent presence: security for its maritime and fishing fleets and for the increasingly important warm water sea route between Vladivostok and the Black Sea ports; support for its friends and expansion of its influence within the region; and as a check on U.S. naval power, particularly submarines, directed against the U.S.S.R. itself. Under such circumstances, the chances for the Indian Ocean to emerge as a "zone of peace" are unlikely. At best, we can hope for a negotiated reduction of naval force levels in the Indian Ocean as part of a more general arms control agreement between the United States and the Soviet Union.

RELATIONS WITH THE MIDDLE EAST

From the time of independence, India has courted the Muslim nations of the Middle East. Its interest initially was the product of three main concerns. First, India sought to establish close relations with "progressive" Arab states and to identify itself with the Palestinian cause in the Arab-Israeli dispute in order to prevent Muslim unity in support of Pakistan. Second, with a large Muslim majority, India sought good relations with the Islamic world to secure its own image, both internationally and domestically, as a secular state in which the rights and position of Indian Muslims are fully protected. India's domestic concern was not only to give the Muslim minority a greater sense of security, but in the context of democratic politics, the governing Congress party looked to the Muslim vote as one of the critical elements of its electoral base. A third element in India's relations with the Middle East was Nehru's quest, joined by Egypt's Nasser, for Afro-Asian solidarity, the foundation of today's Non-Aligned Movement. Each of these elements, modified by the course of events, remains an important ingredient in India's concern for the Middle East. But India's involvement in the region has been extended and deepened over the past decade by economic concerns--access to oil; trade and investment; and remittances from Indian workers in the Gulf states--and by concern over the expanded superpower presence in the Indian Ocean.

India, heavily dependent upon imported oil, has bee deeply affected by the two major rounds of petroleum price increases in 1973 and 1979. Petroleum imports--more than two-thirds from the Middle East--have consumed as much as 70 percent of India's foreign exchange earnings and has been the principal factor in India's rising trade deficit and declining foreign currency reserves. India's dependence upon imported oil is being cut back dramatically by increased domestic production as well as by reduced consumption growth (affected mainly by higher pricing for petroleum products). Domestic oil production increased by 54 percent in 1981-82 and 32 percent in 1982-83. Where India imported 64 percent of its crude for domestic consumption in 1979-80, it imports only 47 percent today, and, with excellent prospects for further increases in domestic production, oil imports should continue to decline over the next five years. Nevertheless, India will remain heavily dependent on petroleum imports and thus vulnerable not only to a possible new round of price increases, but to the danger of lost access to oil arising from superpower confrontation in the Indian Ocean, political instability in the region, and war between states in the Middle East--either another Arab-Israeli war or war between Muslim nations.

The Iran-Iraq war underscores India's vulnerability. Faced with the loss of its oil supply from its two main sources, India was able to make up the shortfall on the spot market and by a shift to Gulf states suppliers, but the conflict between Iran and Iraq was costly to India not only in its scramble for new petroleum sources, but in lost Indian construction contracts in the two countries, lost remittances from Indian workers suddenly returned home, and lost markets for Indian exports.

The Middle East is a rapidly expanding market for Indian manufactured goods and technology, and India has become increasingly active in construction projects, agricultural development, and in such joint ventures as luxury hotels. India is also seeking increased Middle Eastern investment in India. Prospects for dramatic increases in trade and investment have been tempered by the fall in oil prices, but, even in these tighter times, India has made a major breakthrough with Saudi

Arabia. In 1981, the two nations signed an economic and technical cooperation agreement, and in 1982, during Mrs. Gandhi's three-day visit, India and Saudi Arabia created a joint economic commission. India seeks a long-term contract for Saudi crude, a larger share of the Saudi market for Indian exports (especially engineering goods), and a larger role for Indian consultancy services and technology. India hopes to tap the Saudi Development Fund for an increase in concessional loans and to attract greater Saudi investment in India in joint ventures. India has assured Saudi investors of handsome returns on their investments and free repatriation of profits.

One of India's most vital links to the Middle East is through the more than 300,000 Indians working in the region, most of whom are in the Gulf states. Their annual remittances of an estimated $1.5 billion make a critical contribution to India's foreign exchange earnings and cushioned the widening trade deficit as the price of oil went higher and higher over the past decade. As oil prices have declined, however, remittances have leveled off, and officials in India's Ministry of Finance are bracing themselves for a possible decline as Indian workers return home. It is ironic that while the decline in oil prices gives India the relief of a lower petroleum import bill, it means losses for Indian exports and, most critically, in remittances of hard currency earnings from Indian workers.

India's increasingly important economic ties with the Middle East and its continuing dependence upon Middle Eastern oil imports have deepened the political importance of the region to India and have stimulated a more active diplomatic Indian presence. This was witnessed by the mid-1970s in India's improved relations with Iran under the Shah. And India, although apprehensive about the "contagion" of Islamic fundamentalism under Khomeini, continues to cultivate its Iranian ties. The Soviet invasion of Afghanistan, the U.S. arms commitment to Pakistan, and the buildup of Soviet and American forces in the Indian Ocean gave impetus to one of the major changes in India's stance toward the region--improved relations with Saudi Arabia, once denounced by New Delhi as "reactionary." Saudi money channeled through Pakistan is a major source of finance for the Afghan resistance, and since 1980, by Indian estimates, Saudi aid to Pakistan has amounted to substantially more than $1 billion, including $500 million to finance Pakistan's purchase of the F-16 fighter. While India remains suspicious of the Saudis in the American and Pakistani connections (India, for example, fears Pakistani access to the Saudi arsenal in the event of another Indo-Pakistan war), it is, in part, to counter the emergence of an American-Saudi-Pakistani "strategic consensus" that India has taken the diplomatic initiative in improving relations with Riyadh. Mrs. Gandhi's visit to Saudi Arabia in April 1982 must be counted as a major success in easing mutual suspicion and in modifying, if not wholly dispelling, the Saudi image of India as "pro-Soviet." The joint communique issued on the conclusion of the visit stated that India and Saudi Arabia recognize that the "stability and security of the Gulf region and that of the Indian subcontinent were closely interlinked," and that "the two sides noted with grave concern the increasing escalation of great power presence in the Indian Ocean area against the declared wishes of the littoral and hinterland states of the Indian Ocean." Underlying the Saudi position may be the recognition that India has a vital role to play in the stability of the larger region and that Pakistan's worth to Saudi security would be significantly reduced by Indo-Pakistani hostility. As stated in the joint communique, "consolidation of Indo-Pakistani relations will contribute to security, stability and peace in South Asia and the entire region."

During the next five years, India can be expected to pursue an active foreign policy in the Middle East, with particular concern for Saudi Arabia, the Gulf states, Iran, and Iraq, at the same time it extends its presence into the Indian Ocean as "protector" of the island republics. And India is likely to seek, as well, closer ties with Egypt. No region beyond the subcontinent within the scope of India's major concerns is likely to be more volatile than the Middle East. The wide range of possible events within the region--political instability in the Gulf states; the fall of the Saudi dynasty; civil war in Iran; an expansion of the Iran-Iraq war to the Gulf states; foreign intervention in Mauritius, the Seychelles, or the Maldives or in the littoral states; Soviet pressure on Pakistan; the breakup of Pakistan, with secessionist movements in Baluchistan and Sind; and the spread of Islamic fundamentalism--would all vitally affect Indian interests.

The course of Indo-Pakistan relations also bears directly on India's relations with the Middle East. Another war with Pakistan, depending on the circumstances and the scope of conflict, could entail active Saudi support for Islamabad, and it would seriously undermine India's position both diplomatically and economically. If India were to engage in a preemptive strike against Pakistan's nuclear facilities--a most unlikely scenario--the consequences for India vis-a-vis the Islamic Middle East would be most serious, involving the likely expulsion of Indian workers and possible cutoff of oil.

India's relations with the Muslim world, and especially with the Islamic states of the Middle East, are also affected by Hindu-Muslim communal relations within India. Not just Pakistan, but Iran and the Arab states (particularly Saudi Arabia) have a protective interest in India's 85 million Muslim minority. Deepening communal tension within India, with Islamic revivalism and an awakening Hindu consciousness, poses not only the prospect of social unrest and violence in India but of international tension if the Government of India is unable to protect Muslim lives and property. If the Government itself were to be perceived as "anti-Muslim," the Islamic world could well impose severe sanctions against India.

Communal relations in India have another international dimension. Despite their vast majority, with more than 82 percent of the population, many Hindus fear Islamic resurgence in India, and the conversion of a thousand or so Harijans (untouchables) to Islam in a South Indian village in 1979 caused virtual panic among Hindus convinced that "mass conversions" were being financed by foreign powers. "Gulf money," in their view, is today's Khyber Pass through which Muslims seek to gain domination over India. The growth of anti-Arab popular feeling as a byproduct of domestic communal tension would surely have repercussions in India's relations with the Middle East.

RELATIONS WITH THE SOVIET UNION

Over the past twenty years, India's "special relationship" with the Soviet Union has been carefully cultivated to what each regards as mutual advantage. With toasts of friendship, differences have been confronted in the privacy of closed negotiations and discussion rather than in the public forum. The relationship has sometimes been characterized as based on an "identity" of interests in a number of areas, but India shares neither the Soviets' values nor world view. It is rather a "convergence" of their separate interests that has sustained the relationship. Robert H. Donaldson, a specialist in Soviet policy toward South Asia, writes that "Moscow's relationship with New Delhi has been built primarily on a mutual sense of need--a shared perception in each state that the friendship of the other is essential to the preservation of its own security."[6]

For the Soviets, South Asia ranks high in geopolitical priorities. They see India, the predominant power of the subcontinent, as a critical counterbalance to China in Asia and the Third World and as a limit on American presence and influence in the region. In supporting India, the Soviets seek to balance Chinese and American ties to Pakistan, India's principal adversary, while at the same time, they seek to improve relations with Pakistan--cautious in doing so not to alarm the Indians. The Soviet Union also seeks in India, a leader of the Non-Aligned Movement, support for its position on international issues and at least silence in the face of its transgressions. The Soviets have projected their interest in India through diplomatic support, economic and technical assistance, trade, arms transfer, cultural exchange, and high level visits. Brezhnev made two trips to India, the only non-Communist country of the Third World he ever visited. Most critically, the Soviets have sought--and with considerable success--to convince Indians that the U.S.S.R. is a reliable friend whose support and assistance is vital to the realization of India's own objectives.[7]

The importance of the Soviet relationship to India is underscored by the continuity of policy under the Janata Government. When the new Government came to power in 1977, many observers--including those in Moscow--saw in the proclamation of "genuine non-alignment" a cooling of Indo-Soviet friendship if not an ardent pursuit of American favor. Prime Minister Morarji Desai assured the Soviets of India's constancy and reaffirmed the Indo-Soviet Treaty of 1971. Following Gromyko's visit to New Delhi in April 1977, Desai and Foreign Minister Atal Bihari Vajpayee went to Moscow in October of that year.

Most Indians, even those most favorably disposed to the United States, see friendship with the Soviet Union as advantageous--even necessary--for India. They point out, almost as an incantation, that the U.S.S.R., often with its veto power, has supported India in the United Nations on the critical issues of Kashmir, Goa, and Bangladesh. In the 1962 India-China border war, the Soviets adopted a neutrality favoring India, and as the Sino-Soviet rift deepened, the Soviets provided India with an unwritten security guarantee against Chinese aggression. In the Bangladesh crisis of 1971, as the U.S. tilted toward Pakistan and China threatened intervention, India found enhanced security in the Indo-Soviet Treaty of Peace, Friendship and Cooperation. Within the subcontinent, the Soviet Union tries to accommodate its own politics toward other states of the region to Indian interests and objectives.

In aid and technical assistance, although only a fraction of what the United States has provided, the Soviets have been highly visible in their willingness to finance major public sector industrial projects from which the U.S., in part for ideological reasons, held back. Similarly, in arms sales, from the mid-1960s, the Soviets stepped in as a major supplier when the West effectively closed its markets to India. In 1979, during negotiations between the Janata Government and the U.S.S.R. for a $1.6 billion arms sale (concluded in 1980), Prime Minister Morarji Desai stated in an interview with an American news magazine that "if we buy more arms from the Soviet Union, it is the fault of the western countries for not selling to us.[8]

The Soviet involvement in South Asia and its support of India has been sustained by need. By contrast, Robert Donaldson states,

> The United States...has developed very little stake in South Asia. Its interest in the region has been sporadic at best and is usually occasioned by a threat or challenge in an adjacent region (Southeast Asia or the Persian Gulf region). American attention to India and Pakistan, like the military aid program in the region, has been shut on and off periodically in response to specific crises or provocations. Having not <u>needed</u> India (or Pakistan, for the most part) in the pursuit of any of its more vital objectives, the United States has had no particular incentive to establish its presence or develop its influence on the subcontinent.
>
> Understanding this point should help us to avoid being <u>surprised</u> by the substantial Soviet interest and presence in South Asia and by the relatively high esteem in which Moscow is regarded by the states of the region. It might also help us to avoid being <u>alarmed</u> at the Soviet presence in South Asia, having seen that Moscow's considerable investment has by no means won her inordinate influence or turned India into a puppet state, and that much of the Soviet "victory" over the U.S. in the superpower competition in this region has in effect been accomplished by default.[9]

This was written before the Soviet invasion of Afghanistan, but the American response only confirms Donaldson's argument as to the episodic character of U.S. concern for the region. The Soviet presence in Afghanistan, however, has fundamentally changed the nature of the strategic environment of South Asia and the "esteem" in which the Soviet Union is held. In a reenactment of "the Great Game," the Russians are now at the Khyber Pass--and not only Pakistan but India is worried.

India's concern about Soviet intervention in Afghanistan has strained Indo-Soviet friendship, but it has not substantially altered its character. India was miffed in not being consulted by the Soviets in regard to their action in Afghanistan, and the lack of Soviet response to India's private expressions of concern has been a source of continuing irritation. But if the Soviet invasion of Afghanistan changed the nature of the South Asian strategic environment, India viewed the U.S. commitment of arms--notably the F-16 aircraft--to Pakistan as deepening regional tension and posing a threat to India's own security.

India's relationship with the Soviet Union is in large measure the product of its security concerns vis-a-vis Pakistan and China, but India has never been as dependent upon the U.S.S.R. as has been generally believed in the United States nor has the Soviet Union exercised pervasive influence. India, for example, has consistently resisted Brezhnev's 1969 proposal for a "collective security" system in Asia--a system clearly directed against China. India has instead sought improved relations with China, and in 1976, without consulting the Soviets, Mrs. Gandhi took the initiative in upgrading diplomatic relations with Beijing. Soviet discomfort has been expressed by warnings of China's designs in South Asia and, particularly since 1980, of a United States-Pakistan-China axis against India. Soviet publications (and their counterparts in India) have also portrayed Pakistan's offer of a no-war pact as an American-laid trap--leading Mrs. Gandhi in February 1982, without naming the U.S.S.R., to refer to "some who preferred to see that India's relations with Pakistan did not improve."

Since 1971 and the dismemberment of Pakistan, India is the undisputed power of the subcontinent. Although India still regards Pakistan as a security threat, India's military superiority is assured, and some headway has been made toward improving relations between the two nations. A militarily stronger and more self-confident India, together with an easing of tensions with China and Pakistan, have significantly reduced India's strategic dependence upon the Soviet Union--so much so that many analysts argue that Moscow needs India today far more than New Delhi needs the Soviet Union.

Mrs. Gandhi has moved to reduce imbalances in India's relations with the two Great Powers, seeking to improve relations with the United States in her visit in July 1982 and to reaffirm the traditional friendship between India and the Soviet Union in her visit to Moscow in September 1982. But it is noteworthy that this was Mrs. Gandhi's first visit to the Soviet Union since her return to power in January 1980. She had rather obviously avoided going earlier, even to take part in the Moscow celebration of the tenth anniversary of the Indo-Soviet Treaty of Friendship. Indeed, the anniversary was treated very differently in the two capitals. In Moscow, it was a major event; in New Delhi, it passed virtually without recognition.

There may be in all of this an element of personal pique. During the period when Mrs. Gandhi was out of power, she became a "non-person" for the Soviets. During a stopover in Moscow between London and New Delhi, she was met only by middling functionaries, and when Kosygin visited India during the Janata period, he declined Mrs. Gandhi's request for a meeting. Perhaps most galling was the Soviet information service publication of a souvenir booklet celebrating 30 years of Indo-Soviet friendship. Neither Indira Gandhi's name nor photograph appeared--despite the fact that she had been Prime Minister 11 of those 30 years.*

Another source of Mrs. Gandhi's displeasure with Moscow is the Communist Party of India (CPI), the Kremlin's recognized representative of the world Communist movement in India. The CPI had supported Mrs. Gandhi and her Government from 1969 through the Emergency but with her defeat in 1977, the CPI broke the tie, moving closer to the independent and more powerful Communist Party (Marxist), as the CPM moved closer to the CPI by assuming a more pro-Soviet stance on international issues such as Afghanistan and Kampuchea. In the 1980 elections, the two Communist parties supported the Lok Dal-Congress (U) coalition, and since 1980, the CPI has regularly denounced Mrs. Gandhi's "anti-people and anti-democratic" policies. It has joined the CPM in exploring possible alliance of opposition parties, including the "rightist" Bharatiya Janata Party, against the Congress. During her September 1982 Moscow visit, Mrs. Gandhi attacked the cynical opportunism of the CPI and the efforts of left parties in India to weaken and

---

* Several Indians who are well-connected with official circles mentioned the Soviet publication in interviews in New Delhi in December 1982.

destabilize her Government, and she is believed to have brought the matter up in discussions with Brezhnev and Gromyko, asking them to rein in the party and stop its criticism of her Government.

Soon after her return to power, Mrs. Gandhi cut official patronage of the CPI-sponsored Indo-Soviet Cultural Society and called upon Congress party members to resign and to join the new "Friends of the Soviet Union." She also asked Congress members to resign from the All India Peace Council, affiliated with the Moscow-backed World Peace Council.

For their part, the Soviets are not all that happy with Mrs. Gandhi's current tendency to equate the superpowers in her criticism of foreign intervention and of naval presence in the Indian Ocean. And they feel considerable unease with Indian policies on arms diversification and economic liberalization, as they do more generally with India's improved relations with the United States and China. But the Soviets have made a great investment in India, and they view India--and Indira Gandhi--as a critical source of support in the international arena. The Soviets court India with a continuous flow of high official visitors and with new offers of aid, trade, and arms. In July 1983, they made an investment in the next generation of Indian leadership, hosting a visit by Rajiv Gandhi.

India today seeks a more balanced relationship with the superpowers, but while it seeks to improve relations with the United States, it does not do so at the cost of its traditional friendship with the Soviet Union. India seeks to reduce its dependence on the U.S.S.R., but Soviet diplomatic support for India, aid and technical assistance for India's public sector heavy industry, Indo-Soviet barter trade, and the favorable terms for arms purchases are important factors underlying Indo-Soviet friendship that will not be lightly abandoned. There are, however, clear indications that India is seeking to distance itself somewhat from the Soviet Union--to gain greater flexibility, to widen its options, to refurbish its image among the non-aligned nations, and to gain greater leverage with Moscow.

As the Indian economy has grown and diversified, its needs for expanded markets and for access to advanced technology have outgrown Soviet capacity. India recognizes that its desire for high technology--for both industry and defense--cannot be fully met by the Soviets nor can the U.S.S.R. meet India's credit requirements. In both trade and military procurements, India seeks to strengthen its independence through diversification.

That process can be expected to continue over the next five years, but the Soviets remain an attractive partner. They can offer seductive trade deals and arms at comparatively low cost and on highly favorable terms. Moreover, the very nature of India's association with the Soviet Union in both trade and arms sales serves to sustain the relationship at the same time that it imposes an element of strain. G. K. Reddy, a distinguished journalist particularly well-connected to India's foreign policy establishment, has described Indo-Soviet relations as having reached a "plateau." The term is an apt characterization, suggesting that relations are unlikely to be enhanced signficantly nor are they likely to deteriorate. A major caveat, however, relates to the flux of Indo-Pakistani relations. If there is a serious deterioration in relations with Pakistan (particularly if New Delhi perceives the U.S. as bolstering Pakistan), India could well draw closer to the Soviet Union.

Soviet Assistance

Soviet aid (usually in the form of long-term loans at low interest rates) and technical assistance to India have since their beginning in 1955 gone primarily for public sector heavy industry projects--an area of high priority in Indian planning but one to which the West was unreceptive. With high visibility, the Soviets have had a major role in the construction of steel mills (Bhilai and Bokaro), in oil exploration and refining, heavy machinery and electricals, coal mining, and so on.

By the 1970s, with its infrastructural base well established, India began to look to the West for more advanced technology than the Soviets could offer. But while the volume of Soviet aid declined, the U.S.S.R. has sought to maintain its prominent role as the leading source of aid and technical assistance to India's heavy industry and mining sectors. Virtually every high level contact between India and the Soviet Union, whether in New Delhi or Moscow, is accompanied by Soviet offers of credits for new development projects. Some draw little interest, like the recent offer of a Soviet-built nuclear power station, which would involve a technology incompatible with those now used by India. Soviet technology is rarely state-of-the-art, and India would often prefer to go elsewhere, as, for example, in computers and in off-shore oil exploration. But in many areas, what the Soviets can offer is not substantially below the quality available in the United States, Western Europe, and Japan, and it is offered on extremely attractive terms. Continued Soviet assistance in major projects was underscored in May 1983 with the agreement for the second phase of the Visakhapatnam steel project, with Soviet credits of some $1.4 billion for the supply of goods and services. The credits are to be repaid over 20 years at 2.5 percent interest. Unlike loans from the West, Soviet credits to India are repayable in rupees and are directly tied to trade, thus linking the Indian economy closely to that of the Soviet Union for many years to come.

In the past decade, India has been increasingly selective in the projects undertaken with Soviet assistance. The big projects of the 1950s and 1960s are no longer high priority, and in many areas, India is technologically self-reliant--a principal aim of its development efforts--and is itself exporting technology to lesser developed nations. But if India is to improve its productivity and to gain the export capability necessary to meet its balance of payments requirements, it must move to more advanced technologies. To gain access to high technology, to enhance its export potential, and to develop its energy resources, India is today actively seeking selected foreign investment through joint ventures in both the public and private sector. And the West, for its part, is more receptive to collaboration with India's public sector than in the past. In the coming years, this is likely to draw India increasingly toward the West and to reduce the technological dependence on the U.S.S.R. that characterized the early years of India's industrial development. But unless the United States is prepared to relax restrictions on the transfer of technology to India (especially in such fields as computers), it is likely to lose out to Western Europe and Japan. Two factors will continue to make the Soviet Union an important source of technological assistance--at least in those projects that may be unattractive to foreign private investment. One is the terms of transfer, with credits repayable in rupees, a factor that is likely to assume greater importance to India during periods of foreign exchange pressure. The second factor arises out of the nature of Indo-Soviet barter trade and the pressure on India to balance trade through increased purchases or obligation of credits from the Soviet Union.

Indo-Soviet Trade

Trade between India and the Soviet Union is conducted on the basis of negotiated barter agreements involving no hard currencies. This "rupee trade," as it is called, began in 1953 at a level of $1.6 million, reaching nearly $95 million in 1958. By 1981, the Soviet Union had moved ahead of the United States to become India's largest trading partner with trade totalling some $3.2 billion (roughly 14% of India's foreign trade). In the past three years, as international recession, currency fluctuations, and trade restrictions reduced access to western markets, India found a ready market in the Soviet Union. India's exports to the U.S.S.R. today consist mainly of food products (tea, coffee, rice, cashews, pepper), tobacco, leather goods, cotton textiles, jute products, light engineering goods, and such consumer products as household linens, clothing, pharmaceuticals, and cosmetics. Some 75% of India's exports to the Soviet Union are now manufactured and semiprocessed goods and 90 percent of India's exports to the Soviet Union comes from the private sector. The Soviets have turned to India--their major trading partner outside the Communist bloc--both because of increased consumer demand within the U.S.S.R. and because of their own limited hard currency reserves. The Soviets are India's biggest buyers for a number of products, and some industries are almost wholly dependent upon the Soviet market. An extreme case is that of woolen knitwear manufactured in the Punjab, with an estimated 90 percent of production going to the U.S.S.R. Cosmetics are also heavily dependent upon the Soviet market, and, in fact, a number of western companies have entered into collaborative ventures in India with the Soviet market as the principal target.

Such dependency is a matter of concern to many Indian officials. There are extreme fluctuations from year to year in Soviet purchases of given items, and the impact on Indian industry and cash crop agriculture has been destabilizing. Indeed, the unstable pattern of trade has not only made India vulnerable to the weaknesses of the Soviet economy, but has made India vulnerable to Soviet pressure in trade negotiation. Also, whether by Soviet design or simply as a byproduct of Soviet import requirements, the dependency of certain industrial sectors and of specific companies on Soviet markets has created a domestic interest group in India in favor of sustained trade on contractual barter terms with the U.S.S.R. Moreover, some Indian companies find in the Soviet Union a "captive market" for inferior goods that would otherwise have no export market. (In some instances this has led the Soviets--for all the shabbiness of their own consumer products--to complain about the quality of Indian manufactured goods.)

India's principal imports from the Soviet Union are crude oil (supplied primarily from Gulf sources) and petroleum products--together accounting for some 60 to

80 percent of Soviet exports to India. The Soviets aggressively push heavy machinery, which once made up a major portion of India's imports, but India has increasingly less interest in Soviet manufactured goods, either because the products are now made in India or because they do not meet India's needs in technological sophistication. Soviet oil exports are pegged to OPEC prices, and as the world price has fallen, a substantial trade surplus--now standing at $500 million--has grown in India's favor. The Soviets want India to balance the trade through increased purchases of Soviet heavy engineering goods and new projects such as the acquisition of a Soviet-built nuclear power station. The Indians, not surprisingly, would prefer to see the trade surplus reduced through increased imports of Soviet oil. In June 1983, the Soviets agreed to correct the trade imbalance by supplying India more crude and petroleum products, fertilizers, chemicals, drugs, non-ferrous metals, and newsprint.

The rupee trade, for many reasons, is not so attractive as it once was for India. First of all, beyond oil and military hardware (a special case discussed below), there is not that much the Soviets have to offer that India really wants. But oil and arms without payment in hard currency provide a powerful incentive for maintaining the Indo-Soviet trade relationship. Many Indians, however, are not convinced that even this is sufficient to justify continuation of the barter trade. They argue that while some goods exported to the Soviet Union could find no other market, many Indian products exported to the U.S.S.R. could earn foreign exchange for India with which it could purchase oil and advanced technological items. It is a big "maybe" and obviously involves an element of risk in exchanging the security of the rupee trade for the unknowns of the free market. There are, however, elements within the current relationship which--although not yet on a scale to create major problems--are surely irritants. One involves trade diversion--Soviet import of western goods through Indian firms and paid for in rupees. Related to this is the foreign component in many of the Indian products imported by the Soviet Union. In either case, India has to come up with the foreign exhange. Another problem, although probably exaggerated by its critics, is the "switch trade," the Soviet re-export of Indian products for hard currency. In looking to the next five years, Indo-Soviet trade can be expected to grow, as there continues to be room for an enormous increase in Indian exports to satisfy Soviet consumer demand. Given the range of both agricultural and industrial products that the Soviets can acquire from India without expenditure of hard currency and India's continued petroleum import requirements, the barter trade is likely to be sustained at a high level--so long as the Soviets are willing to meet India's import needs rather than push their own export preferences. New agreements will be reached by tough bargaining on both sides, but the disagreements and irritants are not likely to have a substantial affect either on the volume of trade or on the character of Indo-Soviet relations more generally.

It will be primarily through export promotion in the international market, however, that India will seek to expand and diversify its foreign trade. But should India face protectionist barriers and trade restrictions in the West, it will come under increasing foreign exchange pressure. Exchange difficulties for India will almost surely raise the importance of the rupee trade with the Soviet Union and Eastern Europe--thus reinforcing a relationship of dependency that is neither in the interest of India or of the West.

Soviet Arms

Like Soviet technical assistance, the transfer of arms is tied to the barter trade, but the bookkeeping remains a matter of speculation. Soviet weapons are offered to India at relatively low cost, repayable in rupees on easy terms. Particularly important for India, the Soviets have been willing to provide the manufacturing technology, exemplified by the production of MiG-21s in India, dating back to the agreement of 1962. Indian arms procurement from the Soviet Union began in 1960. By 1964, the U.S.S.R. was on its way to becoming a major supplier, and during the 1970s, some 75 percent of India's arms imports came from the Soviet Union.

By the late 1970s, India began to grow uneasy about its dependence upon Soviet weapons. In its quest for independence, India wants to be sure that in time of crisis no nation can hold India "hostage" and deprive it of its military capability. In part for that reason, India began a conscious effort to diversify its sources of arms, but other factors also entered into the decision. In upgrading its weapons systems, India wants the most advanced arms available, and what the Soviets offer is often not up to the mark. Diversification of arms sources would not only give India access to western military technology, but would give India greater leverage with the U.S.S.R. in negotiations for the most sophisticated weapons in the Soviet arsenal.

Aside from Soviet reluctance to share its latest technology with India, however, there have been problems in the Indo-Soviet arms relationship. Delays in the supply of military spares have been a source of constant irritation, and given the major portion of Indian arms from the U.S.S.R., reliance on Soviet spares is a source of vulnerability as well as long-term dependency. Soviet weapons are also not always the bargain they seem. Spares and servicing have sometimes been overpriced. Moreover, in more advanced Soviet weapons manufactured in India, certain critical elements of production have been withheld from the Indians, in effect, keeping India on a short leash of dependence upon the Soviet Union.

Major arms diversification began under the Janata Government, with the acquisition of the Anglo-French Jaguar, and has been sustained since 1980 by the Congress Government, with contracts for the French Mirage-2000 and West German submarines. At the same time that India was entering the western arms market, the Janata Government began negotiation for a new arms agreement with the Soviet Union. The agreement, concluded in 1980 soon after Mrs. Gandhi returned to power, provided \$1.6 billion in credits to India for Soviet weapons--probably substantially more in market value, given the low prices at which the weapons were tagged. In contrast to western weapons purchased with hard currency, the agreement provided for repayment in rupees at 2.5 percent interest over 17 years. (In contrast, the \$3.2 billion U.S. arms package for Pakistan is repayable in dollars at 11 percent interest over 14 years.) The 1980 Indo-Soviet deal involves production of two major new weapons in India: MiG-23 fighter-interceptors to be built at the three factories manufacturing MiG-21s, mainstay of the Indian air force for nearly two decades, and the Soviet T-72 tank, to succeed the Vijayanta and to be built at Avadi. The agreement also included a Soviet commitment to supply India with the high altitude reconnaissance MiG-25 "Foxbat."

India's diversification surely gives the Soviets greater incentive to meet India's weapons requests, but the 1980 agreement by no means slowed India's efforts to diversify its arms sources. Soviet concern over new arms contracts negotiated with Western European suppliers is measured by the March 1982 visit of Defense Minister Dimitri Ustinov, with a delegation that included the Soviet naval and air chiefs and the vice chief of the Soviet Army Staff, together with 30 generals and other high ranking officers. The Ustinov visit prompted speculation of another major arms deal in the offing, with hints that the package might include the MiG-27, the most advanced fighter in the MiG family. Later in the year, the Soviet minister for shipbuilding came to India with an offer to supply the technology for production of Soviet-designed submarines and naval aircraft--both at bargain prices. In July 1983 (while Secretary of State George Schultz was in New Delhi), Indian Defence Minister R. Venkataraman was in Moscow to conclude a new agreement believed to include MiG-27s to be manufactured in India.

India is today engaged in a major defense equipment replacement program. It aims not only at the acquisition of the best available in modern arms but, eventually, to achieve self-reliance in arms production. India now manufactures some 90 percent of its small arms, much of it under license, but for sophisticated weapons, India looks abroad. In the name of "self-reliance," India has sought domestic manufacture/assembly, and this is, in fact, a condition in most Indian negotiations for arms. In addition to the various MiG deals, the Jaguar and Mirage contracts provided for production in India. In the process (whether it is really cost-efficient or not), India has gotten jobs and experience and a degree of manufacturing technology, but they have not gotten "self-reliance," as twenty years' production of the MiG clearly demonstrates. India still relies on the Soviet Union for advances in MiG technology. Given rapid change in high technology and the enormous costs of research and development, "self-reliance" in arms would condemn India's arsenal to permanent obsolescence--a condition that India will never accept given access to more modern arms by less self-reliant neighbors.

If India cannot realistically achieve self-reliance in its defense requirements, it can maximize its independence--and this is India's fundamental purpose--through diversification of arms sources. In the coming years, the Soviet Union will continue to be India's largest single source of arms. As a supplier, it has proven reliable (in contrast to the image of the United States in South Asia), and the Soviets offer weapons at comparatively low cost, on favorable terms, and most critically, with repayment in rupees. But both to ensure India's independence and to acquire technologically superior weapons, India will continue to look to western sources. Indian military preferences, no doubt, include a number of American weapons, but U.S. imposed conditions on arms transfer have been unacceptable to India. Thus, Western Europe, principally France, Britain, and West Germany, are likely to be the sources to which India turns in balancing its Soviet arms acquisitions.

RELATIONS WITH CHINA

India and China, in cautious approach to rapprochement, held their fourth round of talks in New Delhi in October 1983. The next round is scheduled for Beijing in 1984. Each session in what is likely to be a protracted series of discussions has sustained a continuing movement toward improved relations, and while there is no expectation of an early breakthrough on the border question, the dialogue itself has relaxed tensions and contributed to an atmosphere more receptive to a negotiated settlement.

China's world view is dominated by security concerns vis-a-vis the Soviet Union. China fears encirclement by the U.S.S.R. and envisages Afghanistan and Vietnam as pincer claws moving inward. Here India, as the preeminent power of the subcontinent, occupies a crucial geopolitical position. In 1977, as the Janata Government took power with the talk of "genuine nonalignment," Beijing hoped that India could be weaned away from the Soviet Union. In short time that hope had given way to more modest expectations. Today, in seeking to improve relations with India, China hopes to widen India's range of diplomatic options. Although it continues to view India as an apologist for the Soviets (Afghanistan and Kampuchea), China no longer regards India as a proxy for the U.S.S.R. But while it does not expect India to abandon its traditional friendship with the Soviet Union, China would be happy to contribute to a "distancing" in that relationship.

Derived from its principal interest in limiting the Soviet role in Asia and in checking Soviet attempts to forge an Asian collective security system directed against China, Beijing seeks to promote regional cooperation in South Asia as the best guarantor against the expansion of Soviet influence in the subcontinent. Early in 1981, Premier Zhao Zhiyang visited Pakistan, Nepal, and Bangladesh, urging that they patch up their differences with India. Later that same year, Foreign Minister Huang Hua, after his visit to India, went to Sri Lanka and the Maldives where again the message was regional cooperation. Conflict and instability within South Asia has been the open door to superpower involvement in the region--whether the U.S.S.R. or the U.S.--and in this perception, China's interest dovetails closely with India's pursuit of a region free from superpower intervention. China recognizes the reality of India's preeminence within the region, but sees in this the responsibility of a "big brother" for his smaller and weaker siblings. Rapprochement with India is clearly central to China's goals in promoting a South

Asian stability better able to resist Soviet influence. The key relationship within South Asia is that between India and Pakistan, and Sino-Indian rapprochement could improve chances for better Indo-Pakistan relations. But it could also leave Pakistan uneasy about the reliability of China as a friend.

The Chinese interest in rapprochement with India relates to its own domestic concerns, especially with regard to ethnic unrest in Tibet and, more critically in the context of Islamic resurgence and the Sino-Soviet dispute, Xinjiang. The Chinese would like to see the borders settled and the border areas secure. This also bears on long time Chinese concerns that India is meddling in Tibet and supporting dissidents. More positively, the Chinese hope that improved relations with India might be a conducive factor in the return of the Dalai Lama to Tibet.

China talks of Sino-Indian friendship as involving the two largest Asian nations and sees in this potentially enhanced leverage in the North-South dialogue. China has not joined the Non-Aligned Movement, but it has increasingly brought its policies into accord with NAM, and there is little question that China is again seeking to assert its leadership among the non-aligned nations. Rapprochement with India, in settling their long-standing dispute, would enhance China's position--although in the long run, China's more active role among the non-aligned nations will involve competition with India for influence.

China seeks expanded trade and cultural exchange with India, but neither are likely to reach great levels. Border trade is important for those involved, but hardly represents a significant portion of each nation's international trade. While trade has increased between India and China, so has competition for foreign markets, as already seen in textiles, tea, and small machine goods.

It is sometimes suggested that rapprochement would enable each nation to reallocate resources from military to civil/development or, alternatively, to redeploy military forces. Given broader security concerns, it is unlikely that Sino-Indian rapprochement would substantially affect the military budgets of either nation. Both are engaged in programs of military modernization that are the product of a more general concern for defense capability as well as specific threat perceptions related to but distinct from the Sino-Indian relationship--the Soviet Union for China, Pakistan for India.

Any major redeployment of forces as a result of Sino-Indian rapprochement is similarly unlikely. The nature of the Indian terrain on the northern border is such that rapid redeployment of forces from the plains to the border in an emergency would be difficult--although new roads in the Himalayas give India far easier access today than in 1962. Armed forces are thus likely to be maintained at approximately present levels, although rapprochement might enable a pullback from more isolated posts. Chinese military deployment would probably be unaffected by rapprochement, as it is as much concerned with domestic security, and the border provides a useful justification for concentrations of military in ethnically volatile areas.

India, like China, has come to see regional stability as essential to minimize the opportunity for superpower intervention and confrontation in South Asia. Rapprochement with China would reduce the likelihood of Chinese support for India's neighbors in their bilateral disputes with India. Pakistan, for example, might be more amenable to accepting the line of control in Kashmir as the de jure boundary. While Sino-Indian rapprochement might provide added incentive for Pakistan to come to terms with India, it might also leave Pakistan feeling less secure and perhaps more inclined to reach accommodation with the U.S.S.R.

India could expect in rapprochement non-interference by China in Indian domestic affairs. In the late 1970s, as the normalization process began, the Chinese ceased support for tribal insurgents in India's Northeast. Despite continued reports in the Soviet press that the Chinese remain active in arming and training tribals, New Delhi has accepted Beijing's assurances and has found no evidence to suggest Chinese involvement. Given the sensitivity of the region, there is an important gain for India in a rapprochement that would assure Chinese non-interference.

Normalized relations with China would give to India greater diplomatic flexibility, reduce Indian dependence upon the Soviet Union, and--so long as there remains an element of uncertainty--increases New Delhi's leverage with Moscow. The movement toward rapprochement has clearly worried the Soviets and has brought Indian assurances that improved relations with China will not come at the expense of the Soviet Union.

Another interest India has in improved relations with China is its contribution to Asian "solidarity." If India can reach a settlement with China, the position of the Third World in the North-South dialogue may be strengthened and India's image and role within the Non-Aligned Movement enhanced.

But if there are interests for both China and India in normalizing relations, there are also countervailing factors that are likely to impede any rapid movement forward. India remains suspicious of Chinese aims and intentions--support of Pakistan; aid to insurgents in India's Northeast; interests in the border states of Nepal and Bhutan; and perceived hegemonic ambition in Southeast Asia. Indians frequently describe the Chinese as "inscrutable"--the perception like the term itself, no doubt, a legacy of the British--and recall the Chinese "betrayal" in 1962 as proof that the Chinese cannot be trusted. Many Indians view China's current "moderate" foreign policy as a tactical phase in a long-range strategy that seeks a weakened India and Chinese domination in Asia.

India does not view China as an imminent threat, but the potential for conflict remains. Indians continue to express fear of active Chinese military support (augmented now by the Karakoram highway) for Pakistan in the event of another war, or possible nuclear blackmail by China to either shield Pakistan from wartime invasion or to "guarantee" a Pakistani thrust to seize the whole of Kashmir. Given Chinese interests in South Asia and the experience of the 1965 and 1971 Indo-Pakistan wars, neither is a likely prospect. Indians say, however, that it is not a matter of intentions alone, but of Chinese capabilities. India's conventional military capability is today the match of China and probably superior. But it is not so much China alone as the prospect of a Sino-Pakistan combination, with possible support of the United States, that worries India. Nuclear uncertainty, compounded by reports that the Chinese have provided technical assistance to Pakistan's nuclear project, deepens that concern. The Chinese nuclear force may not now pose a major threat to Indian security, but Indian defense analysts are apprehensive about an expanded and modernized Chinese nuclear capability that will bring more of India within target. Of special concern is the long-range prospect of Chinese submarines, armed with nuclear warheads, in the Indian Ocean. While such a force may be designed to give China second strike nuclear capability against the Soviet Union, it would also give China a presence in the Indian Ocean with which it might seek to extend its influence in the littoral states. Basing facilities will be necessary to support any permanent presence, and in the northwest sector, Pakistan might offer its ports to the Chinese.

Chinese capabilities and uncertain intentions mean that, even as India pursues normalized relations with China, New Delhi will continue to look to the Soviet Union to provide a strategic counterweight to China. For this reason, as well as to maximize its leverage with Moscow, India is unlikely to rush toward a final settlement of its differences with China. Indeed, for India and probably for China as well, the process of normalization rather than rapprochement itself may pay the greatest dividends.

Within the context of triangular relations, the tentative movement toward Sino-Soviet detente is being watched closely in New Delhi. Publicly, Indian officials express no apprehension at such a prospect, and some suggest that relaxed tensions between China and the Soviet Union would contribute to world peace and to stability in Asia. Privately, many express unease. No one expects Sino-Soviet detente to involve restoration of close friendship and solidarity. What seems most likely if Sino-Soviet detente is to go forward is an attempt by Beijing to improve relations with Moscow to balance ties with Washington, achieving a kind of equidistance between the superpowers designed to increase Chinese leverage with each and at the same time advance Chinese influence and leadership among the non-aligned nations.

The implications for India would be far-reaching, with both advantages and disadvantages. On the positive side, Sino-Soviet detente would be conducive to further improvement in Sino-Indian relations and a settlement of outstanding differences, including the border dispute. It might also give impetus to rapprochement between India and Pakistan and to greater regional cooperation under Indian leadership. On the negative side, as China's stature grows, Indian leadership and influence in the Third World may decline. Sino-Soviet detente might also bring a decline in the importance of India to the Soviet Union--and, indeed, of South Asia to the course of world politics. A possible Soviet accord with Pakistan, perhaps as part of a settlement on Afghanistan, might reinforce Islamabad's intransigence on Kashmir in refusing to accept the status quo division along the line of control. In strategic terms, rather than promoting improved Indo-Pakistan relations, a Soviet-Pakistan accord in the context of Sino-Soviet detente could imbue India with a sense of isolation and encirclement. India, no longer confident that it could rely on the Soviet security shield, might feel compelled to take its option for nuclear weapons. Thus, in what might have been a more secure strategic environment as a result of Sino-Soviet detente, India's acquisition of "the bomb" would impel Pakistan to follow suit, heightening regional tension and the danger of further nuclear proliferation if not of nuclear war itself.

Over the last five years and even more markedly in the past two years, there has been a shift in Indian public opinion on China. It is reflected in newspapers, in intellectual circles, and, more cautiously, among government officials. It is expressed in support for Sino-Indian rapprochement and a settlement of the border dispute. Especially noteworthy has been the appearance of newspaper articles exploring the bases for compromise in the border dispute, where only a few years ago, any suggestion that India should yield even an inch of its territorial claims was tantamount to treason. Indian public opinion today is receptive to a settlement on the border so long as it is fundamentally a vindication of India's position.

Initially, the Chinese suggested that the border dispute be set aside for future negotiation and that India and China work toward rapprochement in more tractable areas of trade and cultural exchange. India held that full normalization depended upon a resolution of the border dispute and that any discussions toward improvement of relations had to include the border question. The Chinese agreed to open talks on the border, and the Indians agreed to pursue, concurrently, normalization of relations in other areas.

The Chinese feel no urgency to reach a border solution. Any settlement acceptable to India would require China to give up at least a portion of the territory now under its control in Ladakh. The Chinese government may also feel constrained in how far it can go in a negotiated settlement. The Army, particularly, might choose to use a Chinese withdrawal from territories now held as a vehicle for attack against those in power in Beijing. But if China's strategic position in the Aksai Chin is protected, a border settlement would serve China's larger interests at minimal cost.

The Chinese have proposed to settle the border dispute on the basis of a "package deal," in effect, reiterating Zhou En-lai's 1960 proposal of a quid pro quo --Indian acceptance of the Chinese occupation of the Aksai Chin for Chinese recognition of India's claims in the eastern sector on the basis of the McMahon Line. For India, any legitimation of the status quo is unacceptable. India wants the border negotiations to proceed on a sector-by-sector basis, assuming India's rightful claims in the eastern sector and focusing negotiation on the western sector, where the Chinese occupy 14,500 square miles of territory claimed by

India. From the Chinese perspective, this is simply a ploy: What is mine is mine; what is yours is negotiable. The Chinese have not relinquished their claim to the area south of the McMahon Line in the northeast, as its protest in December 1982 over the Arunachal Pradesh dancers at the Asian Games served to remind India.

While the Indians and Chinese negotiating teams prepare for another round of talks, the basis for a settlement is already there. Perhaps all but the most intransigent Indians recognize the strategic importance of the Aksai Chin to China, while the region is of no real value to India save to deny China its vital link between Xinjiang and Tibet. Unlike the crest of the Himalayas to the east, there is no one watershed in Ladakh by which the boundary can be defined indisputably. A pullback by the Chinese from the area beyond the Aksai Chin occupied in 1962 to that held in 1958 or, perhaps, to that held in 1954, at the time of the signing of the "Panchsheel" treaty, could be matched with the selection of the crest of one of the inner ranges as the basis for border demarcation. The Chinese would retain the Aksai Chin, while territories of Ladakh seized by China in 1962 would be returned to India.

A border settlement will require at least three other elements: first, adjustments in the central sector, agreed by most analysts to be relatively easy; second, Chinese recognition of the McMahon Line or, if not by that name (an imperial residue), the crest of the Himalayas which it follows in the eastern sector; and third, Chinese acceptance of Sikkim as a part of India. An additional complicating factor in a Sino-Indian border settlement is the unresolved Kashmir dispute between India and Pakistan. At a minimum, India would expect Chinese neutrality on the question, but the issue is complicated by the 1963 border agreement between Pakistan and China. Because it involves disputed Kashmir territory, India has never accepted Pakistan's legal right to settle the boundary. In a Sino-Indian border agreement, this can be set aside pending final resolution of the status of Kashmir, so long as Chinese neutrality in the dispute is guaranteed.

There is today an increasing willingness in India to reach a compromise along the lines suggested above. Details vary, but many Indians--journalists, academics, politicians, and officials--offer similar scenarios for a border settlement. There is a recognition that China will never give up the strategically vital Aksai Chin, that the region in any case lacks a defined boundary, and that India has much to gain in resolving the dispute. Although the military might be expected to oppose any compromise which would confirm Chinese control of the Aksai Chin, their honor--and that of Nehru--would be redeemed by a negotiated settlement that returned to India those territories taken in war and, at the same time, conferred legitimacy on the watershed principle by which India seeks boundary definition in the Himalayas. In India, the opposition political parties are divided, both between and within the parties, on the China question. The Communist Party (Marxist) supports rapprochement and a border settlement; the Moscow-affiliated Communist Party of India (CPI) is opposed. Within the Janata Party, Madhu Lamaye, regarded as pro-Soviet, warns of China's perfidy, while Subramaniam Swamy is India's leading advocate of improved relations with China. Within the Bharatiya Janata Party, Atal Bihari Vajpayee, who served as Minister of External Affairs under the Janata Government, supports efforts to reach a border settlement, while his Hindu nationalist colleagues in the RSS are generally critical. And H. N. Bahuguna, leader of the Democratic Socialist Party, would likely see anything less than complete Chinese withdrawal from the Aksai Chin as a sacrilege to Nehru's memory.

The Congress party is similarly divided, but even those favorable to a compromise with China on the border remain uneasy as to whether a solution is yet politically acceptable. Advisers close to Mrs. Gandhi remain distrustful of Chinese intentions and wary of the political consequences of a border settlement. Any settlement confirming Chinese occupation of the Aksai Chin would be vulnerable to attack by elements of the opposition--the CPI, the pro-Soviet lobby (Madhu Lamaye, H. N. Bahuguna, etc.) and the extreme right. And many in the opposition who otherwise favor a settlement might find it politically expedient to attack a compromise--and Mrs. Gandhi--for not getting a better deal for India.

While a border solution could surely be proclaimed as a victory for India, there are inevitably those who would attack it as a "sell out." It is very unlikely that Mrs. Gandhi would take the political risk in the period preceding the next parliamentary elections, scheduled to be held by January 1985. If a non-Congress coalition comes to power, the division on the China question and the vulnerability of the Government to defection will make a settlement on the border dispute very unlikely. The prospect would more likely be for continued discussions with China, relaxed tensions, but no breakthrough. If Mrs. Gandhi returns to power with a secure parliamentary majority, she would be in a strong position to accept a negotiated settlement on the border. There is good reason for doing so, once the Indian political climate is favorable, for the longer the Chinese retain control over the area now under their occupation, the less likely they are to relinquish any portion of it. Moreover, the Chinese are now more receptive to a negotiated settlement than they have been before and the time may now be ripe--as it may never be again--for India to secure a return of the territory in Ladakh seized during the 1962 border war, a demarcation of the border in the middle sector, Chinese recognition of Sikkim as a part of India, and, in the eastern border sector, Chinese acceptance of the McMahon Line as the de jure boundary. This would be a significant achievement for India and it is within reach over the next five years.

A resolution of outstanding differences between India and China, however, will still leave the world's two most populous nations as rivals for influence in the Third World and as competitors for international markets and for access to concessionary loans. This rivalry is likely to grow in the next five years.

OTHER BILATERAL RELATIONS

Over the past six years, beginning with the Janata Government and continuing under Indira Gandhi, India has pursued closer and more active relations with Southeast Asia, Japan, Saudi Arabia and the Gulf States, and with Western Europe.

Southeast Asia

Despite geographic proximity and cultural ties, India has not accorded Southeast Asia high priority in its foreign relations. Its principal goal is to minimize the presence and influence of external powers in the region. Since 1975, this concern has focused on China, and India's support for Hanoi, including its ill-calculated recognition of the Heng Samrin regime in Kampuchea, is, in part, an effort to strengthen Vietnam as a counterweight to Chinese influence in Southeast Asia.

The growing economic and political power of the ASEAN states provided the incentive for India to seek closer relations with the region, and the new Janata Government in 1977 initiated a flurry of diplomatic activity. A link to ASEAN would balance New Delhi's ties with Vietnam, thus refurbishing India's non-aligned image and, at the same time, perhaps enabling India to assume the role of intermediary in an accommodation between Vietnam and ASEAN. In bilateral relations with the ASEAN states, India signed agreements on trade, culture, and maritime boundaries, and the level of Indian economic activity in Southeast Asia--particularly in Malaysia and Singapore--expanded rapidly. India's efforts to associate itself with ASEAN as an "observer" at the meeting of the regional organization, however, soon foundered with Mrs. Gandhi's return to power on the issue of Kampuchea.[10]

India's recognition of the Heng Samrin regime set back India-ASEAN relations and particularly irritated Indonesia and Malaysia, whose own efforts to reach a settlement on Kampuchea were undermined by the Indian action. Mrs. Gandhi had returned to power in January 1980 on a platform that included recognition of Heng Samrin, but it was another six months before India moved. There is considerable speculation as to the timing, for it was hardly to India's benefit. It aborted India's long-sought attendance at the ASEAN foreign ministers meeting; it strained relations with China, coming as it did just after the announced visit of the Chinese foreign minister to India; and, following so soon after the Vietnamese incursion into Thailand, it could hardly have angered the ASEAN states more. It resulted in a hardening of positions by both ASEAN and Vietnam, and China, rather than being checked in its influence, probably gained greater leverage in the region. India surely underestimated the ASEAN reaction and also the degree to which--coupled with India's position on the Soviet invasion of Afghanistan--the recognition of Heng Samrin compromised India's non-aligned position.

There are a number of contending theories as to the timing, but for all the speculation on the recognition of Heng Samrin, very few Indians--even those least sympathetic to Mrs. Gandhi--believe that the decision was made in response to Soviet pressure. It was a decision, however ill-considered or ill-timed, that was taken in judgment of India's interests. It was taken in the belief that acceptance of the Heng Samrin regime and an end to external support for Pol Pot will enable Vietnam to withdraw its troops from beleaguered Kampuchea. India believes that international isolation has forced Vietnam into a dependence upon the Soviet Union with which Hanoi feels great discomfort: To break that isolation will enable Vietnam to assert its independence from Moscow. Finally, India believes that a strong Vietnam is essential to prevent the expansion of Chinese influence in Southeast Asia.

In the fall, 1981, India reached out again to ASEAN, with visits by Indira Gandhi to Jakarta and Manila, by Foreign Minister Narasimha Rao to Kuala Lampur, and by President Sanjiva Reddy to Jakarta. But for all the talk of cooperation, there is little prospect for a basic change in India's relations with Southeast Asia over the next five years. India can be expected to continue support for Vietnam as the counterweight to China and, through the Non-Aligned Movement and other international forums in the North-South dialogue, to seek cooperation with ASEAN. India has not pressed the issue of Kampuchea in the United Nations, and in the 1983 Non-Aligned Conference, India succeeded in defusing the question of Kampuchea's representation by keeping the seat open. As chair of the Non-Aligned Movement for the next three years, Mrs. Gandhi faces the enormous task of holding the disparate association together, and in emphasizing South-South cooperation, contentious issues, such as Kampuchea, are likely to be shelved. And India is not likely to take the initiative at this point in seeking to mediate a settlement on Kampuchea. Time is probably on New Delhi's side, as the Heng Samrin regime is consolidated and the claims of Pol Pot (or Sihanouk) further lose credibility.

While India has been unable to find political accommodation with ASEAN, it has pursued closer economic ties. Over the past decade, trade and joint ventures have grown rapidly. About a third of India's joint ventures abroad are in the ASEAN states, led by Malaysia, but results are mixed and prospects limited. Nearly a third of the joint ventures in Malaysia, for example, have failed--largely as a result of small and inexperienced Indian companies rushing in for quick profits. Ventures involving India's big industrial houses have had considerably more success, but the high expectations of even two years ago for joint ventures with ASEAN have been moderated. India also faces a severe trade deficit with Southeast Asia. Over the past five years, imports from ASEAN have far outpaced Indian export growth. The next five years will involve increasing efforts to bring trade into greater balance, with increased Indian exports--heavy machinery, for example--and a likely cutback of imports from ASEAN.

Japan

For more than three decades, India's relations with Japan have been minimal, but New Delhi is now making a concerted effort to forge links with Asia's economic giant. Mrs. Gandhi stopped in Tokyo on an unofficial one-day visit on her return from the United States to

India in July 1982--her first visit to Japan in 13 years--and Prime Minister Nakasone has accepted an invitation to visit New Delhi. In May 1982, Indian Finance Minister Pranab Mukherjee visited Japan, ending his stay with the pronouncement that "India will increasingly look to Japan for technology in the future." And it is India's search for technology that is Japan's principal draw.

Indo-Japanese trade is at a very low level, with imports from India accounting for less than 1 percent of Japan's total imports. The two-way trade in 1981 totaled only $2 billion, but this is targeted to reach $5 billion by 1986. India's more liberal economic policy eases restrictions on both imports and investment, and the Japanese are showing interest in expanded trade and in joint ventures in India and with Indian firms in third countries. Japan is also increasing loans and grant aid to India.

There are now some 400 Japanese industrial projects in India. The major collaboration involves the Suzuki Motor Company, with 40 percent equity, in the Indian public sector Maruti Udyog for the production of 100,000 vehicles a year--the realization of Sanjay Gandhi's ill-fated efforts to manufacture a small car. Nissan has also signed on for a joint venture with an Indian private firm to produce small trucks. And India looks to Japanese technology for its infant micro-electronic industry.

Beyond access to technology, India sees in Japan potential support in the North-South dialogue. At the May 1983 economic summit at Williamsburg, Nakasone stated that "there can be no prosperity of the North without the prosperity of the South," to which New Delhi responded with encouragement for a more active Japanese role in the development efforts of the Third World.

Western Europe

Aside from its historical tie with Great Britain, India has not had especially close or extensive relations with other nations of Western Europe. That is rapidly changing. India looks to Europe--particularly Britain, France, and West Germany--and to the European Economic Community for expanded markets for Indian exports, for loans (and support in multilateral lending agencies), for investment in joint ventures in India and in third countries, and for access to high technology. India also sees in Europe, especially France, an important source of support in the North-South dialogue.

Moreover, India looks to Europe in its efforts to gain greater diplomatic flexibility and to diversify its sources of arms. All of these factors portend an increasing importance for Europe in India's international relations.

Although the developing nations, collectively, are the European Economic Community's major trading partner in both imports and exports, India's share of the community's external market is less than 1 percent. India is making a concerted effort to enlarge and diversify that share, but given intense competition and EEC protectionism, trade is not likely to expand significantly. Joint ventures, however, may be more promising, and greater collaboration may be facilitated by the 1981 Indo-EEC agreement on commercial and economic cooperation and the Indo-EEC Joint Commission formed in 1982. Under its liberalized industrial policy, India seeks foreign investment as a source of capital and as a means of acquiring modern technology. New Delhi regards Western Europe as its most promising source of high technology. Even when India might prefer U.S. technology, the opportunity costs in approval and licensing procedures, delay, and uncertainty, together with restrictions, increasingly lead India to look to Europe.

India also looks to Europe as a source of credit and for support in its access to concessional loans through the World Bank, the IMF, and other multilateral lending agencies. As U.S. policy is to graduate India to hard loan windows and to commercial banks, India views European support as critical in sustaining its development efforts during a period of probable foreign exchange pressure over the next five years. France, for example, played a major role in securing the $5.7 billion IMF loan for India in the face of U.S. opposition.

Western Europe (and France most prominently) is also positioned to play an important role in the North-South dialogue for a new international economic order. Mitterrand spelled out the French position in terms of self-interest: "I regard solidarity for development with the whole of the Third World as the key to our common future and a necessity for us. Helping the Third World, we help ourselves to overcome the crisis."

In all of this, the "French connection" has become increasingly important. In 1981, France targeted three nations of the developing world for special attention: Algeria, Mexico, and India. Even before Mitterrand, however, France had begun to pay increasing attention to India, as evidenced by President Giscard d'Estaing's visit to India in January 1980. For India, France is especially attractive for its high technology, its eagerness to do business, and its political independence of the superpowers. In a November 25, 1982 interview for Le Matin (Paris), Indira Gandhi stated, "We readily welcome French assistance particularly since, unlike other countries, no political strings are attached to it and we are fairly sure that we will not be let down over spare part supplies should the need arise."

The French economic presence in India is still relatively small. India accounts for only 0.4 percent of France's total foreign trade, and in investment in India, France is far behind Britain and West Germany. But investment and French technological assistance is rapidly expanding. Out of the 1980 Giscard visit, the French are building one of the world's largest aluminum plants in Orissa and arranged financing through a $680 million Eurodollar loan. And India is seeking French assistance in telecommunications, oil exploration, coal extraction, nuclear power generation, and helicopter and missile production.

In modernizing its armed forces, India has turned to Western European suppliers both in a conscious effort to enhance its independence and flexibility through diversification of arms sources and, most critically, in the search for advanced weapons technology. Beginning in 1979, India has made a series of major arms purchases from Europe: the Anglo-French Jaguar, the British Sea Harrier, the French Mirage 2000, new generation Exocet and Mantra missiles from France, and the Germany SSK-1500 submarine. In July 1983, virtually coinciding with Indian Defence Minister Venkataraman's visit to Moscow, India signed an agreement for the purchase of 20 Sea King anti-submarine helicopters and the latest generation of Sea Eagle missiles from Britain.

France has become India's second largest arms supplier (after the Soviet Union), and the purchase of the Mirage 2000 is a downpayment on future access to French military technology. Europe (and perhaps France most readily) is prepared to meet India's terms, as the United States is not. In shopping for arms, India seeks the transfer of technology. Its conditions have typically involved three stages for the acqusition of weapons: first, delivery of a specified number of weapons; second, co-production in India; and third, transfer of the technology.

India's European arms purchases have a two-pronged political dimension. First, by turning to Europe for arms, India is able to reduce its dependence upon the

Soviet Union, widen its options, and gain greater leverage in Moscow. The Soviets are clearly concerned, but not so alarmed as they would be if India were acquiring American arms. Second, through its arms purchases, India is forging a link with Western Europe which may pay political dividends in enhanced Indian prestige and influence through European support on North-South economic issues and, associated with the Non-Aligned Movement, on global issues of East-West conflict.

INDIA IN INTERNATIONAL FORUMS

India was one of the founding members of the United Nations, and in its foreign policy, has given great importance to international forums as a platform for the articulation and advancement of its national interests. In March 1983, Indira Gandhi took the chair of the Non-Aligned Movement for a three-year tenure. In doing so, India sought to set a more moderate tone and to bring the movement back on course after its loss of credibility under Castro's leadership, with its projection of the Soviet Union as the "natural ally" of the developing world. Yet the sober economic resolution calling for North-South cooperation was paired with a pointedly anti-American political resolution, hardly calculated to warm the industrial nations to the NAM economic appeal. India apparently wanted the West to read the two resolutions separately and to discount the political resolution as an expediency to which India yielded for the higher purposes of the movement's unity.

The irritation the United States no doubt felt at th final product, however, does not diminish the power represented by the Non-Aligned Movement, divided though it may be. With 101 member nations and the outside support of China, it represents more than three-quarters of the world's population. Under India's leadership, it is likely to pursue a pragmatic and well-orchestrated effort for a negotiated new international economic order: increased aid by the industrial nations to the developing world; increased World Bank resources and lending programs; increased quotas and resources for the IMF and less stringent conditions for making funds available to developing nations; easier access for developing country exports to the markets of the industrial world; action to relieve the burden of unmanageable debts among developing countries; and a new, more equitable international monetary system.

From its position as chair of the Non-Aligned Movement, India in the coming three years can be expected to play a prominent role in the international forum--evidenced by Mrs. Gandhi's appearance before the United Nations General Assembly in September 1983. Within a somewhat more limited arena, India's prestige was also enhanced in hosting, for the first time, the Commonwealth Conference in November 1983. In such international gatherings, India is likely to give primary emphasis to economic issues, avoiding or downplaying the political conflicts that divide the developing nations among themselves and link into superpower rivalries. On the economic issues, India will likely eschew strident rhetoric and call instead for cooperation through negotiation. In the political arena, India will seek to maintain an image of "genuine non-alignment," balancing its traditional friendship with the Soviet Union with a continuing if sometimes fitful dialogue with the United States.

India's future role in the Non-Aligned Movement and in the various arenas of the North-South dialogue must be viewed with a certain caution. Many Indians are skeptical of the utility of the Non-Aligned Movement. It may provide a platform for rhetoric, but that in itself may be counterproductive, and whether the NAM can be effective in seeking constructive solutions to world crises--either East-West, North-South, or South-South--is yet to be seen. In the context of the North-South dialogue, India's position as a relatively advanced industrial nation ties many of its interests more to the "North" than to the lesser developed nations of the "South." This accounts, in part, for India's moderation on international economic issues, but it also exposes the potential contradictions likely to emerge among the politically and economically disparate nations of the Third World.

INDIA AND THE UNITED STATES

Relations between Indian and the United States have been broadly characterized by strain, punctuated by periods of friendship and cooperation. Difficulties have been less the product of bilateral conflicts than of problems arising out of differing perceptions of the strategic environment of South Asia. The United States has taken a "global" view, shaped fundamentally by the East-West conflict with the Soviet Union. India's view is regional, and New Delhi seeks to insulate the subcontinent from superpower conflict. Viewing South Asia as a strategic entity, its borders constituting India's defense perimeter, India seeks to exclude foreign powers and to secure its own preeminence in the region.

It has been an assumption of American foreign policy that the U.S. has no vital strategic interests in South Asia as such. American involvement in the region has been episodic and derivative of other interests--notably containment of the Soviet Union and, earlier, of China and, more prominently over the past decade, protection of the vital petroleum resources of the Gulf and their access through the sea lanes of the Indian Ocean. In pursuit of these interests, the United States established an erratic strategic tie with Pakistan that, from its inception, affected the nature and course of the Indo-U.S. relations. Thus, in the 1950s, the U.S. viewed Pakistan as the eastern flank of the "northern tier" and as a critical link in the chain of alliances forged to contain communist expansion in the Middle East and Southeast Asia. In Pakistan's perception, however, it was not the U.S.S.R. but India that posed a threat to its security, and American support was Pakistan's means to attain military parity with its more powerful neighbor. With little sensitivity to the impact of American actions on regional stability, the U.S. contributed to deepened Indo-Pakistani enmity and spurred India to seek closer ties with the Soviet Union. For some Washington officials then, as later in the wake of the Soviet invasion of Afghanistan in December 1979, India simply did not count. In their judgment, there was not much that India could do either <u>for</u> or <u>to</u> the United States.

While opposing great power interference in South Asia, India has a perhaps greater antipathy to indifference. Nothing has been so galling to India than the perception of some American officials that India--the world's second most populous nation, a civilization of great cultural richness, and a leader among the nonaligned nations--can be relegated to "benign neglect." India aspires to recognition as a power that matters. That China should be so recognized and India not is especially galling and was surely a factor in India's decision to demonstrate nuclear capability in its 1974 test. Perhaps one reason that Indians have so often portrayed the U.S. as actively opposing India's interests--that the U.S. seeks to "contain" India and restrict its independence, that it strives to weaken and destabilize India--is that this may be easier to accept and deal with than being ignored.

But India does matter and in the coming years is likely to assume increasing importance in the world arena. Its size and growing economic power, its military strength and diplomatic leadership destine India to middle power status comparable with that of China. Within South Asia, India is the keystone of stability. A strong, stable, secure, and independent India is absolutely essential to the peace and stability of South Asia as a whole. If the United States has one foremost interest in the region, it is in India's political stability and national integrity.

If the expansion of Soviet influence in South Asia is to be contained, it will not be by Pakistan alone, armed with the latest in American weapons, but by regional cooperation with India as its centerpiece. India is the strongest and politically the most stable state in South Asia. Indian weakness and instability would affect the whole of South Asia, opening the region to external interference and potential armed conflict. China might seek to extend its influence in Nepal, Bhutan, and Bangladesh, to again support tribal insurgency in India's Northeast, and to assert militarily its claims south of the McMahon Line. The Soviets would no doubt seek to draw India into a web of dependency and might seize the opportunity to exert greater pressure on Pakistan, perhaps fomenting ethnic unrest and creating a Soviet client state in Baluchistan.

Pakistan may be a "frontline state" as it now faces Soviet-occupied Afghanistan, but Pakistan's security depends upon India. Pakistan on its own would be unable to resist Soviet aggression, and the added strength of the American Rapid Deployment Force would hardly match Soviet logistical advantage and conventional military power. Any attempt by the United States to meet Soviet superiority in such a situation through the use of tactical nuclear weapons is most unlikely, as it would almost inevitably extend the conflict beyond the region. The most credible deterrent to Soviet military action against Pakistan is Indo-Pakistani detente and a common commitment to regional security. A direct move by the Soviets against Pakistan is not an imminent threat, but Soviet subversion of Pakistan national unity--support for Baluch, Pathan, and Sindi separatism--is a potential danger, although there is no evidence today of such Soviet activity. Here again India's role is critical. A united and secure Pakistan is in India's interest. The breakup of Pakistan would open the region to foreign intervention--the extension of Soviet influence, if not control, in Baluchistan and Chinese penetration via the Karakoram Highway into the Gilgit Agency of Kashmir. The danger of great power confrontation in Southwest Asia would be heightened and India's own security would be threatened. And the breakup of Pakistan would also carry the danger that the contagion of separatism would spread to India. The clearest message to the Soviets not to interfere in Pakistan would again be Indo-Pakistani detente.

United States support for Pakistan remains today the most serious source of tension between New Delhi and Washington. India wants a secure Pakistan and recognizes the need for modernizing Pakistan's armed forces, but India is apprehensive about enhanced Pakistani military capability insofar as it exceeds what New Delhi judges to be Pakistan's legitimate defense requirements and, most critically, as it is linked with an external power. Many Indians are convinced that as a quid pro quo for the F-16, the United States sought basing facilities in Pakistan. Any extension of bases by Pakistan to the United States--naval facilities at Gwadar, air bases, surveillance operations, or the prepositioning of arms and supplies for the Rapid Deployment Force--would seriously affect U.S.-Indian relations and would exacerbate tension between India and Pakistan.

India would not likely compromise its non-aligned status by extending comparable basing facilities to the Soviet Union, but it would probably lean heavily on Pakistan, perhaps with aid and encouragement to Pakistan's political opposition. The opposition, especially in Sind, would likely oppose a U.S. military presence as reinforcing military rule and Punjabi domination, and insofar as the U.S. is identified with the military regime, a change of government will entail a loss of whatever basing facilities the U.S. was able to secure and a cooling of U.S.-Pakistan relations.

India will regard any substantial increase in the quantity or quality of U.S. arms to Pakistan as a threat to its own security and as destabilizing to the region. Of particular concern is the introduction of military technology beyond the level already within the region. India has the will and resources to maintain the current ratio of arms superiority, but the increased sophistication of Pakistan's weapons may also bring India closer to taking the nuclear weapons option. Without giving a "veto" to New Delhi, American consultation with India (and Pakistan) regarding all arms transfers to the subcontinent might assuage Indian fears and, at the same time, promote a greater degree of trust between India and Pakistan. The deterioration of Indo-U.S. relations that followed the 1980 offer of U.S. military assistance to Pakistan was at least in part the product of Washington's failure to consult New Delhi.

South Asia is widely regarded as the most likely region in the world for nuclear proliferation. India has demonstrated capability but has chosen not to take the option to develop and deploy nuclear weapons. Pakistan is, by all indications, engaged in a clandestine nuclear program directed toward the development of a weapons capability. Pakistan's apparent determination to push forward underscores the limits of American leverage. The F-16 delivery schedule may postpone a Pakistani nuclear test (although Pakistan is probably not as far along in its program as once believed), and Pakistan will remain vulnerable to the cutoff of American military spare parts--perhaps a sufficient contingency to foreclose actual testing altogether so long as India does not move beyond its present nuclear status. Upgraded Pakistani conventional military capability, as it provides a greater sense of security, may reduce the incentive to go nuclear, but the increased sophistication of Pakistan's armed forces may itself propel India toward nuclear weapons so as to maintain undisputed military superiority.

America's response to the challenge of nuclear proliferation in South Asia must address the insecurities of both Pakistan and India that make nuclear weapons so tempting. The U.S. response must be to preclude proliferation so far as possible by reducing its attraction. Sanctions after the fact will have little effect save to reduce further what leverage we do have. It is in Indo-Pakistani detente that the dangers of proliferation are most likely to be reduced, and American interests here, just as in limiting the expansion of Soviet influence in South Asia, are best served by promoting rapprochement between India and Pakistan--even when it will likely involve a reduced American presence in the region.

Within the larger strategic environment of the Indian Ocean, the United States and India share the ultimate goals of ensuring open sea lanes and access to Gulf oil, the independence of the littoral states and their freedom from external interference, and the avoidance of great power confrontation. The U.S. and India, however, take very different approaches that are likely to bring the two nations into periodic conflict in the coming years. Given the geographic proximity of the Soviet Union to the Indian Ocean region, its presence in Afghanistan and the Horn of Africa, and its buildup of naval forces, the United States seeks to maintain a balance of power. India, joined by most of the littoral states, seeks a "zone of peace" free from the presence of external military powers. But clearly, if the U.S. were unilaterally to reduce its forces in the Indian Ocean, the states of the region would be more vulnerable to Soviet pressure. The U.S. and the U.S.S.R.

each have vital strategic interests in the Indian Ocean and are unlikely to forego any presence in the region--and, in any case, the Soviet Union by virtue of its geographic position is a permanent presence. While a balanced superpower presence in the Indian Ocean may give the littoral states, including India, more room for maneuver than the predominance of either the U.S. or U.S.S.R., the instability of the nations of the region invite potential confrontation as the Americans and Soviets each may be tempted to intervene to either protect or advance their interests.

India, much to Soviet displeasure, has increasingly equated the U.S. and U.S.S.R. in its condemnation of the buildup of external military power in the Indian Ocean. Though no less concerned about Diego Garcia, American naval forces, or the potential for U.S. intervention (e.g., in destabilizing the Marxist Government in Maritius), India is likely to pursue a measured effort, with a moderate tone, to secure the reduction of forces by both the United States and the Soviet Union. This will likely be manifest in the continued projection of its own presence in the Indian Ocean region and by diplomatic efforts (as in Saudi Arabia in 1982) to marshal the littoral states against extending base facilities to external powers. The danger the Indian Ocean poses to Indo-U.S. relations arises out of the volatility of the region and the potential for American intervention in response to a threat to its perceived interests, particularly insofar as it involves Pakistan.

After a low in U.S.-Indian relations in 1980-1981, both India and the United States have sought to improve relations, to downplay differences of strategic perception and to accentuate the positive. Mrs. Gandhi's visit to Washington in 1982 was an important atmospheric breakthrough, providing a more optimistic prospect without unrealistic expectations. U.S.-Indian relations over the next five years are likely to be affected by the periodic strains of East-West and North-South conflict, but India has compelling interests in keeping relations with the United States on a reasonably steady course and, if possible, in improving relations. The U.S. is a major market for Indian goods, a source of investment, technology, and aid, and India and the United States are being drawn closer together by the increasing number of Indians resident in this country.

Although trade with India is less than 1 percent of America's total foreign trade, the United States is India's second largest trading partner (after the Soviet Union), accounting for approximately 13 percent of

India's exports and 12 percent of its imports (1980-81). Over the past five years, Indian exports to the U.S. have grown and diversified, with an increasingly large share devoted to such manufactured products as hand-tools, bicycles, castings, electronic components, etc. India's new push for export led growth draws India to seek an expanded American market, but while increased trade represents an important element in closer relations between India and the U.S., trade is a potential source of acrimony. U.S. quota restrictions and other trade barriers to cotton textiles, steel products, and industrial fasteners (nuts and bolts), for example, have drawn strong Indian protests, and the protectionist mood in the United States, as reflected in political rhetoric, could lead to the imposition of new restrictions. At a time when India is seeking to expand exports--in accordance with the advice of the IMF and the World Bank, as well as its own economists--restricted American markets would hardly reinforce India's more liberal economic policy nor would it heighten "the magic of the marketplace" extolled by President Reagan. Trade barriers against Indian goods would, moreover, probably draw India into closer trading ties with the Soviet Union.

India's imports from the U.S. have grown at an even faster rate than exports and have contributed to a widening trade deficit. There is already some pullback in imports, and increasing pressure on foreign exchange may bring more rigid controls. If India is unable to expand exports, it can be expected to impose new import restrictions, and there is already a demand to do so by some Indian businesses that see their protected markets threatened. The Government of India has resisted pressure to turn back economic liberalization, but the policy is itself limited and cautious. India has selectively relaxed import controls and eased the licensing process, but it has by no means thrown open its huge market--some 70 million middle class consumers--to international competition.

There are significant opportunities for increased American exports to India, and short of a new wave of protectionism, the two-way trade between India and the United States should continue to expand over the next five years. But beyond protectionism, the U.S. has thrown up another barrier that is an irritant in Indo-U.S. relations. Much of what India most wants from the United States is high technology. Approximately 70 percent of India's computer imports, for example, come from the U.S., but American security restrictions on the export of the most sophisticated technologies and the opportunity costs in license procedures have led India to turn increasingly to Western Europe and Japan for high technology. The long-term consequences may be to close out the United States from a growing market and to weaken an important link between the U.S. and India.

America's economic ties with India have perhaps greatest potential in investment through joint ventures. India's new economic policy seeks to attract foreign investment in targeted areas of high technology, energy-related fields, and production for export. The conditions for collaboration--equity participation, taxation, return on investment, repatriation of profits, etc.--are attractive. But the "ghosts" of IBM and Coca Cola, which left India during the period of the Janata Government, continue to trouble potential American investors, and the image of India as the "permit raj," with bureaucratic delays and endless red tape, is difficult to counter, even as controls are relaxed and procedures streamlined. Efforts by government agencies of both the U.S. and India, by the Indo-U.S. Business Council, the Indo-American Chamber of Commerce, and the Overseas Private Investment Corporation (OPIC) are beginning to pay off with increased interest in joint ventures in India among American firms, especially among middle-sized enterprises. American investment in India now stands at some $600 million, second after the British, but it is only 0.3 percent of the total U.S. foreign investment. Over the next five years, given India's favorable investment climate, the number of collaborations should increase, but there is little prospect for a massive inflow of capital.

India's principal goal at this point is technology transfer through joint ventures, but a continuing trade imbalance, a decline in foreign remittances, and reduced access to concessional loans may make the inflow of investment capital itself increasingly attractive. This would likely draw attack from the political opposition on both the left and right as a "sellout" to the multinationals,* but there is a very broad base of support in India for expanding foreign investment. Socialist ideology is on the wane, and rhetoric is often hollow. How the United States responds in terms of trade and investment will be an important determinant

---

* That India is aiming its efforts to attract investment primarily at middle-sized firms has a significant political consequence. Because of their lower visibility, these companies are less likely to draw the notice of the political opposition, and because they are not great multinational corporations, they pose no threat of domination to the Indian economy.

in whether India's new economic policy succeeds and can be sustained. While prospects for continued liberalization of the economy are probably most favorable under a Congress party Government, a non-Congress coalition, were one to come to power, would be unlikely to make a sharp reversal. One aspect of India's political stability, arising from its pluralism, has been an essential continuity of policy, both foreign and domestic. A possible change in Government with the next parliamentary elections, to be held before January 1985, would probably leave the basic thrust of current economic policy intact. In a world of interdependence, economic autarky is simply not a realistic option.

One of the major factors drawing India toward the United States, Western Europe, and Japan is access to credit. Direct aid has today been largely supplanted by loans, and the United States is the largest single contributor to the major multilateral lending agencies--the International Monetary Fund, the World Bank, and the Asian Development Bank. India has in the past been the largest recipient of concessional loans of the International Development Association (IDA), the World Bank's "soft loan" window, drawing some 40 percent of its funds yearly. At a time when the United States is reducing its contributions to IDA, China is coming in as a new member, its share of low-interest loans coming out of what otherwise might have gone to India. India's share of IDA funds has now been reduced to some 25 percent. India's call for increased contributions to IDA has gone unheeded during economic recession, although the Western European members have maintained the level of their commitments.

The squeeze on India, however, is also a matter of policy. The United States seeks to reserve concessional loans for the poorest developing countries and to graduate more advanced nations like India to the hard loan windows of the World Bank and to the commercial banks. The commercial banks are pushing the policy, as they are eager to make loans to India--a nation with a low debt service ratio and a record of no defaults. New Delhi's response is that the U.S. is punishing India for its fiscal responsibility, its good credit rating, while rewarding the profligate with concessional loans.

Many people in India--and many who should know better--see U.S. policy as a deliberate attempt to weaken India and thwart its efforts to develop economically. Beyond the American position on IDA, they point to U.S. opposition to the $5.7 billion IMF loan to India, U.S. opposition to India's application for a World Bank loan for oil exploration in the

Krishna-Godavari basin, and reported U.S. efforts to deny India access to loans from the Asian Development Bank. In the case of the IMF loan, the U.S. believed that India's balance of payments problems did not justify so large an amount (the largest IMF loan ever granted) and that it was sought for development programs. On the World Bank loan, it was U.S. judgment that the project was sufficiently sound to sustain the higher interest loans of commercial banks. As for the Asian Development Bank, given the enormity of India's requirements, Indian access would squeeze out the smaller Southeast Asian nations for which the Fund was principally created. India received the IMF and World Bank loans, and U.S. opposition--however principled it may have been--was a gratuitous affront to India. The issue of the Asian Development Bank continues to rankle.

The U.S. policy to wean India from concessional loans has been ill-timed, for India is being forced into the commercial loan market at a time when loans may not be so readily available. In the wake of the crisis precipitated by the near default of debt-burdened nations in 1982, the banks are now skittish and, with the IMF, are trying to stave off defaults with rescheduled interest payments and new loans. For its part, so as not to fall into the debt trap, India has become more selective in international loans. But by the mid-1980s, as India begins to repay the IMF loan, India's debt service ratio will rise rapidly, making access to concessional loans all the more critical. The United States can work with New Delhi in efforts to ensure India's continued access to a mixture of concessional and commercial loans, but if U.S. policies effectively deny India access to soft loan windows, Indo-U.S. relations are likely to be in for rough times.

For the past five years, from the passage of the 1978 Nuclear Nonproliferation Act, Indo-U.S. relations have been troubled by fundamental differences of interpretation in regard to the contractual obligations of the United States in the 1963 agreement on the Tarapur nuclear power plant. The Reagan administration averted a major confrontation by arranging for the supply of enriched uranium fuel for the reactor (to have been delivered by the U.S. under the terms of the agreement until 1993) by a third party--France. In the face of India's continued unwillingness to extend full-scope safeguards to all nuclear facilities throughout the country and to comply with the specifics of the Nuclear Nonproliferation Act, the U.S. Congress in 1983 sought to bar the supply of spare parts to the Tarapur plant. The capstone of Secretary of State Shultz's visit to

New Delhi in July 1983 was an arrangement for a third party--West Germany later agreed--to supply the parts, with the U.S. agreeing to meet requirements if the parts cannot be secured elsewhere.

Opposition in the U.S. Congress to the arrangement was reflected in August 1983 in resolutions introduced in the House and Senate stipulating that in order to receive spare parts, India must provide reliable assurances that it is not engaged in a nuclear weapons program and that it will not explode another nuclear device. The resolution also called for the extension of the International Atomic Energy Safeguards to Tarapur provided for in the 1963 agreement after the agreement lapses in 1993.

Of particular concern in Congress is the Indian Government's proposal to reprocess spent fuel from Tarapur, now more than 140 tons and an increasingly worrisome storage problem. India's capacity to develop nuclear weapons does not depend on reprocessing Tarapur's spent fuel nor would the plutonium obtained be a likely weapons component. U.S. sanctions against India would be unlikely to influence Indian nuclear policy, save possibly to strengthen the pro-bomb lobby and to push India into a rigid adherence to its present position. India has thus far resisted the nuclear weapons option and, unless confronted by a nuclear Pakistan, will most likely maintain its status as having demonstrated capability without exercising the option to develop and deploy nuclear weapons. But given the intensity of feeling on nonproliferation in Congress and in the American press (as expressed, for example, in the periodic editorials of the Washington Post and the New York Times) together with India's fierce sense of independence, the probability for serious fallout between the U.S. and India over the issue in the next five years is very high.

Potential conflict between the U.S. and India over such issues as American arms to Pakistan, concessional loans, or nuclear nonproliferation will be mediated to some degree by India's desire to maintain and improve economic relations with the U.S. for trade, investment, technology, and loans and to maximize diplomatic flexibility by balancing relations with the two superpowers. But tension between the U.S. and India is also mediated by the growing Indian community in the United States--now some half a million. The importance of the Indian community--largely upper income, highly educated, and heavily professional--should not be underestimated. It is likely to shape a more positive image of India in the United States, but more significantly, it will deepen and extend the personal bond between the U.S. and India. It is difficult to find anyone among India's elite classes who does not have family and friends in the United States either as permanent residents or students. Indians have always distinguished between the American people and the policies of the U.S. government, and they can be expected to do so in the future--criticizing U.S. policy at the same time they eagerly seek an invitation to visit or admission for a son or daughter to an American university. But personal ties and the positive images of American society that they sustain cushion some of the bumps in Indo-U.S. relations and perhaps provide added incentive for India to seek improved relations with the United States.

The basic character of Indian foreign policy is not likely to change over the next five years, whatever leadership changes may occur. Continuity has been the hallmark of Indian foreign policy, and India can be expected to maintain its traditional friendship with the Soviet Union even as it pursues rapprochement with China, closer ties with Western Europe, and improved relations with the United States. Both India and the U.S. have an interest in improved relations. India does--and should--matter to the United States. As chair of the Non-Aligned Movement and a leader of the Group of 77 in the United Nations, India speaks for much of the developing world in the North-South dialogue. In its call for cooperation through negotiation, India's stance is one of moderation not confrontation. The United States and India see the world differently, but they share common goals in seeking peace, political stability, and economic development for the Third World. India is the keystone of stability in South Asia, and the security of the region is fundamentally dependent upon the strength and stability of India.

NOTES

1. Shashi Tharoor, Reasons of State: Political Development and India's Foreign Policy under Indira Gandhi, 1966-1977, New Delhi: Vikas, 1982, p. 144. Tharoor argues that Haksar brought the Prime Minister's Secretariat to the center of foreign policy decision-making.

2. Ministry of External Affairs, Report, 1966-67, New Delhi: Government of India, 1967, p. 83.

3. Interview, New Delhi, April 19, 1982.

4. For a fascinating scenario, see Ravi Rikhye, *The Fourth Round: Indo-Pak War 1984*, New Delhi: ABC Publishing House, 1982.

5. *India Today*, August 31, 1983, pp. 14-15.

6. "Soviet Security Interests in South Asia," in Lawrence Ziring, ed., *The Subcontinent in World Politics: India, its Neighbors, and the Great Powers*, Revised Edition, New York: Praeger, 1982, p. 184.

7. *Ibid*., p. 185.

8. *U.S. News and World Report*, June 19, 1979.

9. "The Soviet Union in South Asia: A Friend to Rely On?" *Journal of International Affairs*, Winter-Fall 1980-1981, p. 258.

10. For an account of these efforts, see Leo Rose, "India and ASEAN: Much Ado About Not Much," in Robert A. Scalopino and Jusuf Wanandi, eds., *Economic, Political, and Security Issues in Southeast Asia in the 1980s*, Berkeley: Institute of East Asian Studies, University of California, 1982, pp. 93-107.